THE INTELLECTUAL MILIEU
OF
JOHN DRYDEN:

STUDIES IN SOME ASPECTS OF
SEVENTEENTH-CENTURY THOUGHT

LOUIS I. BREDVOLD

CENTRAL WYOMING COLLEGE
LIBRARY
RIVERTON, WYOMING 82501

ANN ARBOR PAPERBACKS
THE UNIVERSITY OF MICHIGAN PRESS

PR
3423
B7
1956

Copyright © by the University of Michigan 1934
First edition as an Ann Arbor Paperback 1956
Second printing 1959

A. M. McCLEARY
BOX 393
WOOSTER, OHIO

Manufactured in the United States of America

PREFACE

IT IS not my purpose in this volume to present a comprehensive or complete study — either biographical or critical — of John Dryden and his work. My investigation has been limited to two closely related subjects: Dryden's characteristic thought and its background in the seventeenth century. Much of this background is unfamiliar to students of literature, and some of it is inaccessible except in the more important libraries of Europe; I have therefore felt compelled to describe and illustrate it in some detail. If any readers of this volume should be interested in *Geistesgeschichte*, they will perhaps more readily approve of this extensive study of Dryden's intellectual milieu; others, whose interest in this volume will depend exclusively on the light it throws on Dryden, I must beg to read on trustfully and with patience; when they come to the end they will, I hope, feel rewarded for their toil.

As I have had to include the results of much "spade-work," my study has acquired a monographic character. I have accordingly adopted a method predominantly historical, with only some tentative suggestions as to what bearing my findings might have upon the interpretation and evaluation of Dryden's work as literature. Biographical questions also enter the discussion casually from time to time. But, in general, it has been my main concern here to present a series of facts as I see them; if my statement of them wins acceptance, it will then be time to say more regarding their consequences and implications.

I am happy to record my obligations to the John Simon Guggenheim Foundation for a fellowship in 1929–30, which, with a sabbatical leave granted by the University of Michigan the same year, made possible the collection of material for this study. My colleague, Professor Louis A. Strauss, has read my work in manuscript and given me most helpful comment. Professor George Boas, of The Johns Hopkins University, very kindly helped me expunge some errors in the second chapter, and Father J. J. Daly, S.J., of the University of Detroit, did me a similar service with the fourth; but I fear neither of these friendly critics will be entirely satisfied with what I have let stand. The third chapter, which appeared originally in *Modern Philology* for May, 1928, is reprinted, with some revisions and additions, with the kind permission of the editors.

Finally, it is a pleasure to acknowledge my indebtedness to Dr. Eugene S. McCartney, editor of the University of Michigan Publications, for his helpful and searching criticism of my manuscript.

CONTENTS

NOTE

Unless otherwise indicated, all references to Dryden are to the most nearly complete edition available, by Sir Walter Scott and George Saintsbury (1882–93); in some cases I have preferred to quote the poetry from the edition by John Sargeaunt (1910) and the essays from the edition by W. P. Ker (1900), because of the superiority of these editions textually.

THE INTELLECTUAL MILIEU
OF
JOHN DRYDEN

CHAPTER I

INTRODUCTION

DRYDEN has received generous recognition for his stylistic achievement, for the way in which he has put the stamp of his genius upon the language of England, in both prose and poetry. Dr. Johnson's famous dictum that "by him we were taught *sapere et fari*, to think naturally and express forcibly," appears to be also the standard critical opinion of our own day. Thus Mr. Bonamy Dobrée, in an essay occasioned by the tercentenary of Dryden's birth, states that the "chief work" of his "long, patiently arduous life consisted in creating a language fit for civilized Englishmen to use."[1] And Mr. T. S. Eliot has expressed the opinion that "it is hardly too much to say that Dryden found the English speechless, and he gave them speech; and they accordingly acknowledged their master; the language which we can refine, enrich, distort or corrupt as we may, but which we cannot do without. No one, in the whole history of English literature, has dominated that literature so long, or so completely. And even in the nineteenth century the language was still the language of Dryden, as it is to-day."[2] If this criticism errs, it is on the side of generosity, and it is possible that some of the credit here given to Dryden may in the future be distributed more equitably among his contemporaries and predecessors.

But the content of Dryden's work, his cast of mind, and his intellectual equipment have received little attention, except in disparagement. Mr. Allan Lubbock, for instance, has recently asserted that Dryden's "whole body of work can be explained as the

---

[1] *Variety of Ways* (Oxford, 1932), p. 9.
[2] *John Dryden* (New York, 1932), p. 24.

child of a deep enthusiasm, which made him attach but little importance to religion or politics, or even to many aspects of literature itself. What excluded everything else was the love of expression for its own sake. He devoted himself therefore to increasing the efficiency of his instruments."[3] That is to say, Dryden was an expert craftsman with an uninteresting mind. But this is the judgment of the twentieth century; readers in the past have been able to say more for Dryden. Roscommon found weighty things in *Religio Laici:*

> Let free, impartial men from Dryden learn
> Mysterious secrets of a high concern,
> And weighty truths, solid convincing sense,
> Explained by unaffected eloquence.[4]

Or, if Roscommon's praise is ruled out as the partiality of a friend, there is the passage in Walter Savage Landor's verse letter to Wordsworth:

> Our course by Milton's light was sped,
> And Shakespeare shining over head:
> Chatting on deck was Dryden too,
> The Bacon of the rhyming crew;
> None ever crost our mystic sea
> More richly stored with thought than he;
> Tho' never tender nor sublime,
> He wrestles with and conquers Time.[5]

We need not infer from these lines that Dryden should, in Landor's judgment, be placed among the great philosophical poets, with Lucretius and Dante, with whom he assuredly does not belong. But the confession of so discerning a reader as Landor may remind us that there are stores of thought in Dryden's work which should not be ignored in an explanation and appraisal of his literary achievement. There is, indeed, something anomalous in a criticism which concerns itself with natural thinking and forcible expression without deigning to note *what* is thought and expressed. Such criticism is either sophistical itself, or applicable only to sophists. And the unpleasant assumption underlies much of the criticism, much even of the praise, of Dryden, that he was a sophist and to be dealt with accordingly; that, with the possible exception of some

---

[3] *The Character of John Dryden*, Hogarth Essays (London, 1925), p. 6.
[4] Dryden, *Works* X, 34.   [5] Landor, *Works* (London, 1853), II, 667.

of his literary criticism, his mind was neither sincere nor significant nor interesting.

This depreciation of Dryden's mind is in large measure due to certain preconceptions — long current — regarding his moral and intellectual character, which must be dealt with briefly before we enter upon the proper subject of this study. There are at least three such common preconceptions which the student encounters as obstacles in his approach to Dryden: that Dryden was a hireling, whose political and religious affiliations were determined by bribes and pensions; that in his most serious work he never rose intellectually above the level of ephemeral journalism; and that the inconsistencies and contradictions with which his work abounds are conclusive evidence of a lack of intellectual character and significance.

I

Dryden's pensions as Poet Laureate and Historiographer Royal were constantly harped upon in his own time by hostile pamphleteers, and they have since then inspired suspicion in many of his biographers and critics — with the exceptions of Malone, Scott, and Saintsbury. Very little was known about them, but such fragmentary information as came to light from time to time was always given the most sinister interpretation. The full facts are now in print,[6] and many of these insinuations can be proved gratuitous. The time has come when it is possible to reconsider the question of Dryden's character, both intellectual and moral, with a more open and receptive mind.[7]

The poet should be heard in his own defense; he has important testimony to give regarding the moral and intellectual seriousness of his nature. Perhaps he replied too seldom to the contemporary pamphleteers who vilified him. "Anything, though never so little," he wrote in his old age, "which a man speaks of himself, in my

[6] In the *Calendar of Treasury Books* for the reigns of Charles II and James II.

[7] The present author has attempted two studies in this direction: "Political Aspects of Dryden's *Amboyna* and *The Spanish Fryar*," *Essays and Studies in English and Comparative Literature*, in University of Michigan Publications, Language and Literature, VIII (1932), 119–132; and "Notes on John Dryden's Pension," *Modern Philology*, XXX (1933), 267–274.

opinion is still too much."[8]   He had too much dignity to be egotistically voluble, but he often spoke incidentally about his work and himself with admirable candor, without either false modesty or false pride. These passages in his writings merit some attention from any critic who engages to explain the poet's personality.

It would appear from some of them that Dryden regarded himself as a man of greater moral dignity than tradition since his time has allowed him. Two passages may suffice to illustrate this point. In *A Discourse concerning the Original and Progress of Satire* (1693), addressed to the Earl of Dorset, he questions the legitimacy of the lampoon, "a dangerous sort of weapon, and for the most part unlawful." But possibly, he continues, we may be permitted to use it in revenge,

. . . when we have been affronted in the same nature, or have been any ways notoriously abused, and can make ourselves no other reparation. And yet we know, that, in Christian charity, all offences are to be forgiven, as we expect the like pardon for those which we daily commit against Almighty God. And this consideration has often made me tremble when I was saying our Saviour's prayer; for the plain condition of the forgiveness which we beg is the pardoning of others the offences which they have done to us; for which reason I have many times avoided the commission of that fault, even when I have been notoriously provoked. Let not this, my Lord, pass for vanity in me; for it is truth. More libels have been written against me, than almost any man now living; and I had reason on my side, to have defended my own innocence. I speak not of my poetry, which I have wholly given up to the critics: let them use it as they please: posterity, perhaps, may be more favourable to me; for interest and passion will lie buried in another age, and partiality and prejudice be forgotten. I speak of my morals, which have been sufficiently aspersed: *that* only sort of reputation ought to be dear to every honest man, and is to me. But let the world witness for me, that I have been often wanting to myself in that particular; I have seldom answered any scurrilous lampoon, when it was in my power to have exposed my enemies: and, being naturally vindicative, have suffered in silence, and possessed my soul in quiet.[9]

Dryden quite evidently was not afraid in his own time to lay public claim to some of the nobler virtues.

[8] *Essays*, ed. W. P. Ker (Oxford, 1900), II, 80.   [9] *Ibid.*, pp. 79–80.

In our second passage Dryden defends his sincerity in the matter of party loyalty. Accused as he was of having been hired to write *The Duke of Guise*, he replied in his *Vindication* (1683):

... If I am a mercenary scribbler, the Lords Commissioners of the Treasury best know: I am sure, they have found me no importunate solicitor; for I know myself, I deserved little, and, therefore, have never desired much. I return that slander, with just disdain, on my accusers: it is for men who have ill consciences to suspect others; I am resolved to stand or fall with the cause of my God, my king, and country; never to trouble myself for any railing aspersions, which I have not deserved; and to leave it as a portion to my children, — that they had a father who durst do his duty, and was neither covetous nor mercenary.[10]

Such a reply Dryden's Whig enemies presumably regarded as sheer effrontery and hypocrisy; but the facts regarding his pension bear him out. From 1677 to 1684 he received annually only one half of his stipulated pension; and the payments were neither hastened nor increased on account of his political services. There is no evidence that the government offered him any inducement to write on politics. We may reasonably assume that he wrote as he did because he believed that his own security as an Englishman along with that of the nation depended on the defeat of the Whigs. In this spirit, certainly, he addressed the Earl of Rochester in the dedication to *The Duke of Guise* (1683):

... If ever this excellent government, so well established by the wisdom of our forefathers, and so much shaken by the folly of this age, shall recover its ancient splendour, posterity cannot be so ungrateful as to forget those who, in the worst of times, have stood undaunted by their king and country, and, for the safeguard of both, have exposed themselves to the malice of false patriots, and the madness of a headstrong rabble. But since this glorious work is yet unfinished, and though we have reason to hope well of the success, yet the event depends on the unsearchable providence of Almighty God, it is no time to raise trophies, while the victory is in dispute; but every man, by your example, to contribute what is in his power to maintain so just a cause, on which depends the future settlement and prosperity of three nations.[11]

Rochester, as first lord of the Treasury, was in a position to know to what degree Dryden's Tory zeal was mercenary; if Rochester

[10] *Works*, VII, 173–174.   [11] *Ibid.*, p. 16.

thought the poet was to be purchased for a price, that price was merely the regular payment of one half of the annual pension of the Laureate.[12]   Mercenary men know better how to reap their reward.   Everything points rather to Dryden's deep devotion and dignified loyalty to the Tory cause, which he identified with the best interests of his king and his country.

II

It would seem difficult enough for any man, in such an unsettled age as the seventeenth century in England, to have remained indifferent to the political and religious embroilments of his age.   But Dryden was first of all a poet, and he considered it fatal for a poet to cut himself off from the intellectual life of his age and nation. His statement of the qualifications necessary for the practice of poetry should be a fair indication of the nature of his own intellectual regimen.

Dryden's career as a man of letters turned out vastly different from what he wished it.   His creative energy was diverted from his great ambition, to write an epic, and dissipated in a multitude of miscellaneous tasks.   If we must find a flaw in his character, this is perhaps the great and serious one, that, in spite of his love for literature and his desire for fame in it, he was not heroic enough to achieve what he himself, correctly or incorrectly, thought should be his greatest work.   But there can be no question of his deep desire to write an epic, or of his considered preparation for that task.   It was a task which he understood to involve extensive learning and ripe wisdom as well as genius.   In the realm of literary theory Dryden was still, in some respects, in the afterglow of the Renaissance; he considered the great epic the supreme achievement of the mind of man.   The epic poet, as any reader of Sidney

---

[12] Dryden's famous undated letter to Rochester, appealing for "half a year of my salary" or "some small employment . . . either in the Customs, or in the Appeals of the Excise, or some other way," apparently brought him no results.   The John Dryden who was appointed, on December 17, 1683, as Collector of Customs in the port of London, was not the poet: see Charles E. Ward, "Was John Dryden Collector of Customs?" *Modern Language Notes*, XLVII (1932), 246–249, and *Calendar of Treasury Books, 1689–1692*, p. 1886.   It should be observed also that Dryden's letter to Rochester appears to have been an isolated appeal, made only in circumstances of dire extremity.

and Spenser would know, must be a legislator, a moralist, a philosopher; as Sidney said, he is the monarch of all sciences. In this old humanistic tradition of the Renaissance, which required the man of genius to acquire learning and judgment, Dryden had been educated, and he was never able to unlearn this lesson.

"I am of opinion," he said in the *Defence of an Essay of Dramatic Poesy* (1668), "that they cannot be good poets, who are not accustomed to argue well. False reasonings and colours of speech are the certain marks of one who does not understand the stage; for moral truth is the mistress of the poet as much as of the philosopher; Poesy must resemble natural truth, but it must *be* ethical."[13] In 1674 he excluded Settle from the communion of orthodox and true poets, because he lacked learning, because he was a sottish "mere poet":

Fanciful poetry and music, used with moderation, are good; but men who are wholly given over to either of them, are commonly as full of whimsies as diseased and splenetic men can be. Their heads are continually hot, and they have the same elevation of fancy sober, which men of sense have when they drink. So wine used moderately does not take away the judgment, but used continually, debauches men's understandings, and turns them into sots, making their heads continually hot by accident, as the others are by nature; so, mere poets and mere musicians are as sottish as mere drunkards are, who live in a continual mist, without seeing or judging any thing clearly.

A man should be learned in several sciences, and should have a reasonable, philosophical, and in some measure a mathematical head, to be a complete and excellent poet; and besides this, should have experience in all sorts of humours and manners of men; should be thoroughly skilled in conversation, and should have a great knowledge of mankind in general. Mr. Settle having never studied any sort of learning but poetry, and that but slenderly, as you may find by his writings, and having besides no other advantages, must make very lame work on't; he himself declares, he neither reads, nor cares for conversation; so that he would persuade us he is a kind of fanatic in poetry, and has a light within him, and writes by an inspiration; which (like that of the heathen prophets) a man must have no sense of his own when he receives; and no doubt he would be thought inspired, and would be reverenced extremely in the country where Santons are worshipped.[14]

[13] *Essays*, ed. W. P. Ker, I, 121.   [14] *Works*, XV, 406–407.

These were not mere transient principles, professed only for the castigation of Settle. "It requires Philosophy," he wrote in 1677, "as well as Poetry, to sound the depth of all the passions." [15] And in 1679, referring to the necessity for a dramatist or an epic poet to know the "manners" of men, this knowledge, he said, is "to be gathered from the several virtues, vices, or passions, and many other commonplaces, which a poet must be supposed to have learned from natural Philosophy, Ethics, and History; of all which, whosoever is ignorant, does not deserve the name of poet." [16] In 1693 he described the qualifications of the poet who "may build a nobler, a more beautiful and more perfect poem, than any yet extant since the Ancients":

. . . a man, who, being conversant in the philosophy of Plato, as it is now accommodated to Christian use, (for, as Virgil gives us to understand by his example, that is the only proper, of all others, for an epic poem,) who, to his natural endowments, of a large invention, a ripe judgment, and a strong memory, has joined the knowledge of the liberal arts and sciences, and particularly moral philosophy, the mathematics, geography, and history, and with all these qualifications is born a poet; knows, and can practise the variety of numbers, and is master of the language in which he writes. [17]

In an epic poet, he says a few pages on, "one who is worthy of that name, besides an universal genius, is required universal learning." [18] Such were the comprehensive qualifications of an epic poet, as Dryden understood them in an age before specialization.

Not that Dryden was a great scholar comparable to Gray or Milton, or that he set himself the hard task of keeping up with all the mathematical discoveries of the seventeenth century; what is contended here is that Dryden had a generous conception of the learning necessary to a poet and that his intellectual interests, thus closely integrated to his calling, were both wide and genuine. "Every page," said Johnson, who surmised that Dryden acquired his extensive knowledge rather from conversation than from reading, "every page discovers a mind very widely acquainted both with art and nature, and in full possession of great stores of in-

[15] *Essays*, ed. W. P. Ker, I, 183.   [16] *Ibid.*, p. 214.
[17] *Ibid.*, II, 36.   [18] *Ibid.*, p. 43.

tellectual wealth." [19] We must not be deluded by the charming small talk of the study which Dryden so often gives us — the careful balancing of the advantages and disadvantages of rhyme, the problem of the comic subplot, the synaloephas of Chapman's *Homer*, the "turns" of Mr. Waller and Sir John Denham to which Sir George Mackenzie had called his attention, the examination of tropes and figures and catachreses — we must not be deluded into supposing that his vital intellectual, or even artistic, interests were narrowly confined to matters of style and language. Dryden said often enough that style is more than technique, that "it must proceed from a genius, and a particular way of thinking"; his discussions of the styles of Lucretius, Horace, Juvenal, and Persius, touching as they do on the lives, social and political circumstances, personal characteristics, and philosophical tenets of these authors, are illustrative of both his theory and practice; and they might well be taken as models for appreciations of the style of Dryden himself. For Dryden believed that the man of letters must study many subjects besides style. He not only knew his *belles lettres*, but ranged extensively among the most unliterary books; he has a wealth of quotation, allusion, and anecdote, much of it from obscure sources as yet untraced by any editor of his work. To describe such a man as a mere polisher of phrases, and devoid of wide-ranging and serious intellectual interests, is a grave error in criticism; it is to give the reader exactly the wrong clue.

III

Dr. Johnson, who was by temperament and reading one of the best qualified critics Dryden has ever had, has remarked that "his compositions are the effects of a vigorous genius operating upon large materials." [20] It is the purpose of this study to inquire into the intellectual traits of that genius, and into the nature of the materials upon which it operated. It is our purpose to discover to what extent and in what ways Dryden was intellectually representative of his age; to ascertain what his essential temperament was, and to find what currents of thought in his time were es-

[19] *Lives of Poets*, ed. Birkbeck Hill (1905), I, 417.   [20] *Ibid.*, p. 457.

pecially congenial to him; in short, whether he belonged to any significant intellectual milieu.

Changeableness is beyond dispute one of the dominant characteristics of his mind. But we must be careful not to conclude hastily that this observation is in itself a moral appraisal; it may be profitable to adopt a more neutral procedure than the time-worn one of dwelling on Dryden's inconsistencies in criticism, religion, and politics, and explaining them as prudential accommodations to changing fashions. We shall better understand the nature of his mind if, to begin with, we consider some less important episode, such as cannot by any chance raise suspicions of a sordid motive. A passage in the dedication to *Aureng-Zebe* (1676) may serve. Some of the ladies had criticized as unnatural the conduct of Indamora and Melesinda in the last act. The problem was not one of vast importance, but Dryden gallantly consented to examine their representations:

That which was not pleasing to some of the fair ladies in the last act of it, as I dare not vindicate, so neither can I wholly condemn, till I find more reason for their censures. . . . I have made my Melesinda in opposition to Nourmahal, a woman passionately loving of her husband, patient of injuries and contempt, and constant in her kindness, to the last; and in that, perhaps, I may have erred, because it is not a virtue much in use. Those Indian wives are loving fools, and may do well to keep themselves in their own country, or, at least, to keep company with the Arrias and Portias of old Rome: Some of our ladies know better things. But, it may be, I am partial to my own writings; yet I have laboured as much as any man, to divest myself of the self-opinion of an author; and am too well satisfied of my own weakness, to be pleased with anything I have written. But, on the other side, my reason tells me, that, in probability, what I have seriously and long considered may be as likely to be just and natural, as what an ordinary judge (if there be any such among those ladies) will think fit, in a transient presentation, to be placed in the room of that which they condemn. The most judicious writer is sometimes mistaken, after all his care; but the hasty critic, who judges on a view, is full as liable to be deceived. Let him first consider all the arguments, which the author had, to write this, or to design the other, before he arraigns him of a fault; and then, perhaps, on second thoughts, he will find his reason oblige him to revoke his censure. Yet, after all, I will not be too positive. *Homo sum, humani a me nihil alienum puto.* As I am a man, I must be changeable: and sometimes the gravest of us all are so, even upon ridiculous accidents. Our minds are perpetually wrought on by the temperament of our bodies; which makes me suspect, they are nearer allied, than either our philosophers or school-divines will allow them to be. I have observed, says Montaigne, that when the body is out of order, its companion is seldom at his ease. An ill dream, or a cloudy day, has power to change this wretched creature, who is so proud of a reasonable soul, and make him think what he thought not yesterday. And Homer was of this opinion, as Cicero is pleased to translate him for us —

> Tales sunt hominum mentes, quali pater ipse
> Jupiter auctifera lustravit lampade terras.

Or, as the same author, in his "Tusculan Questions," speaks, with more modesty than usual, of himself: *Nos in diem vivimus; quodcunque animos nostros probabilitate percussit, id dicimus.* It is not therefore impossible, but that I may alter the conclusion of my play, to restore myself into the good graces of my fair critics; and your lordship,[21] who is so well with them, may do me the office of a friend and patron, to intercede with them on my promise of amendment.[22]

Were ever fair ladies so perplexed by banter? And could anything be more characteristic of Dryden?

But, in small affairs as in great, Dryden's hesitancy is something more positive than indecision; it is less a weakness of will than a richness and suppleness of intellect. Dryden dearly loved a debate; he ornamented his plays with stretches of resonant argument, and his genius sustained both sides with such impartiality that we are often puzzled which is intended to receive the palm of victory. There are those who regard as the final test of an idea its coherent relation within a unified system. Dryden preferred to see it tested in a vigorous combat with its opposite, each side putting forth its utmost force. He wrote, accordingly, not treatises, but essays and dialogues. Three of his most important works are in the latter form, in spite of the fact that in each case Dryden had a partisan interest. In *An Essay of Dramatic Poesy* Neander is his spokesman; but the ideas of Neander are presented with no more force and art than those of the other three interlocutors.

---

[21] The Earl of Mulgrave.   [22] *Works,* V, 197–200.

Political ideas are expressed in *Absalom and Achitophel* very largely by discussion and argument, and no one can say that the Whiggism there presented, whatever its morality may be, is intellectually contemptible. The plan of *The Hind and the Panther* permitted of a vigorous recapitulation of the arguments used on both Catholic and Anglican sides in the enormous pamphlet war of the time. And one might add that *Religio Laici*, even though not a debate, is a balancing of conflicting ideas, and that, Protestant though it be, it gives a clear and forceful expression of the main Catholic criticism of the Protestant doctrines regarding religious authority. As Dr. Johnson has observed, Dryden's mind was "always curious, always active." His apparent indecision is evidence, not of weakness, but of strength, of energy, of a versatile understanding. It is his distinction and his virtue.

This is only to speak after Dryden. He has himself told us that his temper was the opposite of the dogmatic and the magisterial, the traits of Hobbes and Lucretius, from whom he carefully distinguished himself in the Preface to *Sylvae* (1685):

If I am not mistaken, the distinguishing character of Lucretius (I mean of his soul and genius) is a certain kind of noble pride, and positive assertion of his opinions. He is everywhere confident of his own reason, and assuming an absolute command, not only over his vulgar reader, but even his patron Memmius. . . . These are the considerations, which I had of that author, before I attempted to translate some parts of him. And accordingly I laid by my natural diffidence and scepticism for a while, to take up that dogmatical way of his, which, as I said, is so much his character, as to make him that individual poet." [23]

It would be easy to multiply passages to show that Dryden understood the skeptical and diffident nature of his own mind. But more than that, Dryden recognized that his temperament found support and expression in a philosophy; he has repeatedly claimed kinship with skeptical tendencies in ancient and modern thought. Regarding the *Essay of Dramatic Poesy* he declared that

. . . my whole discourse was sceptical, according to that way of reasoning which was used by Socrates, Plato, and all the Academics of old, which Tully and the best of the Ancients followed, and

[23] *Essays*, ed. W. P. Ker, I, 259–260.

which is imitated by the modest inquisitions of the Royal Society. That it is so, not only the name will show, which is *an Essay*, but the frame and composition of the work. You see it is a dialogue sustained by persons of several opinions, all of them left doubtful, to be determined by the readers in general.[24]

Such was his defense of the *Essay* in 1668. In his Preface to *An Evening's Love* (1671) he asked, "Why should there be any *Ipse dixit* in our poetry, any more than there is in our philosophy?" Finally, in the Preface to *Religio Laici* (1682) he tells us explicitly that he was "naturally inclined to skepticism in philosophy."

Such was the intellectual cast of Dryden. His contact with philosophical skepticism enabled him to rationalize his natural diffidence of temper. Though he has no claim to originality as a thinker, he did possess a loose group of ideas and philosophical doctrines which he understood and to which he felt himself affined. They constitute an essential part of his personality, both as a man and as a writer; to them Dryden was attracted by his "genius," his "particular way of thinking," and through them his intellectual character was formed. Their pervasive influence is evident wherever Dryden made any important intellectual decisions, whether in politics, religion, or philosophy — most evident, perhaps, in his conversion to Catholicism. They drew him quite naturally into certain currents of thought of the century. He lived in an age of philosophical skepticism; every reader of any pretensions to cultivation knew Montaigne and Charron intimately, and almost every scholar had read Sextus Empiricus. Neither Dryden nor his age can be fully understood apart from this Pyrrhonism, diffused in every department of thought, lending itself to the most diverse purposes, appearing sometimes in strange guises and in the most unexpected places.

[24] *Ibid.*, p. 124.

CHAPTER II

THE TRADITIONS OF SKEPTICISM

i Greek   ii Medieval and Christian   iii The sixteenth century:
Montaigne   iv The seventeenth century: Pascal
v The seventeenth century: Browne

SKEPTICISM [1] in the seventeenth century cannot be appreciated as an historical force if it is defined narrowly as a philosophical system. It was protean in nature, as much a group of tendencies as a system. It had popular as well as learned traditions, and it appealed to the most heterogeneous authorities, both ancient and modern. Primarily it was, of course, the philosophy of Pyrrho, the reputed founder of the Greek sect, which had been transmitted to the modern world through the writings of Sextus Empiricus. But in the welter of Renaissance thought this Greek philosophy was frequently associated with various other traditions of a disruptive or anti-rational nature, which under its influence might in this way be further developed and clarified. Thus the warnings issued by Solomon and St. Paul and the Church Fathers against the vanity of worldly knowledge might lead the pious Christian apologist to a respectful reading of Sextus Empiricus. Various medieval developments, such as Nominalism and mysticism, had already popularized a distrust of the reason as an organ of religious knowledge. Among other influences of a disruptive nature may be mentioned the influx of Arabian thought and the attacks on Aristotle and on the syllogism. We may therefore expect the skepticism of the sixteenth and seventeenth centuries to

[1] It should be understood that the "skepticism" discussed in this volume is not the same as "religious unbelief." It is philosophical skepticism, that is, anti-rationalism. But inasmuch as it advanced a theory regarding the possibility or impossibility of knowledge, it had its applications to all realms of thought, to ethics, politics, science, as well as to the theory of Christian evidences. It is, of course, these numerous and various applications, more than the basic theory of knowledge, which command the attention of the student of the seventeenth century.

be of innumerable kinds and shades; it was as complex and various as a climate.

Many of these developments do not interest the metaphysician who is concerned with skepticism purely as a dialectic; he would reject them as not skeptical at all in the strict philosophical sense. But the historian is not permitted to be so selective in his method. Ideas which in their origins were unrelated may by the accident of history come to be associated, and thus sometimes gain in profundity, sometimes even receive new significance and intention. If the study of the history of ideas is to illuminate literature, it must concern itself not only with those major developments which attained a high degree of clarity and consistency, but also with those which to the philosopher seem second-rate and immature, even those which he would discard as mere unphilosophical prejudices.

These observations are particularly applicable to the study of skepticism in the general culture of the sixteenth and seventeenth centuries. Skepticism existed in that age in all possible forms of immaturity and development, and one form of it might even appear in opposition to another. Its adherents were often at variance with one another, and sometimes with themselves. The skeptical argument might by the same man sometimes be pressed hard to its logical conclusion, sometimes be moderated to a mild form of anti-rationalism. To limit an historical investigation to skepticism full blown is to pluck the one bright flower and ignore the rest of the plant.

I

Not until the eighteenth century, however, did modern skepticism make any profound advance over the essential dialectic of the Greeks. The whole argumentative procedure relied on in the seventeenth century was to be found in the writings of Sextus Empiricus, who lived about 200 A.D., and who, coming thus late, gave something like a summary statement to five hundred years of Greek skeptical philosophy. The history of the sect was obscure, but its great names enjoyed a considerable reputation and authority, vague as it was, when the school again became influential in the Renaissance.

The most celebrated was, of course, Pyrrho of Elis, who, after taking part in Alexander's campaign to India, settled in his native city and taught that seeking after knowledge is vain, and that indifference to all philosophical assertions is the only way to peace of mind. Against every proposition, according to Pyrrho, the wise man will balance its contrary and consequently, by showing the futility of both, arrive at the happy state of imperturbability (*ataraxia*). But the main interest of Pyrrho was in his ethical teaching, to which this argument was the preparation. He held that, since no moral standard can be established by reason, the wise man will conform to the laws and conventions he finds about him. Thus the first great skeptic was, like many of his successors, a conservative in social and political matters. But he left no philosophical writings, and it is difficult to decide precisely how far he developed the doctrine of skepticism.

Arcesilaus and Carneades, who represent the New Academy, wrote treatises which have been lost. Their doctrines, ascertainable to some degree from Cicero and Diogenes Laertius, represent a milder form of skepticism. A return to a more rigorous Pyrrhonism appeared with Aenesidemus, but his works have also been lost. The writings of Sextus Empiricus are, therefore, with the exception of fragments quoted by ancient authors, the sole literary remains of Greek skepticism; his two treatises, *The Pyrrhonic Hypotyposes* and *Against the Mathematicians*, exercised upon the modern world the force and fascination of a philosophical novelty.

In these treatises the Renaissance found the most thorough and systematic demonstration yet attempted of the relativity of all knowledge, and of the futility of philosophizing. All knowledge, such was the argument, is built up from sense impressions, and who can test the reliability of the senses? Such imperfect examination of them as it is within our power to make — a comparison of men with one another and of men with lower animals — tends only to show that our senses are defective and can give us but an inadequate, and often false, impression of the world about us. In support of this contention the skeptics gathered abundant examples: the square tower appears round from a distance; the straight stick appears crooked in water; the sick and the well palate taste differently; such phenomena as meteors are terrifying only because they are rare; and hundreds of others. The skeptics therefore concluded that our impressions of phenomena, though admittedly real, cannot be regarded as genuine knowledge of things as they are. Having established this basic principle, they naturally went further and attacked also all deductions from sense impressions, all forms of dogmatic or confident assertion, whether in logic, in ethics, or in medicine. They pointed to the inconsistencies and contradictions among philosophers and scientists as sufficient demonstration that no one doctrine can be regarded as more true than another, and that the search for criteria of truth is only an attempt to know the unknowable. In the place of such stiff dogmatism — and the ancient skeptics were especially given to criticizing the high authoritative manner of the Stoics — these doubters adopted more humble formulas of expression: "I know nothing"; "Nothing can be known with certainty"; "Perhaps yes, perhaps no." In this state of equilibrium, of suspended judgment, with calm resignation to the unknowableness of truth, the skeptics sought for that inner peace which is the only attainable intellectual satisfaction.

Like Pyrrho, most of the other Greek skeptics were primarily interested in the consequences of their argument for ethics. Any science of ethics was obviously impossible. The philosophers have never agreed on the *summum bonum;* no moral pronouncement has ever been made to which one cannot juxtapose its opposite; the Persians permit sons to marry their mothers; the Egyptians, brothers to marry their sisters; the Greeks forbid both such marriages. Gods of all varieties are worshiped with equal sincerity by the different peoples of the world. The skeptic is unable to affirm that one is preferable, in any absolute sense, to another. He balances one against the other, and concludes that all man can know is that he can know nothing.

However upsetting these doctrines were, their practical outcome was the very opposite of revolutionary. For since true knowledge is unattainable, it is futile to argue or quarrel over it, to sacrifice comfort or life for it; it is as well to conform to the custom of the country, to worship the gods as they are worshiped by the others; neither you nor anyone else can demonstrate that you would be wrong. Conduct yourself as a prudent man of sense and live as others live. In the modern world, as among the Greeks, the Skeptic has often been a traditionalist, conservative in temper, a defender of the established order in politics and society, and a conformist in religion and practical conduct.[2]

II

Throughout the Middle Ages the skeptical philosophy of antiquity remained practically unknown. Some echoes of it from Cicero, Augustine, and the *Noctes Atticae* of Aulus Gellius can be traced in the *Polycraticus* (Book VII) of John of Salisbury, in Henry of Ghent, and in Siger of Brabant, all of whom *per contra* demonstrated the necessity of believing in the efficacy of the reason; but their discussions are superficial, and their knowledge of ancient skepticism is necessarily extremely vague and fragmentary. A curious manuscript of the *Hypotyposes* of Sextus Empiricus, in a bad Latin translation, dating from the Middle Ages, has indeed been found in the Bibliothèque Nationale,[3] but it is an isolated phenomenon. The Middle Ages did not even know the names of Pyrrho and Sextus Empiricus.

Nevertheless that period was not without its own forms of anti-rationalism. That ambitious effort to explain the whole universe in one coherent intellectual system, which reached its highest level in the philosophy of Aquinas, provoked the vigorous and penetrating criticism of Duns Scotus and William of Occam; and this opposition of Nominalism to the orthodox and official philosophy of Realism stimulated in the late Middle Ages some very important developments of an anti-rationalistic nature. For the Nominalists, although they were not skeptics, tended to minimize the importance of reason in religious experience and to separate the spheres

[2] The best account of Greek skepticism, and the one to which I am chiefly indebted, is the famous volume by Victor Brochard, *Les Sceptiques grecs* (Paris, 1887; reprinted 1923).

[3] See Charles Jourdain, "Sextus Empiricus et la Philosophie Scolastique," *Excursions historiques et philosophiques à travers le Moyen Âge* (Paris, 1888), pp. 201–217. To this essay I am indebted for the information in this paragraph.

of theology and philosophy; theology, they began to say, is not a science. The certitude of faith is of a different kind from that of reason. Such argument naturally moved in the direction of skepticism, in the direction of "fideism," an error which the Church began to condemn as early as 1348.[4] The irrepressible, though condemned, Nominalists thus left a legacy of anti-rationalism for a later age to appropriate and use in its own way.[5]

These Nominalists were, on the whole, pious and sincere Christians, some of them notable mystics; they separated reason and faith only in order to liberate the latter. But there were others who made the same cleavage with a more ambiguous purpose, whose pretence to a pious intention was only a cover and an excuse for a free exercise of philosophical speculation. By drawing a distinction between theological and philosophical truth they could assert a doctrine as true philosophically, though, with submission to ecclesiastical authority, they would admit that it was false in theology. This conception of the double truth, introduced into European thought in the thirteenth century by Averroës,[6] was sen-

---

[4] The "philosophical errors" of Nicholas d'Autricourt, recanted by him in 1348, are given by H. Denzinger, *Enchiridion Symbolorum*, 10th ed. (Fribourg, 1908), pp. 221–222. They include the following: 1 . . . Quod de rebus per apparentia naturalia quasi nulla certitudo potest haberi; 9 . . . quod certitudo evidentiae non habet gradus; 10 . . . quod de substantia materiali alia ab anima nostra non habemus certitudinem evidentiae; 11 . . . quod excepta certitudine fidei non erat alia certitudo nisi certitudo primi principii vel quae in primum principium potest resolvi.

[5] It may be worth repeating here that medieval thought continued to be studied throughout the sixteenth and seventeenth centuries. Its forms and phraseology were part of the idiom of the time. Thus even Abraham Cowley identified that tree in the garden of Eden whose forbidden fruit brought all our woe, with the *Arbor Porphyrii*, which bore the fruit of Realism:

"That right *Porphyrian Tree* which did true *Logick* shew,
Each *Leaf* did learned *Notions* give,
And th' *Apples* were *Demonstrative* . . .
The onely *Science* Man by this did get,
Was but to *know* he nothing *Knew*. . . ."

In this "railing against the dogmatists" Cowley shows not a trace of Sextus Empiricus; he speaks as a belated Nominalist, denouncing the Realists. See his poem, *The Tree of Knowledge*, in *Poems*, ed. A. R. Waller (Cambridge, 1905), p. 45.

[6] In 1277 a large number of heretical doctrines taught at the University of Paris were formally condemned, including many Averroistic propositions which asserted the distinction discussed here: "Anima separata non est alterabilis se-

sationally popularized early in the sixteenth century by Pomponazzi (1462–1525), professor of philosophy at Bologna, who, defending himself against the charge of heresy, answered: "I believe as a Christian what I cannot believe as a philosopher." Henceforth this defense became notoriously common among the emancipated wits of the Renaissance; it became a commonplace of sophistication. But the theory of the double truth was not confined to the proponents of dangerous new speculation; it proved also to be a useful weapon for the orthodox. Although condemned by the Lateran Council of the 19th of December, 1512, it appeared frequently among French Catholic writers after 1540 who engaged in a polemic against the new Protestant appeal to the judgment of the individual.[7] Thus this heresy, somewhat developed under the influence of the newly revived skeptical thought of antiquity, was pressed into the service of the Church, to demonstrate the dangerousness of confiding in the judgment of the individual and to teach the reason to bow submissively to the authority of faith.[8]

Some authority for this argument was to be found in Christian doctrine and the Church Fathers. From the time of St. Paul the Christian religion had had to establish itself in opposition to Greek and Roman philosophy; and the early leaders of the Church could appeal to many a text in St. Paul to prove that pride of intellect must be vanquished before the soul can admit that true knowledge which is from God. It must not be supposed that St. Paul and most of the Fathers were philosophical skeptics; but the fact was

---

cundum philosophiam, licet secundum fidem alteretur. — Quod naturalis philosophus simpliciter debet negare mundi novitatem, quia nititur causis et rationibus naturalibus: fidelis autem potest negare mundi aeternitatem, quia nititur causis supernaturalibus. — Quod creatio non est possibilis, quamvis contrarium sit tenendum secundum fidem. — Quod resurrectio futura non debet credi a philosopho, quia impossibilis est investigari per rationem. Error, quia philosophus debet captivare intellectum in obsequium fidei." — See Ernst Renan, *Averroès et l'Averroïsme*, pp. 273–275.

[7] Henri Busson, *Les Sources et le développement du rationalisme dans la littérature française de la Renaissance (1533–1601)*, (Paris, 1922), has studied thoroughly the influence of the Paduan School on French thought, and frequently emphasizes the fideistic development due to it. See, e.g., pp. 55, 258, 384–385, 428, and 435, n. 1.

[8] M. Busson therefore counts among the representatives of Paduan fideism, not only Montaigne, but also La Mothe Le Vayer and Pascal. See *op. cit.*, p. 619.

not lost on modern skeptics that it was possible to collect a multitude of passages from these high authorities to show that skepticism, of all philosophies, was the best introduction to the mysteries of religion. La Mothe Le Vayer devoted some pages to this subject in his *De la vertu des payens* (1642); contending that pagan philosophies can be of real value to the Christian life, provided they are "circumcised," he comes in turn to the sect of skepticism:

However, though it is undeniable that this Philosophy [Skepticism] needs, like the others, to be purged of many faults, even of its impiety, which requires a pretty rigorous circumcision; nevertheless I also believe that, after such abridgment, this philosophy is possibly one of the least contrary to Christianity and the one which can accept most submissively the mysteries of our Religion. What obliges me to make such a statement is principally the outcry of all the Church Fathers against the dogmatic philosophers, whom they have generally denominated the Patriarchs of the Heretics. . . That is why Saint Gregory, distinguished by the cognomen of Theologian, says that these dogmatists have been to the Church as Egyptian plagues, by which it has been afflicted in every possible way. In fact, people like Decius and Julian, or the other famous persecutors, have never made the Church suffer so much by open use of force as have many of the learned and famous philosophers by their subtle disputes and by the guile of their writings. But everyone knows that they were prompted to that sort of thing chiefly by that presumption and obstinacy, of which Skepticism is so much the declared leading enemy that it may be called for that reason a philosophy favorable to the Faith, because it destroys that which is most contrary to this mediator of our salvation. For Saint Paul has repeated nothing so often in all his Epistles as the warning to flee from the vanity of learning and the delusions made use of by the philosophers when they base their opinions on axioms and on elements of the material world which have nothing in common with the doctrine of Jesus Christ. Such advice he gave to the Romans, the Hebrews, the Ephesians, the Galatians, and in general to all those whom he honored with his letters. But the Skeptics have never spoken more vigorously against the pride of the Dogmatists than he did to the Corinthians, advising them that it is necessary to be foolish and ignorant according to the World to be wise and understanding according to God, in whose sight the greatest learning and the most acute sapience appear only as pure folly. For, so this sacred Vessel continues, if anyone thinks that he truly knows something, he does in fact not know even in what manner he should know that which he must know. In all soberness, it is fairly difficult to pay the deference due to these Apostolic precepts without valuing highly the modest suspension of opinion of the Skeptics, and without detesting the arrogance of other sects in maintaining the infallible certainty of their maxims. . . . We are saying here only what is in conformity with the best theology, for that of Saint Denis expounds nothing more explicitly than the feebleness of our intellect and its ignorance regarding all divine matters. . . . I also find the opinion of Saint Augustine very weighty on general moral questions. He shows in Book XVIII of his *City of God* that we should rather receive from Divine Authority those precepts which determine what is vice or virtue than rely on human reason, which is neither powerful enough nor uniform enough to command universal obedience. There is no act so vicious, as he well observed, that it has not been approved by some philosopher, and no act so virtuous but that some members of this profession have condemned it. . . . Such are the considerations that have made me think so favorably about a philosophy which I do not believe is more an offender than others, provided one compels it to yield that deference which all philosophies owe to Holy Theology, and provided that, as a hand maiden only, it is called along with the others into the service of this divine mistress.[9]

Among the Patristic influences Augustinianism was by far the most important for the fideistic tendencies of the sixteenth and seventeenth centuries. The nature of Augustine, as well as his influence on Christian thought, was, of course, far from simple; he represented also an intellectualism which found its greatest expression in Thomas Aquinas. But he has stimulated in all ages a religious feeling which, in its fervent leaning on a personal God, was not only unintellectual but often anti-intellectual. This pietism of Augustine found its disciples in certain evangelical and mystical movements within medieval Catholicism, in Protestantism in general, and particularly Calvinism, and in the Jansenist movement in France in the seventeenth century. The Augustinian doctrine of grace, according to which the intellectual as well as the moral faculties of man are in their present fallen state totally useless toward salvation, had both in Augustine and among his followers an effect parallel to philosophical skepticism. In the Protestant churches, however, where the appeal of the Church had to be to the intelligence, and even the learning, of the individual, by way

[9] Trans. from *Œuvres* (Paris, 1656), I, 646–649.

of opposition to the authority of the Roman Catholic Church, this fideism could not easily pass into a complete Pyrrhonism. But in many Catholic writers, such as Pascal, the transition from Augustinianism to skepticism was natural and unchecked. In fact, one can find in Augustine himself a fideism and authoritarianism definitely based on skeptical principles; Catholic controversialists in the sixteenth and seventeenth centuries could easily quote, for the purposes of embarrassing his avowed Protestant disciples, statements that he believed in the Gospel only because of the authority of the Church.[10]

But the doctrine of the fall of man, even when it was given a milder interpretation than the Augustinian, might find useful support in the skeptical argument. A book which enjoyed considerable reputation among English Catholics in the seventeenth century was Thomas Fitzherbert's *Treatise concerning Policy and Religion*.[11] This Catholic gentleman of Staffordshire, living in exile after 1588, devoted himself to the Church, first in Spain, then in Rome, where he ultimately entered the priesthood. In the dedication of the *Treatise* to his son, he asks him to observe in it especially three points, "the natural imbecillity of man's wit," "the course of God's providence in the affaires of men," and "the severe Iustice of God in the punishment of sinne." It is the first point that concerns us, and particularly Fitzherbert's grounds for his doctrine. "To the end," he says, "that the natural infirmitie of man, and his ignorance may the better appeare, the cause therof is first to be considered, for so we shal the better understand the effect." He first states the theological doctrine:

Therefore although man at his first creation, had al the powers of his soule vigorous, & perfect in their nature, prompt, and readie to the execution of their functions, as his reason & vnderstanding cleare, his wil and affection ordinate, and inclyned to good, and his

[10] Such remarks as "Ego vero evangelio non crederem, nisi me catholicae [ecclesiae] commoverat auctoritas." See Adolf von Harnack, *History of Dogma*, English translation (London, 1898), V, 77 ff. On the similarity of Pascal to Lactantius and Augustine see Edouard Droz, *Le Scepticisme de Pascal* (Paris, 1886), pp. 282–296.

[11] First published in parts, 1606 and 1610, and reprinted in 1615, 1652, and 1696. The British Museum has a copy of the last edition, which was once owned by Mary of Modena.

sensual powers so bridled by original iustice, that they yealded due obedience to reason: yet when original iustice was lost by the fal of our first father Adam, and the light of Gods grace extinguished, not only reason was much weakened, and the wil disordred, but also the sensual powers so corrupted, or rather infected, that they haue euer since runne head-long to their obiects with such violence, that they commonly draw the wil after them, ...

Then follows the appeal to skepticism, not as set forth by Sextus Empiricus in this case, but the skepticism of the New Academy which Fitzherbert had learned from Cicero:

Hereto I may adde also another reason of the error in mans vnderstanding, to wit, the difficultie of the obiect therof, for that truth, (which is the obiect of the vnderstanding) is not only in-uolued, and wrapped like the kernel of the nutte, in so many shells & rindes of abstruse doubtes and difficulties, that many times it is hardly found, but also it is so incountred with falsehood and error, disguised with the shew & apparence of veritie, that the best wittes are often deceaued therewith; and therefore no maruaile if the wisest men of the world doe many times goe astray, stumble, & fal into the obscuritie of the manifold, and intricate doubtes, questions, controuersies, perplexities, & vncertaine euentes that daylie occurre in humaine affaires.

This the wisest Philosophers did so wel consider, that many of them affirmed; that nothing in this world can certainly be knowne and vnderstood, by reason of the error in mans senses, imbecilitie of their wittes, breuitie of their liues, and the obscuritie of truth; of which opinion were Socrates, Plato, Democritus, Anaxagoras, Empedocles, and al the new Academicks; [12] in so much that Socrates was iudged by the Oracle, to be the wisest man then liuing, because he was wont to say, *Hoc solum scio, quod nihil scio. I know only this, that I know nothing;* wherto Archesilaus added, that not so much as that could be knowne, which Socrates said he knewe, to wit: that he knewe nothing. And although these Philosophers may seeme to haue exceeded in exaggerating the ignorance of man (thereby to represse, & correct, as it may be thought, the presumption that many men had of their owne knowledge, & wisdome) yet they sufficiently signified therby, their conceit of the weaknes of mans iudgment, and imbecilitie of his wit.[13]

Fitzherbert refuses to go the whole distance with the more extreme skeptics, but, like the later La Mothe Le Vayer, though less deeply

[12] In margin: "*Cicero. Acad. quest. lib. 1. & 2.*"   [13] Ed. 1615, pp. 3–5.

read in the subject, he regards a moderate Pyrrhonism as an excellent preparation for the Evangel. His book provides us with one more bit of evidence as to the wide diffusion and almost inevitable growth of fideism at this time.

It is therefore not surprising that, when ancient skepticism was rediscovered and popularized in the sixteenth century, it was readily assimilated by such medieval and patristic traditions and its new argumentative resources turned to old and familiar polemical purposes. It provided an armory of weapons for those who thought that anti-rationalism or fideism was the soundest defense of religion. But they were dangerous weapons even to the side that used them; they were officially condemned by the Roman Catholic Church. Nevertheless her apologists continually employed them against Protestantism and rationalism, the two most dangerous enemies of the Roman Catholic Church in the Renaissance. And thus the arguments of Pyrrho and Sextus Empiricus appeared on the same page with appeals to St. Paul and the Fathers, in defense of the Christian religion in general and of the Roman Catholic Church in particular. The renowned exponents of this apologetic in the sixteenth century were Francis Pico della Mirandola, Francis Sanchez, and Montaigne, and in the seventeenth, Charron, La Mothe Le Vayer, Pascal, and Huet. Within this tradition, also, lies what is most characteristic in Dryden's ideas on religion.

III

The bibliography of Sextus Empiricus does not suggest any wide diffusion of his thought before 1700. The Greek text of his treatises was first printed at Geneva in 1621, and this *editio princeps* sufficed for all Europe until the edition of Fabricius in 1718.[14] More important in its influence was the publication by Henri Stephen of his own Latin translation of the *Hypotyposes* in Paris in 1562, which was reprinted in 1569 with a Latin version of the *Adversus Mathematicos* by Gentian Hervet. Thomas Stanley published an English translation of the *Hypotyposes* in his *History of*

---

[14] Neither does it appear to have been easily accessible in manuscript form in the sixteenth century. The few manuscripts extant have been described briefly by Herman Mutschmann, in his edition of Sextus Empiricus (Leipzig, 1912–14).

Philosophy (1655–61; second edition, 1687), and a French translation was made by Samuel Sorbière (1615–70). These few
publications, most of them coming so late in the period, do not
indicate any momentous skeptical revival. Perhaps many readers
contented themselves with the succinct but definite descriptions
of skeptical doctrine in Diogenes Laertius, and many others with
Cicero's exposition of the thought of the New Academy. But the
real explanation seems rather to be that the *ipsissima verba* of the
ancient writers were eclipsed and rendered superfluous, at least for
the general reader, by the celebrated works of their Renaissance
disciples. All the arguments and proofs of Sextus Empiricus were
to be found restated there, along with a multitude of startling new
ones collected by modern wits in an age when the knowledge of
the world was ever expanding. The diffusion of skepticism in this
period is explained by the popular acceptance of such writers as
Montaigne and Charron. But it began before Montaigne, even
before anything by Sextus had appeared in print.

Gian-Francesco Pico della Mirandola, nephew of the renowned
Giovanni Pico, became alarmed over the growth of humanism,
with its tendency to exalt pagan thought and neglect Christianity.
He therefore published in 1520 an assault on the human reason
and human learning: *Examen Vanitatis Doctrinae Gentium et
Veritatis Christianae Disciplinae, distinctum in libros sex: quorum
tres priores omnem philosophorum sectam universim, reliqui Aris-
toteleam et Aristotelis armis particulatim impugnant, ubicumque
autem christiana et asseritur et celebratur disciplina*. He divided all
philosophers into three groups: the dogmatists, who affirm; the
academics, who deny and therefore are but negative or inverted
dogmatists; and the skeptics or Pyrrhonians, who neither affirm
nor deny, but doubt. He declared himself an adherent of the last
sect, and borrowed his whole method of argument from Sextus
Empiricus, whose work he had met with in manuscript. Man is
ever changeable, and his senses are deceptive; we can never get beyond our sensations to test them; all the sciences and arts abound
in contradictions which demonstrate their unreliability and futility. There is only one truth given to man the authoritativeness
of which the intellect is unable to question, and that is the truth of

revelation. Skepticism thus emancipates us from the vanity of pagan science and inducts us into Christian truth and discipline.[15]

Ten years after Pico's *Examen* there appeared a less philosophical, but also more popular, book with the same purpose: *De Incertitudine et Vanitate Scientiarum et Artium atque Excellentia Verbi Dei Declamatio*, by Cornelius Agrippa von Nettesheim. For two centuries this attack on the presumption of human learning reached a wide European public, both in the original Latin and in vernacular translations. Montaigne borrowed generously from it. But it is not truly Pyrrhonian, and possibly derives rather from the *docta ignorantia* of Nicholas of Cusa (1401–64) than from Pico and Sextus Empiricus. Its importance lies chiefly in that it was regarded by its later readers as an addition to the literature of *paradox*, a literary *genre* which frequently became a vehicle for skeptical thought and added to the spicy flavor of the modern skeptics, from Montaigne down.[16]

Between Agrippa and Montaigne there was in France — as M. Busson has shown — a continuous discussion of the vexing problem of the relation of philosophy and religion, of reason and faith. Under the influence of the Paduan school, this discussion frequently terminated in fideism, sometimes passing into the milder skepticism of the New Academy; as regards ancient influences, it owed more to Cicero than to Sextus Empiricus.[17] In the light of this continuous tradition we can more readily understand the almost simultaneous appearance of two essays of similar

[15] This account is based on Fortunat Strowski, *Montaigne* (Paris, 1906), pp. 124–130. Strowski thinks Montaigne had read Pico's book, but Pierre Villey finds no evidence for this supposition. See his *Les Sources et l'évolution des Essais de Montaigne* (Paris, 1908), II, 166.

[16] In the 1603 reprint of the French translation of Agrippa's book the title is changed from *Déclamation* to *Paradoxe*. La Mothe Le Vayer thought that paradoxes, although they had been written by philosophers of other sects, were peculiarly appropriate to skepticism: "Je recognois ingenuëment qu'il n'y a personne qui preste son oreille plus volontiers que moy aux opinions extraordinaires, et qu'avec ce que j'y puis avoir de naturelle disposition, ma Sceptique m'a beaucoup aydé à me donner cette inclination particuliere aux sentimens paradoxiques; comme celle qui sçait mieux que toute autre Philosophie les convertir à son advantage." — *Dialogues . . . par Oratius Tubero* (Frankfort, 1716), I, 327. Cf. also I, 171.

[17] Busson, *op. cit.*, throughout, but in particular pp. 109, 112, 262, 419–423, and 619–621. Also Villey, *op. cit.*, I, 89, and II, 169 ff.

tendency, Montaigne's *Apology for Raymond Sebond* (1580) and the *Quod Nihil Scitur* (1581) by Sanchez, professor of medicine at Montpellier.

Of these Montaigne's essay is of course the more important; it became the classic and standard exposition of modern skeptical thought. The shadow of his authority extends over the thought and literature of the whole seventeenth century, in England as well as in France.

Notwithstanding its title, the *Apology* is less related to Sebond's rationalistic defense of religion than it is to Sextus Empiricus. Montaigne considers two objections which had been made to Sebond's treatise. "The first thing he is reproved for in his Booke, is, that Christians wrong themselves much, in that they ground their beleefe upon humane reasons, which is conceived but by faith, and by a particular inspiration of God." [18] Montaigne replies that we should not receive our religion in mere sottishness, and be "Christians by the same title, as we are either Perigordians or Germans. . . . A goodly faith, that beleeves that which it beleeveth, onely because it wanteth the courage not to beleeve the same." [19] But faith must illuminate reason; and faith, "giving as it were a tincture and lustre unto Sebonds arguments, make them the more firme and solid: They may well serve for a direction and guide to a young learner, to lead and set him in the right way of this knowledge." [20] Thus the first objection is disposed of in ten pages.

But "some say his Arguments are weake, and simple to verifie what he would; and undertake to front him easily. Such fellowes must somwhat more roughly be handled: for they are more dangerous, and more malicious than the first. . . . The meanes I use to suppresse this frenzy, and which seemeth the fittest for my purpose, is to crush, and trample this humane pride and fiercenesse under foot, to make them feele the emptinesse, vacuitie, and no worth of man: and violently to pull out of their hands, the silly weapons of their reason; to make them stoope, and bite and snarle at the ground, under the authority and reverence of Gods Maj-

[18] *Essays*, trans. Florio, Tudor Translations (London, 1893), II, 130.
[19] *Ibid.*, pp. 135–136.   [20] *Ibid.*, p. 138.

esty." [21] This reply to the second objection requires more than two hundred pages. And here the rationalism of Sebond is forgotten; the dialectic of Sextus Empiricus takes its place.

"Let us then see whether man hath any other stronger reasons in his power, then Sebondes, and whether it lie in him, by argument or discourse, to come to any certainty." [22] Montaigne begins with a lesson in humility. "Presumption is our naturall and originall infirmitie." Presumption has led man to assume that he is master and lord of creation. But he cannot demonstrate that he is superior to animals. "When I am playing with my Cat, who knowes whether she have more sport in dallying with me, than I have in gaming with her? We entertaine one another with mutuall apish trickes. If I have my houre to begin or to refuse, so hath she hers." [23] Montaigne fills pages with amusing illustrations of how animals display "a very subtill spirit" and men do not, until the reader is indeed content to escape being placed in a category lower than the beasts.

But man possesses learning, which is surely a legitimate source of pride. Montaigne does not think so; learning is always dangerous and often useless. "I have in my daies seen a hundred Artificers, and as many labourers, more wise and more happie, than some Rectors in the Universitie, and whom I would rather resemble. Me thinks Learning hath a place amongst things necessarie for mans life, as glorie, noblenesse, dignitie, or at most as riches, and such other qualities, which indeed stead the same; but a far-off, and more in conceipt, than by Nature." [24] Learning puffeth up, whereas "onely humilitie and submission is able to make a perfect honest man. Every one must not have the knowledge of his dutie referred to his own judgment, but ought rather to have it prescribed unto him, and not be allowed to chuse it at his pleasure and free-will: otherwise according to the imbecilitie of our reasons, and infinite varietie of our opinions, we might peradventure forge and devise such duties unto our selves, as would induce us (as Epicurus saith) to endeavour to destroy and devoure one another.... The opinion of wisdome is the plague of man." [25]

[21] *Ibid.*, p.139. [22] *Ibid.*, p. 140. [23] *Ibid.*, p. 144.
[24] *Ibid.*, p. 188. [25] *Ibid.*, p. 189.

In no sphere of life is pride of intellect more dangerous, or humility more profitable, than in religion. For "it is not by our discourse or understanding, that we have received our religion, it is by a forreine authority, and commandement. The weaknesse of our judgment, helps us more than our strength to compasse the same, and our blindnesse more than our cleare-sighted eies. It is more by the meanes of our ignorance, than of our skill, that we are wise in heavenly knowledge." [26] Here Montaigne arrives at the heart of his subject and devotes some pages to a eulogy of Pyrrhonism as not only the wisest, but the most honest, of all philosophies. "Whosoever shall imagine a perpetuall confession of ignorance, and a judgement upright and without staggering, to what occasion soever may chance; That man conceives the true Phyrrhonisme." [27] It is, we learn, a comfortable philosophy; it not only gives us an inner tranquillity, but it also makes us tractable and enables us to live at peace with our neighbors, our government, and our established religion.

It is better for us to suffer the order of the world to manage us without further inquisition. A mind warranted from prejudice, hath a marvellous preferment to tranquility. Men that censure and controule their judges, doe never duly submit themselves unto them. How much more docile and tractable are simple and uncurious mindes found both towards the lawes of religion and Politike decrees, than these over-vigilant and nice wits, teachers of divine and humane causes? There is nothing in mans invention, wherein is so much likelyhood, possibilitie and profit [as in Pyrrhonism]. This representeth man bare and naked, acknowledging his naturall weaknesse, apt to receive from above some strange power, disfurnished of all humane knowledge, and so much the more fitte to harbour divine understanding, disannulling his judgment, that so he may give more place unto faith: Neither misbeleeving nor establishing any doctrine or opinion repugnant unto common lawes and observances, humble, obedient, disciplinable and studious; a sworne enemy to Heresie, and by consequence exempting himselfe from all vaine and irreligious opinions, invented and brought up by false Sects. It is a white sheet prepared to take from the finger of God what form soever it shall please him to imprint therein.[28]

[26] *Essays*, II, 204.   [27] *Ibid.*, p. 210.   [28] *Ibid*, pp. 211–212.

One may ask how a Pyrrhonist could with such confidence designate certain "Sects" as "false"; but the answer is that Montaigne had no taste for revolutions and reformations.

It is not wise to look for too definite an organization in an essay by Montaigne. But the *Apology*, notwithstanding its confusing exuberance of detail and illustration, does move consistently in one direction and with definite steps, as M. Villey has shown.[29] It moves toward a complete Pyrrhonism. The climax of the argument is a systematic attack on reason itself, for which Montaigne borrowed the destructive dialectic of Sextus Empiricus. He seems to have felt some misgivings about popularizing this dialectic, which should be used against the rationalistic enemies of religion, he says, only as a last resort. "You for whom I have taken the paines to enlarge so long a worke (against my custome) will not shun to maintaine your Sebond, with the ordinary forme of arguing, whereof you are daily instructed, and will therein exercise both your minde and study: For this last trick of fence, must not be employed but as an extreme remedy. It is a desperate thrust, gainst which you must forsake your weapons, to force your adversary to renounce his, and a secret slight, which must seldome and very sparingly be put in practise."[30] But Montaigne himself did not set an example of sparing use of the skeptical dialectic; it was too necessary to his temper of mind, too closely intertwined with his characteristic thought. It was the basis, not only of his philosophy of faith, but also of that quite different philosophy of his which made the *Essays* the *livre de chevet* of the "libertines," the philosophy of "Nature."

Montaigne had been, to begin with, a disciple of the Stoics, whose doctrine sustained so many elevated minds in the Renaissance. Under their influence he composed his first essays, which are doubtless less read than any other part of his work. But about 1576 he discovered Sextus Empiricus, probably in the 1562 translation by Henri Stephen.[31] His enthusiasm over his discovery was so great that early in 1576 he struck a medal to celebrate it; he decorated the walls of his tower study with mottoes from Sextus;

---

[29] *Op. cit.*, II, 185.   [30] *Essays*, Tudor Translations, II, 275.
[31] Villey, *op. cit.*, I, 218.

and he wrote the *Apology*. Aside from the *Apology*, however, the consequence of this intellectual crisis seems to have been mainly a new orientation in Montaigne's ethical thought. His experience was something like a delivery from an intellectual prison, the prison of Stoicism, in which he had never been at ease. He ceased to be a dogmatist in philosophy, in politics, in ethics, and became henceforth a follower of "Nature" — not the rigorous and normative conception of the Stoics, but his own nature, "supple et ondoyant." And thus the same skeptical argument which humbled the refractory reason before the inscrutable mysteries of religion, also served to liberate Montaigne and his disciples from a servitude to rigoristic ethics. "I study my selfe more than any other subject. It is my supernaturall Metaphisike, it is my naturall Philosophy. . . . Oh how soft, how gentle, and how sound a pillow is ignorance and incuriosity to rest a well composed head upon. I had rather understand my selfe well in my selfe, than in Cicero." [32] After 1576 Montaigne became the supreme exponent of Naturalism, the libertine Naturalism of the Renaissance. The *Essays* which so profoundly influenced the religious thought of Pascal inspired also the unedifying verse of Theophile, who imitated so perfectly both the temper and the ideas of Montaigne:

> I agree that everyone should always follow nature; her empire is pleasant and her law is not harsh. . . . I think that everyone would have sufficient mother wit if he followed the unconfined course which nature prescribes. . . . Never set yourself in opposition to the laws of nature. [33]

They became the bible of the sophisticated *beaux esprits* against whom Pére Garasse felt so bitter, and whose doctrine he has succinctly stated:

> There is no divinity or sovereign power on earth other than NATURE, which we are obliged to satisfy in everything, not refusing to our bodies or our senses anything that they desire from us in the exercise of their powers and natural faculties. [34]

Some of Montaigne's disciples were fideists, and some were libertines. And some of the libertines, when the heats of youth were

[32] *Essays*, III, 338–339.

[33] Trans. from Theophile, *Œuvres complètes*, ed. Alleaume (Paris, 1866), *Notice*, p. lxvi.

[34] *Ibid.*, p. xl.

over and religion became a more pressing concern, quite naturally accepted their faith on fideistic principles.

IV

Similar paradox obtains in the vogue of *De la sagesse*,[35] by Pierre Charron. Charron was a priest, and his intention was to present a Christian Stoicism. But he was also a friend and an admirer of Montaigne, and he incorporated in his book the wisdom of Pyrrhonism as well as that of Stoicism. Moreover, as he explained in his preface, divine wisdom did not come within the limitations he had chosen for his subject; he adopted the tone of a man of the world. No doubt the lesson of Stoicism was not entirely neglected by some readers, but the success of the book was among the *beaux esprits*, who read in it what was to their liking. Others attacked it as dangerous to religion; in his *Petit traité de sagesse*, first published in 1606, three years after Charron's death, he vigorously defended his skeptical attitude:

But to press [these Roman Catholic critics of Skepticism] further and show them that they do not well understand their business, I will inform them that this principle of mine, which it pleases them to call Pyrrhonism, is something more serviceable to piety and divine working than any other whatever, and very far from clashing with them, serviceable, I say, as much for the generation and propagation of piety as for conversion. Theology, even like mysticism, teaches us that to prepare the soul properly for God and his working, and to qualify it to receive the impression of the Holy Spirit, we must empty it, cleanse it, strip it, and denude it of all opinion, belief, inclination, make it like a white sheet of paper, dead to itself and the world, so that God may live and operate in it. . . . From which it appears that to plant and install Christianity in an unbelieving and infidel people, such as the Chinese are at present, it would be an excellent procedure to begin with these propositions and persuasions: that all the learning of the world is but vanity and falsehood; that the world is confused, torn, and debased by fantastic ideas fabricated in its own mind; that God has indeed created man to know the truth, but man can not know it unaided, not by any human means, unless God him-

[35] Printed in 1601 and frequently reprinted in the seventeenth century. English translation by Samson Leonard, 1606, 1615 ?, 1620 ?, 1630, 1658, and 1670; by George Stanhope, 1697 and 1707.

self, whose bosom is the abode of truth and who has bestowed on man the desire for truth, unless God himself reveal it, as he has done: but to prepare oneself for this revelation and make room for it, one must first renounce and expel all opinions and beliefs in which the mind has been already engaged and steeped, and approach truth with an understanding naked and cleansed and humbly submissive. Having fought and won this point and having converted people into something like the Academics and Pyrrhonians, one should bring forward the principles of Christianity, as delivered to us from Heaven, brought us by its Ambassador, completely assured of divine authority and confirmed at the time by so many miraculous proofs and undeniable witnesses.[36]

Thus Charron reconciled his book to the Faith and to his own conscience; but the faithful feared the treatise as seductively pagan, and left it to the *esprits forts*. [37]

The tradition and influence of Montaigne continue in the writings of François La Mothe Le Vayer (1583–1672), an intimate friend of Mlle. de Gournay, Montaigne's adopted daughter. In 1630 he published five *Dialogues faits à l'imitation des anciens* under the pseudonym of Orasius Tubero, followed in the next year by four more. They are at the same time libertine and fideistic. Le Vayer had read both Montaigne and Sextus Empiricus, and a whole library besides. His references are encyclopedic. But all his reading only convinced him more firmly of the futility and error of scientific dogmatism, including moral legislation and speculation. The familiar accent of Montaigne is recognizable at once:

After the Emperor Claudius had taken his niece Agrippina in marriage, incest was declared permissible by the Senate. And we are forced to admit that what is incest in our day was innocence in the early age of the world. The voyages of Americo Vespuccio have informed us that in all the West Indies no regard was paid in this matter to' blood relationship; Marco Polo maintains the same concerning the East Indies; and the Druses of Lebanon still live in this manner. As for the alleged observance of any such restriction by animals, we see every day that dogs, cats, and other such animals demonstrate the contrary.[38]

[36] Trans. from *Petit traité* (Paris, 1646), pp. 46-48.
[37] See Fortunat Strowski, *Pascal et son temps* (Paris, 1907), I, 159 ff.; and F. T. Perrens, *Les Libertins en France au XVIIe siècle*, 2d ed. (Paris, 1899), pp. 61-67.
[38] Trans. from *Dialogues* (Frankfort, 1716), I, 157.

Thus the Law of Nature and of Nations, which enjoyed such high authority in ethics and politics in the seventeenth century, is dissipated into a chimera. But Revelation must not be subjected to this sort of comparative study; the rôle of skepticism ends when it has led us to the portals of faith.

As for the charge that the Skeptical Philosophy is incompatible with Christianity, I am so far from yielding in any way to this slander that I glory in having led my mind and understanding to what would best prepare it for our true religion and render it capable of the mysteries of our faith. It must be understood that when we deny the verity and certitude which each practitioner wants to assert for his own science, and that by this denial we make all sciences suspect of vanity and deceit, we nevertheless say nothing prejudicial to our Christian Theology; although it also may sometimes improperly and after a fashion be denominated a science, still the most holy Doctors agree on the point that it is not really a science such as would require clear and evident principles from our understanding, in matters on which it derives almost all its principles from the mysteries of our faith, which is truly a gift from God, far surpassing the reach of the human mind. That is why, although in the sciences we accept easily the evidence for the principles known by our intellect, in our Theology we assent to divine principles by the direction of our will alone, which submits itself to God in all matters, in which submission consists the merit of the Christian Faith.[39]

In reading these disciples of Sextus Empiricus one is frequently led to recall the Nominalist doctrine that truth is not derived from Eternal Reason in God, but from His mysterious and incalculable will, and therefore is not subject to argument or reducible to any intellectual system.[40]

Le Vayer was a heavy writer and of the second rank at best; oblivion has overtaken his once famous work. But the next name in the succession of Montaigne is illustrious; Pascal was a brilliantly original genius. His *Pensées*, published posthumously in 1670, has always ranked as a classic of religious literature, and in the mind

---

[39] *Ibid.*, pp. 332–333.

[40] Mention may be made of the posthumous *Traité philosophique de la faiblesse de l'esprit humain* (1723), by Daniel Huet (1630–1721), bishop of Avranches. It is fideistic without any tendency toward libertine thought. But it comes too late to have any significance for this study.

of the modern reading public stands apart as something unique. His insight and feeling, his profundity, and his power of disturbing our most secret complacencies are his own. But, although he was not, like Montaigne and Le Vayer, conspicuously a man of books, he was nevertheless, by virtue of two important facts, definitely a product of the tradition we have been following: he was a disciple of Montaigne, and his religious orientation was in the Jansenist, that is, in the Augustinian, tradition. The stern spiritual discipline to which Pascal, in his Jansenist fervor, submitted himself, shielded him from the libertine tendencies in Montaigne. What attracted him to the *Essays* was the humility, the confession of ignorance, the psychological demonstration of the nullity of man, all of which accorded perfectly with the Jansenist doctrine of Grace. Montaigne's easy and mundane reduction of man to the level of animals was not, except in tone, inharmonious with the Augustinian view of the depravity of man. Though the Jansenists themselves were not Pyrrhonists, their greatest disciple had no difficulty in engrafting skepticism upon their characteristic doctrines. But what he borrowed from Montaigne was also transformed. He borrowed Montaigne's description of human nature, but not his complacent acceptance of the humiliating facts; doubt was not for Pascal a soft pillow, but a bed of suffering; he was intensely aware of the miseries of humanity, miseries in which he perceived also the grandeur of man above all creation. In suffering, he believed, the religious experience has its origin; in the miserable man divine grace may operate, to exalt and purify and sanctify. Such ministration to minds diseased was a phenomenon not very closely studied by Montaigne. Pascal raises in his readers the profoundest inquietudes, but he is also tenderly cautious not to leave them in despair. "It is equally dangerous," he says, "to man to know God without knowing his own wretchedness, and to know his own wretchedness without knowing God." [41]

It is no doubt necessary to speak with caution of the Pyrrhonism of Pascal; he was also a mathematician and physicist, and a born dialectician. A great scientist and reasoner is not likely to disavow completely his own distinguished powers. Pascal in-

[41] *Pensées*, trans. W. F. Trotter, Everyman's Library (London, 1931), p. 162.

deed recognized that reason has its place even in religion, but its dominion is not universal. "If we submit everything to reason, our religion will have no mysterious and supernatural element. If we offend the principles of reason, our religion will be absurd and ridiculous." [42] Even the submission of reason in religion should be a rational submission: "Reason would never submit, if it did not judge that there are some occasions on which it ought to submit. It is then right for it to submit, when it judges that it ought to submit. . . . There is nothing so conformable to reason as this disavowal of reason." [43] Notwithstanding such passages, we are justified in including Pascal among the fideists, most certainly, and in a general sense also among the Pyrrhonists. How thoroughly he had assimilated the argument of the *Apology for Raymond Sebond* is evident in the *Entretien avec M. de Saci*. And although he must have discarded promptly many of the *naïvetés* which figure so largely in the dialectic of Montaigne, his use of Pyrrhonism as a preparation to faith is essentially the method of his master. In his religious philosophy Pascal was neither a rationalist nor an intellectualist; he did not submit his faith to the authority of reason, nor did he think it possible to systematize it by force of intellect. His anti-rationalism in the higher levels of his thought becomes at once clearer if he is contrasted with Descartes, or with such a Cartesian as Malebranche. Pascal found fault with Descartes for wanting to think *always* as a geometrician, even when establishing philosophical truths in support of religion. To raise such a structure Pascal regarded as base flattery of the human reason, and as providing atheists with a false and an easily attacked conception of a religion which, in fact, does not pretend to be either clear or rational or demonstrable by argument. In the Scriptures, cries Pascal, God is called *Deus absconditus*. To perceive how strikingly opposite Pascal's thought was to Cartesianism, one has only to open the *Traité de morale* by Malebranche, published fourteen years after the *Pensées*:

The *Reason* which enlightens man is the *Word* or the wisdom of God himself. . . . The Reason I speak of is infallible, immutable,

---

[42] *Ibid.*, p. 78.   [43] *Ibid.*, pp. 77–78.

incorruptible. It should always govern; God himself observes it. ... Evidence, intelligence, is better than faith. For faith is passing, but intelligence endures eternally.[44]

The doctrine of the *Logos*, one of the most fertile and ascendent in Christian thought, was not incorporated into Pascal's projected apology for Christianity; one wonders what his commentary would have been on the opening of the Fourth Gospel. The fact seems incontrovertible, however one may choose to qualify the statement of it, that Pascal belongs in the tradition of Pyrrhonism.

v

Except Pascal, these French writers had, to a greater or less extent, also an audience in England and contributed to the pagan culture, the cynicism, the naturalistic ethics which gradually were diffused throughout English society, at least in the upper strata, before 1660. Their influence is traceable in the English literature of the time. But their peculiar fideistic argument seems not to have appealed widely to Englishmen of the early seventeenth century. The Anglican Church did not take a position which could be easily defended with the weapons of Pyrrhonism; it was at this time becoming more and more rationalistic. The *Apology for Raymond Sebond* and Hooker's *Ecclesiastical Polity* represent two divergent and irreconcilable types of religious thought. Among English Catholics, as will be seen in a later chapter, there developed a tradition of fideistic apologetics, but its influence was not great in the early part of the century.

It is therefore an occasion for surprise when we find one Anglican, Sir Thomas Browne, writing in his *Religio Medici* on the subject of Christian skepticism. But Browne did not pretend to anything official; he had merely written a private confession of faith, which he was forced to publish in 1643 because of previous unauthorized printings from an imperfect manuscript copy. His little book, he explained in the preface, was "a private Exercise directed to my self" and "what is delivered therein, was rather a memorial unto *me*, than an Example or Rule unto any other."

[44] Trans. from *Traite de morale*, ed. Henri Joly (Paris, 1882), pp. 1, 20.

The book immediately had a great vogue, not only in England, but on the Continent, where in a Latin translation it was appreciated for its substance rather than its style. It was no nine days' wonder; twenty years later a friend of Pepys declared that "in all his life these three books were the most esteemed and generally cried up for wit in the world — *Religio Medici*, Osborne's *Advice to a Son*, and *Hudibras*."[45] During the latter half of the century the book received the flattery of a host of imitative titles, among them *Religio Laici*, which is related to it in substance as well as in name.

Browne's basic skepticism as well as his informal essay style is suggestive of Montaigne.[46] He had the easy tolerance, the distrust of reasoning, the sense of the fluidity of opinion, which characterized the author of the *Essays*. He was content with his own religion, and content to let others retain theirs. "I could never divide myself from any man upon the difference of an opinion, or be angry with his judgement for not agreeing with me in that from which perhaps within a few days I should dissent myself."[47] Disputes and arguments, Browne thought, are no more reliable than pitched battles in settling doubtful points. "A man may be in as just possession of Truth as of a City, and yet be forced to surrender; 'tis therefore far better to enjoy her with peace than to hazard her on a battle." This unheroic attitude was not due to timidity, but to a conviction that truth had little to do with reason.

We do but learn to-day, what our better advanced judgements will unteach to-morrow; and *Aristotle* doth but instruct us, as *Plato* did him; that is, to confute himself. I have run through all sorts, yet find no rest in any: though our first studies and *junior* endeavours may style us Peripateticks, Stoicks, or Academicks,

---

[45] Pepys, *Diary*, Jan. 27, 1664.

[46] Joseph Texte, "La Descendance de Montaigne," *Études de littérature européenne* (Paris, 1898), pp. 51–93. In a manuscript note, preserved in the British Museum, Browne disavowed any obligations to Montaigne: ". . . when I penned that piece I had never read these leaves in that author, and scarce any more ever since." Quoted in Sir Thomas Browne's *Works*, ed. Simon Wilkin (London, 1835), II, 10, n. 6. But direct obligations need not be insisted on; such striking similarity without direct influence is in itself an evidence of the dissemination and vitality of the tradition of thought represented by both writers.

[47] *Works*, ed. Charles Sayle (London, 1904), I, 12.

yet I perceive the wisest heads prove, at last, almost all Scepticks, and stand like *Janus* in the field of knowledge.[48]

Our life is bounded on every side by the unknowable. The wisest understandings are tormented by unanswerable doubts, and we are unable to know one another, nay even ourselves. "No man can justly censure or condemn another, because indeed no man truly knows another. This I perceive in myself; for I am in the dark to all the world and my nearest friends behold me but in a cloud." "Our ends are as obscure as our beginnings; the line of our days is drawn by night, and the various effects therein by a pencil that is invisible.[49]

But Browne, true to the tradition of Montaigne, disciplines and humiliates his insubordinate reason only that Faith may rise triumphant. Within his own nature he observes a constant feud between passion, reason, and faith. "As the Propositions of Faith seem absurd unto Reason, so the Theorems of Reason unto Passion, and both unto Faith." Reason is constantly raising objections, demanding explanations: perhaps the combustion of Gomorrah was due to "an asphaltic and bituminous nature" of the lake; manna is now plentiful in Calabria, and where then was the miracle of the days of Moses? But these attempts to rationalize our knowledge, by seducing our reason, weaken our faith. It is better to remain in our ignorance and believe, than to strive for that knowledge which would make belief unnecessary. "The Devil played at Chess with me, and yielding a Pawn, thought to gain a Queen of me, taking advantage of my honest endeavours; and whilst I laboured to raise the structure of my Reason, he strived to undermine the edifice of my Faith."[50] Browne countered his artful adversary; he undermined his own reason, so that he might raise freely the structure of his faith.

Since I was of understanding to know we knew nothing [he says], my reason hath been more pliable to the will of Faith; I am now content to understand a mystery without a rigid definition, in an easie and Platonick decription. That allegorical decription of *Hermes*, pleaseth me beyond all the Metaphysical definitions of Divines; where I cannot satisfie my reason, I love to humour my

---

[48] *Works*, ed. Charles Sayle, I, 99.   [49] *Ibid.*, pp. 91, 62.   [50] *Ibid.*, pp. 31-32.

fancy. . . . Where there is an obscurity too deep for our Reason, 'tis good to sit down with a description, periphrasis, or adumbration; for by acquainting our Reason how unable it is to display the visible and obvious effects of nature, it becomes more humble and submissive unto the subtleties of Faith; and thus I teach my haggard and unreclaimed reason to stoop to the lure of Faith. . . . And this I think is no vulgar part of Faith, to believe a thing not only above, but contrary to Reason, and against the Arguments of our proper Senses.[51]

In this state of mind, faith becomes easy, it surmounts every difficulty. "Methinks there be not impossibilities enough in Religion for an active faith. . . . I love to lose my self in a mystery, to pursue my Reason to an *O altitudo!*" Scornfully Browne says that " 'tis an easy and necessary belief to credit what our eye and sense hath examined." [52]

Such was the philosophical part of Browne's confession of faith, which the wits of the time of Charles II read so eagerly, along with Butler's burlesque of the Puritans and the grossly cynical and opportunistic *Advice to a Son*. They were all, according to Pepys' friend, cried up for their "wit." The age loved paradoxes better than either philosophical systems or devotional treatises; and Browne was preëminently a man of wit and paradoxes. His confession of faith was not read as a devotional book, neither did it contribute to the scientific and philosophical enlightenment of the century. Notwithstanding his scientific training in medicine, his intellect was neither independent nor accurate nor critical. It cannot be distinguished from his temperament, so completely is it led, turned, directed into devious ways by the demand of his imagination and emotion. Browne is not read for his insight and wisdom, as Pascal is, but only for the charming *naïveté* of his genial self-revelation, the splendor and sublimity of his imagination, and the quaint beauty of his style. He is for us preëminently a *humourist*, in the older meaning of the word.

If Browne was not forward-looking in intellect, it was not because he misunderstood the spirit of his century. In an interesting passage in his *Christian Morals* he refers to the enlightenment of his time:

[51] *Ibid.*, pp. 17–18.   [52] *Ibid.*, pp. 16–17.

Let thy Studies [he writes] be as free as thy Thoughts and Contemplations: but fly not only upon the wings of Imagination; Joyn Sense unto Reason, and Experiment unto Speculation, and so give life unto Embryon Truths, and Verities yet in their Chaos. There is nothing more acceptable unto the Ingenious World, than this noble Eluctation of Truth; wherein, against the tenacity of Prejudice and Prescription, this Century now prevaileth. What Libraries of new Volumes aftertimes will behold, and in what a new World of Knowledge the eyes of our posterity may be happy, a few Ages may joyfully declare.[53]

But his own studies flew upon the wings of the imagination, and his haggard and unreclaimed reason followed submissively. He passed easily and lightly from conjecture to conjecture, surmounting every difficulty merely by the aid of a "surely" or a "no doubt." When he had observed how generally the ancients planted their gardens in the pattern of the quincunx, he had great desire to pursue the antiquity of this mystical design to its origin, perhaps in the first Paradise:

And if it were clear that this was used by *Noah* after the Floud, I could easily beleeve it was in use before it; Not willing to fix such ancient inventions no higher original then *Noah;* Nor readily conceiving those aged *Heroes,* whose diet was vegetable, and only, or chiefly consisted in the fruits of the earth, were much deficient in their splendid cultivations; or after the experience of fifteen hundred years, left much for future discovery in Botanical Agriculture.[54]

Such scholarship was whimsical already in the seventeenth century, the age of Casaubon and Selden. And in philosophy and divinity, as well, Browne's intellect but served his predilections. His belief in immortality, he said, had been "instructed" by the "smattering I have of the Philosophers Stone," and by "those strange and mystical transmigrations that I have observed in Silkworms.[55] He believed in the resurrection because without a belief in a future life he was unable to withstand temptation.[56] His way of thinking was that ancient one which in our time has been given the name pragmatic: "In Bivious Theorems and *Janus*-faced Doctrines," he writes in *Christian Morals*, "let Virtuous considera-

[53] *Works*, ed. Charles Sayle, III, 470.   [54] *Ibid.*, pp. 153-154.
[55] *Ibid.*, I, 58.   [56] *Ibid.*, p. 67.

tions state the determination. Look upon Opinions as thou dost upon the Moon, and chuse not the dark hemisphere for thy contemplation. Embrace not the opacous and blind side of Opinions, but that which looks most Luciferously or influentially unto Goodness." [57] Thoroughly characteristic of him is that passage in *Religio Medici* where, beginning with confessed doubt and ignorance, he is nevertheless, as the discussion proceeds, able to satisfy himself regarding not only the existence of spirits, but even the scholastic definition of their nature.[58]

With his reason thus bound in servitude Browne let his faith and imagination build him a universe to live in, a universe filled primarily with the wonderful. It was constructed to satisfy the longings, whimsicalities, even weaknesses, of the heart and soul of Browne. Without skepticism no one may enter into it, but once past the charmed portal one must be all credulity. It is the world of the imagination, with something of the fascination and unreality of a fairy story. There is no questioning the sincerity of Browne, who lived in a credulous age, when the gravest and most thoughtful men might believe, not only in tutelar spirits and the resurrection, but in witches. Neither may we suspect him of any intention of heresy or dissent; he regarded himself as completely in accord with the Anglican Church. But his distinction was that he saw all things with the eyes of wonder. He nourished his emotions and imagination chiefly upon the mystery of this world and the invisible which transcends it, and his thirty years of commonplace life seemed to him nothing less than a miracle. If, as Donne had said, all divinity is love and wonder,[59] Browne knew half of divinity; all the world to him was wonder. But it is not so certain that he would have understood all that Donne meant by "love." For with all his faith and imagination and charity, the genial and lovable Browne lacked intensity in his personal life. He had none of Donne's "hydroptic, immoderate desires" after learning or wisdom; he never experienced any such revealing spiritual crisis as Pascal, who knew so much better both "les grandeurs et misères

<hr/>

[57] *Ibid.*, III, 483.   [58] *Ibid.*, I, 48–50.
[59] John Donne, *Poetical Works*, ed. H. J. C. Grierson (Oxford, 1912), I, 30. Cf. pp. 81 and 248.

de l'homme." Such intensity of feeling, a longing for the comfort of finding one's weary and broken soul precious in the sight of God, is implied in Donne's definition of divinity as love and wonder. Browne's religion was free from this strain and effort; he solved his problems by the gentle method of dreaming meditation. He played his game with the Devil and won by a paradox. And as he rose to bid adieu, he must have imagined that he saw in the features of his bewildered adversary an involuntary smile of surprise and admiration.

CHAPTER III

THE CRISIS OF THE NEW SCIENCE

i The revival of materialism   ii Hobbes   iii The recourse to Pyrrhonism   iv Dryden and Hobbes   v Dryden and the Royal Society

E VEN the brief and fragmentary survey of skeptical thought
attempted in the preceding chapter has indicated to some
degree how widely it was disseminated and to what diverse purposes it could be applied. More in particular, it appears from the
illustrative passages, which were chosen with special reference to
the religious thought of Dryden, that the poet's approach to religion was thoroughly traditional, and that *Religio Laici* belongs
historically rather to Roman Catholic than to Anglican apologetics.
But at the present stage in our study such conclusions can be only
general impressions, to be examined and documented more carefully in later chapters. It should also be regarded as a reasonable
assumption — though the evidence for this will accumulate as we
proceed — that Dryden actually came in contact with these skeptical developments; he could hardly have avoided it. They permeated English thought after the Restoration. Montaigne, whose
rambling *Essays* began to appear old-fashioned and inartistic to
the contemporaries of Racine and Boileau, arrived at the same
period at the height of his reputation in England.[1] Charron and
Sextus could be read in English translation; *Religio Medici* was
universally admired. The classics of the skeptical tradition found
a responsive public and gave the intellectual tone to the conversation of the wits.

Such a professed adherent of skepticism as Dryden must have
been interested in these manifestations of Pyrrhonism, which were
all about him. But the problem is very difficult, in the case of

[1] Pierre Villey, "Montaigne en Angleterre," *Revue des deux mondes*, 6 Pér.,
Vol. XVII (1913).

such an allusive and unsystematic writer, to determine which of these manifestations most influenced him, and precisely in what sequence. Dryden lived before the age of confessions, and he never troubled to enlighten his readers regarding his own intellectual history. Only after he had turned fifty did he unveil his mind and address the public directly, in his poems on politics and religion. By what paths he arrived at his final intellectual destination, to what influences he was subjected on the way, can be learned only from his scattered and casual references to them, and only by interpreting these in terms of the movement of ideas in his own age. Such documentary evidence for his intellectual biography as can be gleaned from his own writings must be explained and completed by a study of his intellectual milieu. Not until we understand fully the various implications of ideas as they presented themselves to Dryden, can we appreciate his reactions to them and pass judgment on his consistency and significance.

Inasmuch as our method will be to place Dryden's thought in its context in the thought of his period, it seems necessary to proceed by considering one by one the various aspects of it, rather than by attempting a comprehensive treatment of all aspects in a strict chronological order such as is, moreover, in his case often out of the question. We shall therefore seek to define his intellectual cast and temperament by determining what choices and preferences he made among the tendencies of his age, studying in succession his relation to scientific, religious, and political thought. Such an analysis and presentation of Dryden's ideas must of course not be supposed to correspond to "periods" in his life. All the developments here treated successively were going on simultaneously in his mind, were in fact interrelated; and each section of this study must be supplemented by the others to make the portrait of Dryden's mind complete.

It is perhaps because Dryden has not been credited with real intellectual character that students of him have so generally neglected his connection with the Royal Society and his attitude toward the new science of his time. They have, of course, included in their biographical narratives the fact that he was chosen a member of the newly organized Society on November 19, 1662, and admitted at the next meeting, November 26; but with no significance attached except that Dryden must at this time have enjoyed the social status of a gentleman.[2] As to any intellectual sympathy with the new movement, comment has been meager and conflicting; Christie declares that Dryden "had no accurate knowledge" of science, whereas Scott, more generously but equally without documentation, says that "Dryden, who through life was attached to experimental philosophy, speedily associated himself with those who took interest in its progress." In an elaborate study of the new science in relation to literature,[3] Mr. Carson S. Duncan has been cursory, but severe, in his treatment of Dryden. Although he found that the poet had introduced here and there some imagery derived from science — thus obeying, says Mr. Duncan, "the injunction of Bishop Sprat"[4] — yet he found also imagery drawn from such sources as astrology or the Ptolemaic astronomy. "From all which," concluded Mr. Duncan, "it follows that Dryden was not deeply impressed with the new philosophy. It seems never to have occurred to him that it was a serious matter to know the truth about nature, or at least to be consistent about its representation." "Dryden was practically unaffected by the new intellectual impulse."[5] As for the sources of his poetic imagery, Dryden went all his life to both the new and the old science. But he would probably have defended the latter as he does the supernatural in poetry, by an appeal to folklore. "It is enough that, in all ages and religions, the greatest part of mankind has believed the power of magic, and that there are spirits or spectres which have appeared. This, I say, is foundation enough for poetry."[6] Without raising

[2] Edmond Malone, *Critical and Miscellaneous Prose Works of John Dryden*, I (1800), 49–50; Sir Walter Scott, *Life of Dryden*, in *Works*, I, 46–47; W. D. Christie, "Memoir" in the Globe edition of *Poetical Works*, p. xxv; J. Churton Collins, *Essays and Studies* (1895), p. 18. Saintsbury, in his volume in the "English Men of Letters," does not even mention Dryden's membership in the Royal Society.

[3] *The New Science and English Literature in the Classical Period* (Menasha, Wis., 1913).

[4] See Thomas Sprat, *History of the Royal Society*, Part III, sec. xxxv (2d ed., 1702), pp. 413–419.

[5] Duncan, *op. cit.*, pp. 43–45 and 179.

[6] *Essay on Heroic Plays*, in *Works*, IV, 22.

further, therefore, the question of Dryden's knowledge of science as shown in his metaphors and similes, we shall here approach more directly the larger question whether or not "Dryden was practically unaffected by the new intellectual impulse," or whether he at least possessed any characteristic attitudes or ideas which might indicate sympathetic interest in the Royal Society and the new science.[7]

I

First of all, there are two common errors to be avoided in defining the intellectual impulse of the new science. One is to describe it as mainly Baconian in nature, as merely collection and classification of specimens. Bacon's prestige with the Royal Society and his great influence in fostering the inductive method must of course be admitted. The scientists of the seventeenth century were his disciples in their respect for facts and their suspicion of hasty generalization; the gentlemen *virtuosi* collected rarities with truly Baconian zeal. But the most significant element of the new science was not to be found in these collectors' cabinets, so frequently ridiculed in the literature of the time; neither is it to be found in the works of Bacon. The new philosophy of science, or, as it was then called, the "new philosophy of motion," was the result of the application of mathematics to physics and astronomy; and Bacon had entirely ignored mathematics. "In this respect," says Whitehead, "Bacon completely missed the tonality which lay behind the success of seventeenth century science. Science was becoming, and has remained, primarily quantitative." [8]

It is also a mistake to suppose that the profoundest effect of the Copernican system upon general ideas was the shift of the center of the universe from the earth to the sun. The shock of this revela-

---

[7] Mr. Claude Lloyd, in an article on "John Dryden and the Royal Society," *Publications of the Modern Language Association*, XLV (1930), 967–976, called attention to the fact that Dryden did not pay his dues to the Society and was consequently dropped from membership in 1666. Mr. Lloyd accordingly concluded that "there is little need to attempt to reconcile Dryden's 'scientific' beliefs with those of the scientists of his day." Such a conclusion makes some unwarranted assumptions, and, moreover, contradicts the utterances of Dryden himself. See the correspondence evoked by his article in the same *Publications*, XLVI (1931), 951–962.

[8] A. N. Whitehead, *Science and the Modern World* (New York, 1925), p. 66.

tion, great as it had been at first, was not keenly felt in England, at least, after 1660. And during the process of popularizing the heliocentric theory other problems of deeper and more permanent import emerged and became the real storm center. These deeper problems, again, were the result of the application of mathematics to astronomy and physics.

The development of mathematics and its triumphant application to the phenomena of motion constitutes undoubtedly one of the greatest revolutions in the history of thought. It has so completely permeated even the "common sense" view of the world of the average modern man that only by effort can we understand the conception of motion which preceded it. The medieval interpretation was animistic. The Middle Ages asked the question, "*Why* do bodies move?" And their answer was that they move because they have a desire to. Gravitation is due to each thing seeking its appropriate place; nature abhors a vacuum; Kepler, in his *Mysterium cosmographicum* (1597), explained that planets move because they have "moving souls" (*animae motrices*);[9] Gilbert described the magnetic force he had discovered as "of the nature of soul, surpassing the soul of man"; Harvey believed that the motion of the heart and blood is due to "innate heat," which is not fire nor derived from fire; and the blood, he said, is not occupied by a spirit, but is a spirit, "celestial in nature, the soul, that which answers to the essence of the stars . . . something analogous to heaven, the instrument of heaven."[10] Medieval thought sought for the essence of motion as an answer to the question *why* bodies move. As a matter of fact, the new science of the seventeenth century did not answer this question, but only deprived it of its interest. The new science demonstrated that all motion is regular and mathematically measurable, and thenceforth the real question became, "*How* do bodies move?" Thus Kepler, after many years of astronomical calculations, ultimately rejected his "moving souls" as unnecessary. The seventeenth century, as a period in the development of thought, is particularly notable for its many geniuses in the related fields of mathematics, physics, and astronomy, who

---

[9] H. Höffding, *History of Modern Philosophy* (London, 1900), I, 168–169.
[10] T. C. Albutt, *Science and Medieval Thought* (London, 1901), pp. 41 ff.

by a vast coöperative effort added stone to stone in this new philosophic structure, until Newton completed it, a new universe of cause and effect, a vast machine, whose every mystery must be amenable to the laws of mathematics.[11]

Thus arose in a new and much more perplexing and dangerous form the ancient problem of materialism. Even Descartes felt constrained to regard living organisms as machines, although he of course admitted that man has also a "rational soul," and thus established the famous and influential Cartesian dualism. But there were many who accepted the mechanical theory without adding to it this idealistic superstructure which contradicted it. Hence the great popularity in the seventeenth century of the atomistic philosophy of Democritus, Epicurus, and Lucretius, who not only affected the general tone of sophisticated society by stimulating "libertine" thought, but influenced as well the new science.[12] The French philosopher Gassendi combined ancient atomism with the new science of his own day, thereby preparing for Newton's rejection of the vortex theory of Descartes and the foundation of modern atomism. Voltaire, in his *Elements of the Philosophy of Newton*, pointed out, probably not without some malicious satisfaction, the great prestige and importance, in the eyes of the pious Newton, of the materialistic ancient atheists and their modern disciple:

Newton followed the ancient opinions of Democritus, Epicurus, and a multitude of philosophers rectified by our celebrated Gassendi. Newton has several times said to some Frenchmen still living that he considered Gassendi a very upright and enlightened mind, and that he prided himself on being entirely on his side in all matters on which they had discoursed.[13]

[11] See W. Whewell, *History of the Inductive Sciences* (London, 1837), and *Philosophy of the Inductive Sciences* (London, 1840); E. A. Burtt, *The Metaphysical Foundations of Modern Physical Science* (1925), with Bibliography; A. J. Snow, *Matter and Gravity in Newton's Physical Philosophy* (1926), with Bibliography; also the volumes by Whitehead and Albutt referred to in notes 8 and 10.

[12] See F. A. Lange, *History of Materialism* (Eng. trans., Boston, 1877); Kurd Lasswitz, *Geschichte der Atomistik* (Hamburg, 1890); L. Mabilleau, *Histoire de la philosophie atomistique* (Paris, 1895).

[13] Trans. from a quotation by Lange, *op. cit.*, I, 267, n. 12. Gassendi was not in fact an atheist, but outside scientific circles he was regarded with suspicion, and the "libertines" appealed to his authority.

The materialistic implications of the new science, however, were generally received much more hospitably among lay gentlemen, such as cultivated the gay cynicism of "libertine" thought, than among professional men of science. On the other hand, those members of the Royal Society who were doing significant scientific work were also pious men who held dear that religious and idealistic tradition which their scientific work was putting on the defensive. From this dilemma sprang much of the characteristic thought not only of the seventeenth century, but of the modern era. As Whitehead says, "The history of thought in the eighteenth and nineteenth centuries is governed by the fact that the world had got hold of a general idea which it could neither live with nor live without." [14] But the apologetics of the Royal Society will be understood better if we first consider Hobbes, the most distinguished and the most uncompromising of the contemporary adherents of the dreaded materialism.

II

The mental history of Hobbes is typical of the mathematical and physical preoccupations of the seventeenth century. His philosophical awakening came at the age of forty, when he accidentally opened a book of Euclid and became enchanted by the certainty of mathematical demonstration. Along with Euclid he studied Galileo, from whom, it appears, he derived his fundamental mechanical theory, which he proceeded to apply both to the world and to man.[15] Science is the study of causes, but all causes are ultimately reducible to motion. A complete science should begin with a study of simple motions, then proceed to more complex motions in geometry, thence to physics, until we reach the most complex motions in "moral philosophy, in which we are to consider the motions of the mind . . . what causes they have, and of what they be causes." [16] To complete his scheme, Hobbes also insisted that the soul is material, a sort of thin, filmy substance,

[14] Whitehead, *op. cit.*, p. 74.

[15] W. R. Sorley, *History of English Philosophy* (Cambridge, 1920), pp. 49–50. But this early indebtedness to Galileo has been questioned by Frithiof Brandt, *Den mekaniske Naturopfattelse hos Thomas Hobbes* (Copenhagen, 1921), pp. 72–81.

[16] *Elements of Philosophy*, Part I, Chap. VI, especially secs. 5–6 in *English Works*, ed. Sir W. Molesworth, I, 131–132.

which could thus be assumed to be a part of the mechanical world. The customary theological definition of soul as "incorporeal substance" he ridiculed as meaningless. The soul, he said, has dimension as the body has, though he admitted it has no color. In response to his theological critics, Hobbes declared himself willing to accept on faith such incomprehensible beings as God and the angels, though he suggested with fine irony that "the Scripture favoureth them more, that hold angels and spirits corporeal, than them that hold the contrary." [17]

In spite of this thoroughgoing mechanistic view of the world, Hobbes always professed himself a Christian and a submissive adherent of the Church of England as by law established. Obedience to authority, he said, is the cardinal virtue in political and ecclesiastical matters. But it was well understood already by his contemporaries that under this outward acceptance of Christianity he attempted to conceal a nature in which the religious instincts remained undeveloped. His reaction was significant when early in his philosophical career he was asked for comments on Descartes's *Discours*. His own mechanical and materialistic philosophy was already definitely formulated, and he opposed it to the idealism of Descartes. His manner was as tart as his reasoning was keen; he reduced the whole spiritualistic philosophy to corporeal motion, "et ainsi l'esprit ne sera rien autre chose qu'un mouvement en certaines parties du corps organique." [18] Since both men were irritated by their mutual lack of sympathy, their relations never passed beyond an acquaintance. And the philosophy of Descartes, which had so much in common with Plato, Augustine, and Anselm, became for half a century in England one of the most trusted modes of escape from Hobbism and materialism, especially among the Cambridge Platonists and the members of the Royal Society.

For Hobbism spread rapidly, and after 1650 the philosopher of Malmesbury, already past sixty, became for nearly thirty years more the center of a storm of controversy which reverberated

---

[17] *Human Nature*, Chap. XI, secs. 2–5; ed. cited, IV, 59–62.
[18] Descartes, *Troisièmes objections contre les Méditations*, in *Œuvres*, ed. Jules Simon, pp. 198–199.

throughout Europe. That he had many friends and disciples is certain, although some of the names in the long list given by his friend John Aubrey are open to suspicion.[19] His popularity with Charles II and the court was a thorn in the side of his enemies, though it does not appear to have rested entirely on a philosophical basis:

Order was given that he should have free accesse to his majesty, who was always much delighted in his witt and smart repartees. The witts at Court were wont to bayte him. But he feared none of them, and would make his part good. The king would call him *the beare:* "Here comes the beare to be bayted!"[20]

But he enjoyed also the friendship and esteem of such men of letters as Davenant and Waller, and even of Cowley, a member of the Royal Society.[21] On the whole, however, his disciples seem to have been more ready to talk than to write, and his great vogue is best apparent from the number, the seriousness, and the persistence of his opponents.

Hobbes fought indeed alone against all the leading thinkers of his time. Already in 1645 he had entered upon a long controversy with Bishop Bramhall on free-will and necessitarianism.[22] The Cambridge Platonists attacked from various points of view the "mechanic" philosophy of Hobbes. Of these the most important were Ralph Cudworth and Henry More, both of them members of the Royal Society and both declared adherents of the new science. More had said already in 1647 that "it is plain to any man that is not prejudic'd" that Galileo's "System of the world is more naturall & genuine than that of Tycho's."[23] Cudworth objected

[19] *Brief Lives*, ed. A. Clark (Oxford, 1898), I, 365–372.

[20] *Ibid.*, p. 340. This story is told in a quite different manner by Sorbière: "Il a fait peur je ne sçay comment au Clergé de son pays, aux Mathematiciens d'Oxfordt, & à leurs adherants; c'est pourquoy S[a] M[ajesté] me le compara tres-bien à l'ours, contre lequel il fait battre les dogues pour les exercer" (*Relation d'un voyage en Angleterre* [Cologne, 1666], p. 76).

[21] Cowley's ode to Hobbes was published before the Royal Society was founded, but there is nothing to indicate that he did not to the end continue to admire both the opposing parties.

[22] A controversy discussed and deservedly emphasized as "of great importance in the history of seventeenth-century thought" by Marjorie H. Nicolson, "Milton and Hobbes," *Studies in Philology*, XXIII (1926), 409.

[23] *Philosophical Poems* (Cambridge, 1647), p. 390.

only to a materialistic interpretation of the new science. Imbued with the notion that truth is purest at its source in antiquity, he sought there for a truer philosophy. In his erudite work, *The True Intellectual System of the Universe* (1678), he distinguished between the ancient theistic and atheistic·atomisms, the former of which he believed to be derived from Moses. From such heights of learning he felt himself able to weigh and estimate the atomistic science of his contemporaries, who were only reviving ancient doctrine, "and that with no small pomp and ostentation of wisdom and philosophy."

Though directing their polemics especially against Hobbes, both More and Cudworth, significantly, approved of Descartes, even though with some reservations. In the Preface to his treatise on *The Immortality of the Soul*, a treatise refuting Hobbes's doctrine that the soul is material,[24] More declares that he thinks

. . . it is the most sober and faithful advice that can be offered to the Christian World, that they would encourage the reading of Des-Cartes in all publick Schools and Universities. That the Students of Philosophy may be thoroughly exercised in the just extent of the *Mechanical powers of Matter*, how farre they will reach, and where they fall short. Which will be the best assistance to Religion that Reason and the Knowledge of Nature can afford. For by this means such as are intended to serve the Church will be armed betimes with sufficient strength to grapple with their proudest Deriders or Opposers. Whenas for want of this, we see how liable they are to be contemned and born down by every bold, though weak, pretender to the *Mechanick* Philosophy.[25]

Cudworth gives Descartes the high praise of having revived the right kind, the theistic atomism of Moschus, whom Cudworth rashly identified with Moses.

For *Renatus Cartesius* first revived and restored the atomick philosophy, agreeably, for the most part, to that ancient Moschical and Pythagorick form; acknowledging besides extended substance and corporeal atoms, another cogitative incorporeal substance, and joyning metaphysicks or theology, together with physiology, to make up one entire system of philosophy.

[24] *Op. cit.* (London, 1662), Chaps. VIII–XII, pp. 34–49.
[25] *Ibid.*, Preface.

Hobbes, however, he unreservedly condemns, although without naming him:

> But shortly after this *Cartesian* restitution of the primitive atomology, that acknowledgeth incorporeal substance, we have had our *Leucippus* and *Democritus* too, who also revived and brought upon the stage that other atheistick atomology, that makes *senseless and lifeless atoms to be the only principles of all things in the universe;* thereby necessarily excluding, besides incorporeal substance and immortality of souls, a Deity and natural morality; as also making all actions and events materially and mechanically necessary.[26]

These attempts to read Hobbes out of the new scientific movement did not, however, draw him into controversy, any more than did the sermons and pamphlets of "every young Churchman militant," who, as Warburton says, "would needs try his arms in thundering upon Hobbes' steel-cap." But the members of the Royal Society penetrated his armor, stirred him to counterattack, and in mathematics and physics won a whole series of easy victories, each of which seems to have left Hobbes more sore and obstinate than enlightened. He was indeed constantly on the wrong side of scientific questions; he was incompetent enough as a mathematician to try to demonstrate the quadrature of the circle; he rashly contradicted Boyle on the nature of the vacuum. Both as scientist and mathematician he had been discredited in discerning circles even before 1660.[27] It was his reputation and influence with the larger public that made a continued polemic against him necessary. The situation was especially delicate because the royal patron of the new science also showed a marked partiality for this

---

[26] *True Intellectual System* (London, 1743), Book I, Chap. III, sec. 38, pp. 174–175.

[27] See the correspondence of Christian Huygens, in *Œuvres complètes* (La Haye, 1888 ff.); especially the letters from Huygens to J. Wallis, March 15, 1656 (Vol. I, No. 272); and from Huygens to R. Moray, November 4, 1661 (Vol. III, No. 916): "Dans le Dialogue de Monsieur Hobbes je ne trouve rien de solide, mais seulement de pures visions. C'est par faute d'esprit ou par ce qu'il se plait à contredire qu'il ne recoit pas les veritables raisons des effets du vide, qui sont dans le liure de Monsieur Boile. Quand à ce qu'il adjouste de la duplication du cube, je ne l'ay pas voulu regarder par ce que je scay demonstratiuement que la chose est impossible. Et d'ailleurs il y a long temps qu'en matiere de Geometrie Monsieur Hobbes a perdu tout credit aupres du moy."

charlatanical but dreaded enemy of the scientists.[28]   And though dangerous as an enemy, Hobbes would have been far more insidiously dangerous as a friend and member of the Royal Society. The leaders of the new scientific movement could never have admitted the modern Democritus to their ranks without endangering their cause.   Their most subtle and persistent difficulty was to explain to the public the difference between the Hobbists and the members of the Royal Society; to explain how it was possible for Christian scientists to accept the new philosophy of motion and yet escape an atheistic materialism.

III

The Royal Society had of course enemies of all kinds.   They alienated many churchmen and scholars by attacking the Aristotelian scholasticism which still dominated the universities.   Here the Royal Society had to contend with a powerful vested interest, and they fought it vigorously and openly.   But they suffered even more from the suspicion that they were undermining religion. Sprat, in his *History of the Royal Society* (1667), approaches this subject with the statement that it is "the weightiest and most solemn part of my whole *undertaking;* to make a defense of the *Royal Society*, and this new *Experimental Learning*, in respect to the *Christian Faith*.   I am not ignorant, in what a slippery place I now stand; and what a tender matter I am enter'd upon." [29]

Sprat's discussion of the matter is eminently tactful, and also somewhat evasive.   There is none of the direct attack on Hobbes found in More and Cudworth.   The facts about the situation are more easily gathered from Boyle.   This recognized great champion of both religion and science [30] was also one of the chief antagonists, along with Wallis and Ward, of Hobbes, to whom his references

[28] *Œuvres complètes*, letters from Moray to Huygens, September 13 and October 19, 1661 (Vol. III, Nos. 893 and 909). According to Sorbière, Charles II would have liked to have Hobbes elected to the Royal Society (*Relation* [ed. cited], p. 75).

[29] *History*, ed. cited, Part III, sec. xiv, p. 345.

[30] Stillingfleet, in a letter of October 6, 1662, urged Boyle to publish his papers on behalf of Christianity against Hobbes. See Boyle, *Works*, V (1744), 516. See also letters from Peter du Moulin, December 28, 1669 (V, 594); from J. Beale, June 26, 1682 (V, 505); from Cudworth, October 16, 1684 (V, 549) — all indicative of the way Boyle was relied upon to save the day.

are frequent and explicit. In the Preface to *An Examen of Mr. T. Hobbes his Dialogus Physicus de Natura Aeris* (1662) he says he is writing to defend the experimental method which Hobbes scorned. He adds:

> It was also suggested to me that the dangerous opinions about some important, if not fundamental, articles of religion, I had met with in his *Leviathan*, and some other of his writings, having made too great impressions upon divers persons, (who, though said to be for the most part either of greater quality, or of greater wit than learning, do yet divers of them deserve better principles,) these errors being chiefly recommended by the opinion they had of Mr. *Hobbes's* demonstrative way of philosophy; it might possibly prove some service to higher truths than those in controversy between him and me, to shew, that in the Physics themselves, his opinions, and even his ratiocinations, have no such great advantage over those, of some orthodox Christian Naturalists.[31]

In his *Usefulness of Natural Philosophy* (1663) he objects that

> . . . it has long been the custom of such men [i.e. atheists], to talk, as if themselves, and those of their mind, were not alone the best, but almost the only naturalists; and to perplex others with pretending, that, whereas it is not conceivable, how there can be a God; all things are by the principles of the atomical philosophy, made clear and facil.[32]

In the second part of this work (1671) he says:

> I forget not that there are several divines (and some of the eminent ones) that out of a holy jealousy (as they think) for religion, labour to deter men from addicting themselves to serious and thorough inquiries into nature, as from a study unsafe for a Christian, and likely to end in atheism, by making it possible for men (that I may propose to you their objection as much to its advantage as I can) to give themselves such an account of all the wonders of nature, by the single knowledge of second causes, as may bring them to disbelieve the necessity of a first.[33]

[31] *Works*, I, 119. [32] Part I, Essay 5, in *Works*, I, 459.
[33] *Ibid.*, pp. 429–430. Meric Casaubon, no friend to the new science, had expressed this objection in *A Letter . . . to Peter du Moulin . . . Concerning Natural experimental Philosophie, and some books lately set out about it* (Cambridge, 1669). After a lengthy attack on the presumption of the new science, he continues (p. 30): "Now I crave leave to tell you, that it is (as all good things, more or less) very apt to be abused and to degenerate into *Atheism*. Men that are much fixed upon matter and secondary causes and sensual objects, if great care be not taken, may in time, (there be many examples) and by degrees forget that there be such

In 1675 Boyle writes that, whereas atheists had formerly been in the habit of attacking the historical and doctrinal parts of Christian theology, they in this age attacked the very notion of God and religion. "For these libertines own themselves to be so upon the account of the Epicurean, and other mechanical principles of philosophy"; and, he adds, they recognize no authorities except such as "Leucippus, Democritus, Epicurus, &c.," who "explicate things by matter and local motion." [34] "*The modern Atheists*," wrote the Reverend Joseph Glanvill, another member of the Royal Society, "are pretenders to the *mechanick* principles . . . the *modern Sadduce* pretends that all things we *do*, are performed by *meer matter*, and *motion*, and consequently that there is no such thing as an *immaterial* being." [35] Obviously, the scientists of the Royal Society, even though they themselves may have been secure from the charge of atheism, could hardly escape the charge of cultivating a philosophy which led to atheism in others. How did they defend themselves against this charge?

Officially they did nothing. Officially the Royal Society, as Sprat says, "is abundantly cautious, not to intermeddle in *Spiritual things*," and such subjects as God and the soul were not discussed at their meetings. [36] Nevertheless, there was considerable unanimity of opinion among the members. It is well known that Descartes was respected by them as both a philosophical and a scientific genius. Through the Royal Society as well as through the Cambridge Platonists, Cartesianism became a very important element in English idealistic thought in that century. But the members of the Royal Society adopted also another mode of defense against materialism, namely, a critique of the very science

---

things in the world as *Spirits*, substances really existing and of great power, though not visible, or palpable by their nature; forget I say, that there is a God, and that their souls are immortal." In this same year Dr. du Moulin, who was like Casaubon a prebendary of Canterbury, saw his Latin poem in praise of the Royal Society suppressed by the licenser, Dr. Gunning, later Bishop of Ely. See Boyle's *Works*, I, 60, and V, 594.

[34] Preface to *Some Considerations about the Reconcileableness of Reason and Religion*, ed. cited, III, 510.

[35] *Philosophia Pia* (1671), pp. 23, 32.

[36] *History*, ed. cited, Part III, sec. xiv, and Part II, sec. xi, pp. 83 and 347.

they were promoting, a critique which varied all the way from timidity in generalization to philosophical skepticism.

Sprat testifies to the extreme caution of the Society from its very inception. Their motto *Nullius in Verba* was a hit at the tyranny of scholasticism, but it soon became apparent that the tyranny of Epicurus or Democritus, or of any "modern dogmatists," would be equally unwelcome.[37] In fact, no philosopher was accorded the seat of authority, not even Descartes. Companies, Sprat says repeatedly, are to be preferred before single endeavors in philosophical matters, as "exhibiting more wariness, and coldness in thinking, and rigorous examination." Altogether Sprat fears that "to this fault of *Sceptical doubting*, the *Royal Society* may perhaps be suspected, to be a little too much inclin'd: because they always professed, to be so backward from *setling* of *Principles*, or *fixing* upon *Doctrines*." To which Sprat replies that generalizing is for the future, and in the mean time dogmatism is more dangerous than skepticism.[38]

Among the workers in the Royal Society no one was more wary and cold in scientific thinking, more reluctant to dogmatize from the new science, than Robert Boyle. It is therefore particularly important to note that he cultivated this critical, not to say skeptical, attitude toward science with a conscious intent to serve religion. In his *Excellence of Theology* (1673), Part II, section 3, he criticizes the belief that physics has one prerogative over divinity, namely, "the certainty, and clearness, and thence resulting satisfactoriness of our knowledge of physical, in comparison of any we can have of theological matters, whose being dark and uncertain, the nature of the things themselves, and the numerous controversies of differing sects about them, sufficiently manifest." In reply Boyle does not urge the certainty of divinity, but the real uncertainty of science.

That physical certainty [he says] which is pretended for the truths demonstrated by naturalists, is, even where it is rightfully claimed, but an inferior kind or degree of certainty, as moral certainty also is. For even physical demonstrations can beget but a physical certainty, (that is, a certainty upon supposition, that the

[37] *Ibid.*, Part I, secs. xiii–xv, pp. 28–35.   [38] *Ibid.*, pp. 100–109.

principles of physic be true,) not a metaphysical certainty, (wherein it is absolutely impossible, that the thing believed should be other than true). . . . And there are I know not how many things in physicks, that men presume they believe upon physical and cogent arguments, wherein they really have but a moral assurance; which is a truth held by so few, that I have been invited to take the more particular notice of them in other papers, written purposely to show the doubtfulness and incompleteness of natural philosophy; . . . the most even of the modern virtuosi are wont to fancy more of clearness and certainty in their physical theories, than a critical examiner will find.[39]

Boyle, then, sought a reconciliation of the new science with religion by limiting the sphere of reason; he weakened the materialistic interpretation of the new science by emphasizing the uncertainty of science itself.

This criticism of scientific knowledge was carried still further by Joseph Glanvill, whose volume, *The Vanity of Dogmatizing* (1661), was reprinted in 1664 as *Scepsis scientifica*, with a Dedication to the Royal Society which resulted in his election to membership.[40] A passage from this Dedication will explain his purpose and its relation to Hobbes as well as to the new science. The work of the Royal Society, he says, is

. . . the improving the minds of Men in solid and useful notices of things, helping them to such theories as may be serviceable to common life, and the searching out of the true laws of Matter and Motion, in order to the securing of the Foundations of Religion against all attempts of Mechanical Atheism.

For the ingenious World being grown quite weary of Qualities and Formes, and declaring in favour of the Mechanical Hypothesis, (to which a person that is not very fond of Religion is a great pre-

---

[39] *Works*, III, 432. Cf. Burtt, *op. cit.*, pp. 178–182, and Whitehead's discussion of modern science as "predominantly an anti-rationalistic movement" (p. 23). Although passages from Boyle could be patched together to make a criticism of human knowledge almost as complete as that of Glanvill, yet Nourrisson has undoubtedly exaggerated his skepticism in his essay in *Philosophies de la nature* (Paris, 1887), pp. 43–84.

[40] On December 7, 1664, "Lord Brereton presented a book written by J. Glanvill, dedicated to the Society, the dedication of which was read. Mr. Glanvill was proposed candidate by Lord Brereton" (Thomas Birch, *History of the Royal Society*, p. 500). Glanvill was elected and admitted December 14, 1664. *Scepsis scientifica* was licensed for publication on October 18, 1664.

tender) divers of the brisker Geniuses, who desire rather to be accounted Witts, then endeavour to be so, have been willing to accept Mechanism upon Hobbian conditions, and many others were in danger of following them into the precipice. So that 'tis not conceivable how a more suitable remedy could have been provided against the deadly influence of that Contagion, then your Honourable Society, by which the meanest intellects may perceive, that Mechanick Philosophy yields no security to irreligion, and that those that would be gentily learned and ingenious, need not purchase it, at the dear rate of being atheists.

It is impossible and unnecessary here to examine in detail the skepticism of Glanvill. We are concerned more with the occasion of his thought than with an evaluation of it. It must suffice to say that Glanvill has a place in the history of philosophy as an acute and ingenious thinker, whose critique of causation anticipates in some respects that of Hume himself. These scientific skeptics were, indeed, not naïve theorizers; they were versed in the tradition of philosophical skepticism. Boyle knew the work of Sextus Empiricus,[41] and Glanvill shows an acquaintance not only with Sextus, but with such modern disciples as Montaigne and Charron.[42] Perhaps they were also indebted to Sir Thomas Browne, although his imaginative flights and complete humiliation of the reason must have appeared to them rather too uncritical. And yet Glanvill conveyed, in rhythms that recall Browne, a sense of the mystery of the world both in its vastness and in its infinite minuteness, and of the miracle of man among all these unexplainable wonders:

Whatever I look upon within the amplitude of heaven and earth, is evidence of humane ignorance; For all things are a great darkness to us, and we are so unto our selves: The plainest things are as obscure, as the most confessedly mysterious; and the Plants we tread on, are as much above us, as the Stars and Heavens. The things that touch us are as distant from us, as the Pole; and we are as much strangers to our selves, as to the inhabitants of America.[43]

[41] See reference in *A Free Inquiry into the received Notion of Nature*, printed in 1686, but written about 1666 (*Works*, IV, 376 and 359).

[42] Ferris Greenslet, *Joseph Glanvill* (New York, 1900), pp. 95 ff. For references to Montaigne and Charron see *Scepsis scientifica*, pp. 114 and 172.

[43] From "Address to the Royal Society," *Scepsis scientifica*.

Both Glanvill and Boyle, however, refused to be identified with the extreme skeptical position that truth is unknowable.[44] They were far from intending to discourage scientific and philosophic activity. But they believed that he is least likely to go astray who is most keenly aware of the weakness and deception of human faculties. And in "Hobbism" they saw the grand modern illustration of stiff confidence in opinion, of the vanity of dogmatizing.[45]

These controversies reverberated outside the immediate circles of the Royal Society. When Richard Baxter in 1667 defended the doctrine of the immortality of the soul against the "Somatists or Epicureans," he relied, among other arguments against materialism, upon that of Glanvill.[46] He answers twenty objections to the doctrine, of which the first and fundamental is that "Matter and Motion, without any more, may do all that which you ascribe to souls." "And to what Authors," cries Baxter scornfully, "will they send us for the proof of this assertion? Is it to Mr. *Hobs?*" Hobbes, he thinks, has received some "smart castigations" from Dr. Ward and Dr. Bramhall, but he ventures "some general countercharges and reasons, against the *authority*" of the Material-

---

[44] See, for instance, Boyle, ed. cited, I, 374; and Joseph Glanvill, *Scire, or Reply to Albius* (1665), p. 3.

[45] The skeptical attitude toward science was not without later influence. In 1688 Matthew Prior, then at St. John's College, Cambridge, wrote a grandiose ode *On Exod. III. 14. — I Am That I Am*, the theme of which is the inadequacy of reason to understand the world and the necessity of exercising faith and reverence to reach the high abode of the mysterious God who revealed himself to Moses. A few lines will show how definitely Prior applied his critique to materialistic science:

"Man does with dangerous curiosity
These unfathom'd wonders try:
With fancied rules and arbitrary laws
Matter and motion he restrains;
And studied lines and fictious circles draws:
Then with imagin'd sovereignty
Lord of his new hypothesis he reigns."

(M. Prior, *Poetical Works*, ed. R. B. Johnson [London, 1907], I, 23–27.) The *Scepsis scientifica* has again become a familiar and an important conception in the discussions of the present century, as, for instance, in Émile Boutroux, "La Religion et les limites de la science," *Science et religion* (Paris, 1908).

[46] R. Baxter, *The Reasons of the Christian Religion* (London, 1667), pp. 489–604. Passages quoted are from pages 495–498.

ists. His first observation seems to have in view chiefly their opposition to Aristotelianism and the theological definition of the soul, though it may also glance at their ridicule of all idealistic thought, including the Libertine derision of the science of ethics: "When I find men," he says, "dispute against *Man*, and reason against the *power of Reason*, I think *humane interest* alloweth me to be *distrustful* of their sophistry, and to yield no further than I have cogent evidence. If man's *soul* be his *form*, he denieth *man* to be *man*, who denieth him that soul." After this observation, Baxter makes a curious — but in his age a not uncommon — *volte-face:*

I find Philosophers so little agreed among themselves, that it greatly diminisheth their authority and requireth a man who is just to his reason, to make a very accurate trial before he fall in with any of their opinions. . . .

I find the wisest of them so conscious of their ignorance, that they take most for uncertain which they say themselves; and confess they talk but in the dark: which made the *Pyrrhonians* and *Arcesilas* have so many followers; and *Cicero* with the *Academicks* so *over-modest* in disclaiming *certainty* and *confidence*, and writing by Dialogues with so much indifferency and wavering as they did. I need not send you to *Zanchez* his *Nihil scitur*, nor to our *Mr. Glanvil's Vanity of Dogmatizing*, for satisfaction. The learned *Gassendus* his modesty is sufficient, who if he speak of *Occult Qualities*, will ask you, *What Qualities are not Occult?*

"The most who in this age adhere to the *Epicurean* (or *Cartesian*) Hypothesis," Baxter notes, "are the younger sort of ingenious men," and among them Gassendi's authority was almost equal to that of Hobbes; the quotation from Gassendi was therefore adroit, though hardly representative. Baxter was not a Pyrrhonist; but when he had to contend with the prevalent materialistic dogmatism, he was ready to borrow an argument from Sanchez and Glanvill and buttress it with a confession from the foremost among the enemy.

IV

It is now possible to return to Dryden and ask whether he was aware of the developments we have sketched. We should the more expect their influence to be noticeable because they came so largely in the period from 1660 to 1680, the very years when Dryden was equipping himself with those ideas which make his political and religious poems, as a group, a remarkable expression of the conservative temperament. *Religio Laici* and *The Hind and the Panther* constitute the *terminus ad quem* in a study of Dryden's intellectual history. But for material on his development up to 1680 we have to depend quite largely on his dramas.

A valuable clue is given us in the notes collected in 1679–80 by John Aubrey toward a life of Hobbes: "Mr. John Dreyden, Poet Laureat, is his great admirer, and oftentimes makes use of his doctrine in his plays — from Mr. Dreyden himselfe." [47] And although Aubrey was too enthusiastic a friend of Hobbes to be trusted in all matters, yet this note can hardly be without foundation. Its authoritative source is confirmed by the many parallels to the doctrines of Hobbes to be found in Dryden's plays. In political thought, for instance, the monarchical absolutism of Hobbes is also the doctrine of Dryden's stage creatures,[48] and must have been particularly grateful to the ears of the court audience for which Dryden wrote. And yet this resemblance alone would not be decisive proof of indebtedness; a narrow political outlook was almost inevitable in heroic drama, and is common enough in the plays of Orrery, for instance, who has hardly been suspected of an admiration for Hobbes. More conclusive, I believe, and for the purpose of this study, more important, is the frequent reference in Dryden to the dilemma of free-will and necessity — the great ethical problem raised in a new form by Hobbism. In 1664, in his Dedication of *The Rival Ladies* to Lord Orrery, he implies that free-will is a delusion:

Here in [Orrery's plays] is no chance, which you have not foreseen; all your heroes are more than your subjects, they are your creatures; and though they seem to move freely in all the sallies of their passions, yet you make destinies for them, which they can-

---

[47] *Brief Lives*, I, 372. For the date of the notes see Introduction, p. 16.

[48] Mr. Merritt Y. Hughes has pointed out parallels in his article, "Dryden as Statist," *Philological Quarterly*, VI (1927), 334–350; but he relied only on internal evidence, without noting either the remark of Aubrey or Richard Leigh's contemporary accusation that Dryden got his political ideas from Hobbes, in *Censure of the Rota* (1673), p. 19.

not shun. They are moved (if I may dare to say so) like the rational creatures of the Almighty Poet, who walk at liberty, in their own opinion, because their fetters are invisible; when, indeed, the prison of their will is the more sure for being large; and, instead of an absolute power over their actions, they have only a wretched desire of doing that, which they cannot choose but do.[49]

Almanzor, the hero of *The Conquest of Granada* (1670), is troubled by the same problem:

> O Heaven, how dark a riddle's thy decree,
> Which bounds our wills, yet seems to leave them free!
> Since thy fore-knowledge cannot be in vain,
> Our choice must be what thou didst first ordain.
> Thus, like a captive in an isle confined,
> Man walks at large, a prisoner of the mind:
> Wills all his crimes, while Heaven the indictment draws,
> And, pleading guilty, justifies the laws.[50]

A sufficient number of such allusions can be found before 1680 to indicate that Dryden was interested in the subject.[51] Perhaps the most surprising expression of determinism is in *The State of Innocence* (1674), his operatic version of *Paradise Lost*, a philosophical perversion of the epic to which it is hard to believe Milton would have given his consent. In the opera the newly created Adam seems to have an innate understanding of seventeenth-century philosophy. When he first becomes conscious, he rises and paraphrases Descartes' *Discourse on Method*:

---

[49] *Works*, II, 132–133.
[50] *The Conquest of Granada*, Part II, Act IV, sc. iii (*Works*, IV, 190–191).
[51] I have collected the following, with references to the Scott and Saintsbury edition:

> *Indian Queen* (1664), Act II, sc. iii (II, 246)
> *Indian Queen* (1664), Act III, sc. ii (II, 257)
> *The Tempest* (1667), Act III, sc. v (III, 175)
> *Tyrannic Love* (1669), Act I, sc. i (III, 389)
> *Tyrannic Love* (1669), Act III, sc. i (III, 410)
> *Tyrannic Love* (1669), Act IV, sc. i (III, 430)
> *The Conquest of Granada*, Part I (1670), Act II, sc. i (IV, 56–57)
> *The Conquest of Granada*, Part II (1670), Act III, sc. i (IV, 162)

In the Dedication to *Aureng-Zebe* (1676) there is an interesting passage: "Our minds are perpetually wrought on by the temperament of our bodies; which makes me suspect, they are nearer allied, than our philosophers or school-divines will allow them to be."

What am I? or from whence? For that I am
I know, because I think, . . . [52]

But when Gabriel and Raphael are sent down jointly to instruct
Adam in the doctrine of the freedom of the will, they find him a
most reluctant and obstinate scholar.

> *Gabriel.* The Eternal, when he did the world create,
> All other agents did necessitate:
> So what he ordered, they by nature do:
> Thus light things mount, and heavy downward go.
> Man only boasts an arbitrary state.

> *Adam.* Yet causes their effects necessitate
> In willing agents; where is freedom then?
> Or who can break the chain which limits men
> To act what is unchangeably forecast,
> Since the first cause gives motion to the last?

The lengthy discussion appears to have been unsuccessful, for after
his instructors have departed Adam is still lamenting his "hard
state of life" in the divine disposition which has been explained
to him.[53] These pages of argument read like a brief summary of
the famous Bramhall-Hobbes controversy, with Adam, despite his
innocence, taking the part of Hobbes.

But it would be a mistake hastily to infer, from such passages
and from Aubrey's note, the conclusion that Dryden was at this
time a disciple of Hobbes, any more than of Descartes. He must
have been interested in necessitarianism, speculated on its implications, and enjoyed testing out its argumentative strength in
verse. Sympathetic intellectual curiosity is one of Dryden's
marked characteristics. But this very suppleness of his mind
served also to liberate him from the dogmatism and egotism of
Hobbes. In his old age he spoke of Hobbes's translation of Homer
as "bald," adding that he studied "poetry as he did mathematics,
when it was too late." [54] It was a curt dismissal. In 1685, in a
discussion of himself as translator of Lucretius, he incidentally
clearly draws the distinction between himself and Hobbes, both
in temperament and ideas:

[52] *The State of Innocence,* Act II, sc. i (*Works,* V, 133–134).
[53] *Ibid.,* Act IV, sc. i (*Works,* V, 152–156).
[54] *Preface to the Fables* (1700), (*Essays,* II, 252).

If I am not mistaken, the distinguishing character of Lucretius (I mean of his soul and genius) is a certain kind of noble pride, and positive assertion of his opinions. He is everywhere confident of his own reason, and assuming an absolute command, not only over his vulgar reader, but even his patron Memmius. For he is always bidding him attend, as if he had the rod over him, as our poet and philosopher of Malmesbury. This is that perpetual dictatorship, which is exercised by Lucretius; who, though often in the wrong, yet seems to deal *bona fide* with his reader, and tells him nothing but what he thinks; in which plain sincerity, I believe, he differs from our Hobbes, who could not but be convinced, or at least doubt, of some eternal truths, which he had opposed. . . . For there is no doubt to be made, but that he [Lucretius] could have been everywhere as poetical, as he is in his descriptions, and in the moral part of his philosophy, if he had not aimed more to instruct, in his System of Nature, than to delight. But he was bent upon making Memmius a materialist, and teaching him to defy an invisible power: in short, he was so much an atheist, that he forgot sometimes to be a poet. These are the considerations, which I had of that author, before I attempted to translate some parts of him. And accordingly I laid by my natural diffidence and scepticism for a while, to take up that dogmatical way of his, which, as I said, is so much his character, as to make him that individual poet.[55]

These passages, it is true, come too late in Dryden's life to constitute alone any sure indication of his attitude toward Hobbes before 1680. But when they are considered along with his earlier comments on the new science, the Royal Society, and his own distrust of dogmatism, they lose their casual appearance; and the impression grows that Dryden's attitude toward Hobbes must from the beginning have involved reservations and that he must have found himself more naturally on the side of the Royal Society, with its eminent spokesmen Boyle and Glanvill.[56]

[55] *Preface to Sylvae* (1685), (*Essays*, I, 259–260).

[56] A very interesting passage in the *Essay on Heroic Plays* (1672) by no means implies discipleship: "I dare further affirm, that the whole doctrine of separated beings, whether those spirits are incorporeal substances (which Mr. Hobbes, with some reason, thinks to imply a contradiction), or that they are a thinner or more aerial sort of bodies (as some of the Fathers have conjectured), may better be explicated by poets than by philosophers or divines. For their speculations on this subject are wholly poetical; they have only their fancy for their guide; and that, being sharper in an excellent poet, than it is likely it should in a phlegmatic,

V

There can be no doubt of Dryden's real appreciation of the new science. In an *Epistle to Dr. Charlton*, written in 1662, he praises English science, especially Bacon, Gilbert, Boyle, and Harvey. There is the famous apostrophe to the Royal Society in *Annus Mirabilis*, in which, after prophesying remarkable progress in navigation, he adds:

> This I foretell, from your auspicious care
> Who great in search of God and nature grow;
> Who best your wise Creator's praise declare,
> Since best to praise His works is best to know.

Even more direct and forceful are two passages, heretofore strangely neglected, in *An Essay of Dramatic Poesy* (1668). One is a recognition of the remarkable scientific advance after Copernicus:

> Is it not evident [asks Crites, who is otherwise on the side of the Ancients] in these last hundred years (when the study of philosophy has been the business of all the Virtuosi in Christendom), that almost a new Nature has been revealed to us? — that more errors of the school have been detected, more useful experiments in philosophy have been made, more noble secrets in optics, medicine, anatomy, astronomy, discovered, than in all those credulous and doting ages from Aristotle to us? — so true it is, that nothing spreads more fast than science, when rightly and generally cultivated.[57]

Later in the same essay he makes Lisideius allude to "what the philosophers say of motion that, when it is once begun, it continues of itself, and will do so to eternity, without some stop put to it," [58] — which is a simple statement of what was later to become Newton's first law of motion.

But we can go even further. That "natural diffidence and skepticism" which Dryden in 1685 declared part of his character,

---

heavy gownman, will see farther in its own empire, and produce more satisfactory notions on those dark and doubtful problems" (*Essays*, I, 153). A man who held such theories of knowledge and psychology would certainly never have been recognized by Hobbes as a hopeful disciple. Dryden had a very un-Hobbesian interest in the realms of mystery, and he repeatedly defended the use of the supernatural in epic poetry.

[57] *Essays*, I, 36–37.　　　　[58] *Ibid.*, p. 63.

he already in 1668 identified with the skeptical attitude of the Royal Society. When his brother-in-law, Sir Robert Howard, charged him with being "magisterial" in *An Essay of Dramatic Poesy*, his reply was that

... in vindication of myself, I must crave leave to say, that my whole discourse was sceptical, according to that way of reasoning which was used by Socrates, Plato, and all the Academics of old, which Tully and the best of the Ancients followed, and which is imitated by the modest inquisitions of the Royal Society. That it is so, not only the name will show, which is *an Essay*, but the frame and composition of the work. You see it is a dialogue sustained by persons of several opinions, all of them left doubtful, to be determined by the readers in general.[59]

In the true spirit of the Royal Society he asks, in the Preface to *An Evening's Love* (1671), "why should there be any *Ipse dixit* in our poetry, any more than there is in our philosophy?"[60]

That skepticism which separated Dryden from Hobbes and Lucretius was therefore no passing whim; it was both an early and a permanent intellectual characteristic. In the Preface to *Religio Laici* (1682) he confesses that he was "naturally inclined to scepticism in philosophy." He criticizes the Deists, and even some leaders in the Anglican Church, for their confidence in religious rationalism. He says:

Our modern philosophers, nay, and some of our philosophizing divines have too much exalted the faculties of our souls, when they have maintained that by their force mankind has been able to find that there is one supreme agent or intellectual Being which we call God.... They who would prove religion by reason, do but weaken the cause which they endeavour to support: 'tis to take away the pillars from our faith, and to prop it only with a twig.

It was this distrust of reason, this philosophical skepticism, that drove Dryden toward conservatism and authority in religion, and ultimately to the Catholic Church, just as his distrust of the populace was one reason for his increasing conservatism and Toryism in politics.

[59] *Ibid.*, p. 124. Dryden was following Cicero's account in *Academica* in designating Socrates and Plato among the "sceptical." Compare the earlier quotations from Fitzherbert, p. 26, and Baxter, p. 65.

[60] *Ibid.*, p. 138. Cf. also *Defence of the Epilogue* (1672), I, 163.

Fragmentary and meager as the evidence is, it seems nevertheless sufficient to indicate that Dryden was not unresponsive to the intellectual impulses aroused by the new scientific movement. He was deeply interested in the philosophy of Hobbes and over a long period ruminated on the perplexing problem of materialism. But his own temper allied him rather with the critics and enemies of Hobbes, and with their arguments against the Malmesbury philosopher he was unquestionably familiar. The consequence was a profound and permanent stimulus to the skeptical tendency of his nature. It is not contended here that Dryden became a skeptic through his contact with the Royal Society, because he knew Boyle and Glanvill; skepticism could in that age be acquired in many ways. But we can assert that he was interested in the Royal Society, understood its spirit, and recognized that he was likeminded with it; he understood the new philosophy of motion, vaguely perhaps in its scientific aspects, but with an acute interest in its deterministic implications regarding human nature; and he rejected the dogmatic materialism of Hobbes and Lucretius. And when we look for the meaning and importance of his distrust of the reason in *Religio Laici* and *The Hind and the Panther*, or for the interpretation of his ingenuous changeableness in literary opinions, we must go, among other places, to his intellectual adventures with the new science, with Hobbes, and with the Royal Society.

CHAPTER IV

ROMAN CATHOLIC APOLOGETICS IN ENGLAND

THE skeptical tendency, which Dryden betrayed only casually
in his comments on Hobbes and dogmatic materialism, he
expressed fully and explicitly in *Religio Laici* and *The Hind and
the Panther*. The Pyrrhonism that permeates Dryden's ideas on
religion is patent for all to see.

In an earlier chapter we have traced the history of this application of philosophical skepticism to religion and pointed out how
Dryden belongs to an important tradition of Christian apologetics,
a tradition illustrious for its great names and widely disseminated
over Europe. It will be recalled that, except Sir Thomas Browne,
the important exponents of this fideism were Roman Catholics,
and that fideism was particularly serviceable as an argument
against rationalism and Protestantism. Such is the historical fact;
for although such anti-rationalistic thought has often developed
within Protestantism, and in seventeenth-century England was
particularly prolific among the more "enthusiastic" dissenting
sects, it was the Roman Catholic controversialists who used the
argument with real skill and raised it to the level of learning and
philosophy. It was they, and not the less sophisticated leaders of
Dissent, who fully utilized the resources of the Pyrrhonistic dialectic in religious disputes. In the seventeenth century such attack on the authority of the reason came therefore to be recognized
as a distinctly Roman Catholic maneuvre. This statement will
be further supported by a study of the development of Roman
Catholic apologetics in England from 1600 to Dryden's time, with
which the present chapter is concerned.

But one must also remember that whenever this fideistic argu-

ment was pressed very far, it became heresy; and all fideistic developments have been unwelcome to the Roman Catholic Church.
Whenever called upon to render its final judgment, the Church
has always rebuked those who would unduly disparage the human
reason. Thus in a great crisis in the seventeenth century, the rejection by the Church of the doctrine of absolute depravity as it
was expounded by the Jansenists, though it may seem on the surface to have been the triumph of a Jesuit cabal, was a great deal
more than that; it was consistent with the historical position of
a church which has quite uniformly been accused by the more extreme Augustinians of a semi-Pelagianism. The whole central
tradition of the Roman Catholic Church is against the doctrine
that faith is best supported by a philosophical skepticism. The
philosophy of the Church has been the intellectualistic philosophy
of Thomas Aquinas, which, as is admitted by critics and admirers
alike, is one of the most ambitious and magnificent constructions
of the human reason. Not only did Aquinas provide for believers
an intellectual and systematized statement of revealed truth in the
Summa Theologiae, but he met unbelievers on their own ground
of reason with his *Summa contra Gentiles.* Even Protestants have
not hesitated to appeal to this great authority over the empire of
the mind when they needed assistance in their battles against that
anti-intellectualism of the "private spirit" which was always
threatening to disrupt their more conservative churches.[1] And
within the Roman Catholic Church no form of anti-intellectualism
or philosophical skepticism has permanently succeeded against the
fortified position of the Thomistic theology. We have already
seen [2] that fideistic theories were declared heretical as early as
1348, and that the theory of the double truth was condemned in

---

[1] Meric Casaubon, for instance, who distrusted even the "prophecy" of the
Platonic "Theologia mystica," exclaims: " . . . how contrarie to the doctrine of
the best Schoolmen, I appeal to *Thom. Aquinas 2. 2. quaestione 174.* who there very
solidly proveth and asserteth the excellencie of rationall intellectuall Christian
knowledge, above all prophecy: to whom also that excellent Rabbi *Ben Maimon,*
the *Aquinas* of the Rabbins, doth agree in divers places in his *More Nevochim,*
making it (rationall intellectuall Divinitie) the highest degree of Prophesie. . . ."
— *A Treatise Concerning Enthusiasme, As it is an Effect of Nature: but is mistaken
by many for either Divine Inspiration, or Diabolical Possession* (London, 1655),
pp. 118–129.   [2] Page 21.

1277 and again in 1512. Nominalism, though it flourished mightily, was always disapproved of; in the seventeenth century Jansenism was eradicated; and in the nineteenth century, when such fideistic and traditionalistic writers as Lamennais and de Bonald enjoyed a great popular following among French Catholics, their position was repeatedly repudiated by the Church.[3] There is something tragic in the long succession of adherents whose reasons for submission to its authority the Church has been forced to condemn. Newman was among those who suffered from such a philosophical isolation; it is indicative of his affinity with the fideistic traditions that he, like French Modernists of the latter part of the nineteenth century, "dreaded the excesses of Catholic scholasticism and professed little sympathy with the theology of Thomas Aquinas, which has become, under Leo XIII. and Pius X., the official theology of the church."[4]

However often philosophical skepticism has been put to religious and controversial uses by Roman Catholics, it has never received the approbation of the Church. Montaigne's *Essays*, Charron's *Wisdom*, and Browne's *Religio Medici* were all put on the Index.[5] On the whole, fideism and Pyrrhonism has remained a border phenomenon and failed to contribute to the main tradition of the Church. It has had a succession of histories rather than *a* history, and each manifestation of it has been modified by the peculiar circumstances and peculiar controversial exigencies of the moment, as much as by the intellectual turn of its proponents. This is particularly true of that forgotten development in English Catholic apologetics with which we must be concerned, as it has a special importance for the understanding of Dryden.

[3] See A. Vacant et E. Mangenot, *Dictionnaire de théologie catholique* (Paris, 1903—), under *Augustine, certitude,* and *foi,* particularly the analysis of fideism in the last-named article, VI (1920), 179.

[4] Charles Sarolea, *Cardinal Newman* (Edinburgh, 1908), p. 170. This volume gives an admirable discussion of the broad questions here passed over so cursorily. For a bibliography of fideism see Vacant et Mangenot, *op. cit.,* under *crédibilité,* Vol. III, cols. 2308–2309.

[5] Of course not every heretical book is put on the Index, because the controversy, if there is any, is not always carried to Rome for a decision. Many books of questionable tendency have never aroused controversy, and many others have had a local or passing importance and have never been heard of at Rome.

I

The fideistic movement was essentially controversial, and its proponents repeatedly asserted that their arguments were to be understood only as weapons against Protestantism and not as a part of the structure of Roman Catholic theology. Its history is a study in theological strategy; and it is therefore best explained by a survey of the ground held by the opposing Protestant camp.

The Reformation, which began as a protest against abuses, had quickly assumed a more profound aspect, as a protest against the very authority of the Catholic Church. Protestantism, it was discovered, was individualism in religion. This discovery, pressed home by Catholic controversialists, was on the whole unwelcome to the Protestant leaders, who sought to avoid its implications by asserting that the clarity of the Scriptures on essential points of salvation provided a sufficient basis for uniformity of doctrine; on the practical side they even found that the exercise of political power was necessary to prevent their churches from disintegrating into sectarianism. But the question of Church authority became the point of universal dispute, between the state churches and the sects as well as between Protestants and Catholics.

This fundamental question of authority resolved itself naturally into the problems, first, of the sufficiency — even the intelligibility and integrity — of the Scriptures, and, second, of the power and adequacy of the reason of man to deal with matters of religion. In the first department of controversy the name of Cardinal du Perron (1556–1618) stood preëminent, if we may believe his great Huguenot opponent, Daniell Tillenus, professor of divinity in the University of Sedan. "Neyther *Hosius*," he observed, "nor *Peresius*, nor *Soto*, nor *Lindanus*, nor *Camus*, nor *Canisius*, nor yet that Arch-Rabby *Bellarmine*, not any I say, had as yet so mightily clipped this spirituall coyne (as *Gerson* calleth the Scripture) nor obserued so much drosse, nor so many defects in the pure Alley of the lawe of God, written by *Moses*, as the Lord of Perron doth." [6]

---

[6] *A Defence of the Sufficiency and perfection of the holy Scripture. Against the Cauillations of the Lord du Perron. . . . By D. Daniell Tillenus, Professor of Diuinitie in the Vniuersitie of Sedan. . . .* Printed at London by L. S. for Nathaniell Butter. 1606.

It must have been no small matter to stand highest among these critics of the reliability of Scripture who had defamed it, says Tillenus in another place, "with many contumelies, calling it the booke of heretikes, the blacke Gospell, Incke-Diuinitie, Leaden ruler, . . . the apple of discord, *Sphynxes* riddle, a sword in a mad-mans hand, and other like termes." Lindanus, we are told, had even called Tradition "the true Moly conseruing the Christian faith, against the Enchantments of Hereticks, because Catholikes (saith he) would be soone poysoned with these Enchantments (he meaneth the Scriptures) if they did not use the Moly or antidote of Traditions." [7]

In their eagerness to attack the Protestants, Catholic controversialists thus incited scholarly labors in the direction of what has become "higher criticism," and their success was such as to cause serious anxiety, as we shall see, to Protestants and Catholics alike. The greatest representative of this critical scholarship was Father Simon, to whose work we shall return in a later section.

The other problem — of the power of the human mind to establish religious truth and of the adequacy and dependability of individual interpretations apart from tradition — produced in English Catholic propaganda a fideistic movement of ever-increasing importance down to the reign of James II. If it is to be traced to any one source, it must be to a peculiar "method" which Jean Gontery (1562–1616), a Jesuit of Bordeaux, discovered for use against Protestants.[8] This "method" was simply a *reductio ad absurdum* of the Protestant claim to deriving their doctrines from Scripture. Gontery was convinced that they read their own ideas

[7] *Positions lately held by the L. du Perron, Bishop of Eureux, against the sufficiency and perfection of the Scriptures, maintaining the necessitie and authoritie of unwritten Traditions. Verie learnedly answered and confuted by D. Daniell Tillenus.* . . . Printed at London by L. S. for Nathaniell Butter. 1606.

[8] *La Pierre de touche, ov La Vraye Methode povr desabuser les esprits trompez soubs couleur de Reformation. D'icy on descouurira l'incroyable ruse des Ministres faisans à croire aux simples, que les articles de leur confessions de foy Reformée sont exprez dans la parole de Dieu escrite, sans qu'on y en puisse trouuer vne seule clause. D'ou il aperra aussi que toute la Reformation pretenduë n'est qu'une inuention purement humaine, & diabolique. Par le R. P. Iean Gontery de la Compagnie de Iesus. Premiere Partie. Deprauant Scripturas ad suam ipsorum perditionem. 2. Petr. 3. vers. 16* (Bordeaux, 1614), 474 pages. *Seconde Partie de la Pierre de touche,* . . . (Bordeaux, 1614), 204 pages.

into Scripture; he therefore argued that if the Bible is to be the unique source of religious truth it must be read literally, and without drawing of inferences and consequences. "For if that which is not written [explicitly in the Bible] is in it and contained in it, certainly the Alcoran, Arianism, Donatism, Eutichianism, Anabaptism, and Atheism may be found in it; and all the dreamings of shepherds are there. . . . For you grant the liberty to everyone in the whole world (by means of your alleged necessary *implications*) to supply at his pleasure whatever comes into his mind. By this method the son will revolt against his father, the wife against the husband, the subject against the Prince, the valet against the master, the flock against the shepherd, all contending that they find their caprices in the Bible, by the method of necessary *implication*."[9] The appeal to Scripture, he contended, was only a disguised appeal to the individual reader of Scripture, and therefore, was disruptive of all authority. The only feasible alternative was an infallible church, the guardian of tradition as well as Scripture.

Gontery's principle was immediately seized upon by another Jesuit, François Veron (1575–1625), who elaborated it into a method of his own, by which he became in fact the leading Catholic controversialist of his time in France.[10] He was a type of theological writer now happily extinct; a modern reader is likely to be impressed chiefly with his bristling manners, his self-satisfaction, and his rather stupid insistence on putting all argument in rigid

---

[9] Trans. from *Seconde Partie de la Pierre de touche*, pp. 62-63.

[10] *Bref et Facile Moyen par lequel toute personne bien Qv'elle ne soit versée en Theologie, peut par la seule Bible, soit de Geneue, soit autre, & par la Confession de foy de la Religion pretendue, faire paroistre euidemment à toute Ministre qu'il abuse, & à tout Religionnaire qu'il est abusé en tous & vn chacun des poincts de sa pretendue reformation* (Pont-a-Mousson, 1617), 214 pages. Reprinted more than twenty times.

This appeared in expanded form as *Methode Novvelle, Facile, et Solide de convaincre de nullité la Religion pretendue reformée en tovs les poincts controuersez; ov; La destrvction totale de l'heresie; Par la sevle escritvre saincte exposée selon la mesme Escritvre, par les Saincts Peres, seants es Conciles des quatre premiers siecles, de l'impression de Basle, &c.* (Paris 1623), Vol. I, 551 pages; Vol. II, 834 pages; Vol. III, 920 pages.

In the *Avant-Propos* of the larger work he tells how he had been assisted in controversy by Gontery's advice: "Il m'apprend qu'il fallait se tenir sur la deffensive, & obliger les Ministres selon la loy qu'ils s'estoient prescrite à la pure Escriture, qu'ainsi faisant la victoire estoit facile & asseuree en nostre faveur."

syllogistic form. His qualities of mind as well as his style of controversy may be illustrated by a passage from his *Methode nouvelle*, dealing with the subject "How one should reply to the purely philosophical arguments of the [Protestant] Ministers":

We are under no obligation to reply to such arguments, as much because they have promised to reform us according to Scripture, the rule by which [they assert] everything should be examined, regulated, and reformed, as because faith is above human and philosophical reasoning. Who would believe in the resurrection if faith is to be regulated by philosophical axioms? Nevertheless, inasmuch as the truth of the faith is not contrary to the truth of philosophy and human reason, and as we could easily remain the victors in these lists; to win a quick victory (for it is not expedient to drag out this battle) it is necessary to observe three precepts in this our defense. The first is to force the adversary to state his doctrine in direct terms. The second is to confine oneself exactly within the formulations of the [Protestant] defender, denying simply what it is necessary to deny without producing a great many reasons for such negations, and thus oblige the Minister to commit himself to the opposite. The third point is, since it is a question of ratiocination, never to answer him unless he puts his argument in syllogistic form; for as all novices in the art of reasoning know, no deduction has any validity except by virtue of the two propositions to which it is joined. If these people excuse themselves by saying that they are not philosophers, retort on them that in that case they should not be importuning us in a matter in which they are ignorant and in which it is easy to deceive and be deceived by sophistical or plausible arguments. Whoever observes these precepts will quickly silence these Ministers, who, excessively ignorant as they are, would still like to parade a little philosophy before the simple-minded populace. Whoever would reply more at large, however learned he may be, will injure our cause; for, though he may convince the Minister, nevertheless the Minister, having more intelligence than the people listening, if he is impudent and shameless (as such people are), will doubtless always say in reply something that the simple minded cannot understand, and thus these simple listeners will remain uncertain as to who is the victor,—a matter very prejudicial to the good of their souls, which should always be our concern; and our side having so much the real advantage, we are losing too much when we battle in such a way that, although victory is really ours, it is not so understood by the audience; it is not sufficient to win, unless the victory is recognized, and therefore it is necessary to avoid subtleties that raise the combatants beyond the level of the spectators. Thus one may answer in three words, for example, all that du Moulin argues against transubstantiation, in his *Bouclier* [*Shield*], part 2, section 30. One must simply deny his propositions: *that if the parts of a body do not occupy different locations in space, the body can not be material; it must be a spirit; it no longer has the dimension of length; it is more spiritual than a soul; that a body in two places is not one but two bodies,* and similar odd fancies. Just deny them, without discoursing about our negations, etc. Thus we shall soon make these alleged Reformers speechless.[11]

This makes amusing reading to-day, but in his time this "machine de guerre de nouvelle invention," as Veron called it in his dedication to the king, had its effect upon thousands and caused his name to be remembered, with both reverence and execration, for a century. It is true that his argument was essentially destructive; he made no attempt at any direct proof of the truth of Catholic doctrine. But one must remember that Veron, as the Abbé Feret has pointed out,[12] began with the assumption that there must be some church somewhere which could offer to the individual the necessary certitude in faith and authority in doctrine. If Protestantism has no such authority and certitude, the inevitable consequence, according to Veron and his followers, must be that the Catholic Church *does* have it.

It is obvious, however, that this method was susceptible of far greater philosophical development than it received from Veron. In his hands it was as rigid and brittle as his mind, and devoid of any psychological or metaphysical interest. What it needed, what it seemed particularly to call for, was an infusion of that highly developed criticism of human knowledge which the revival of Greek skepticism had made current and which it is curious that Veron should have so completely ignored. But this defect was remedied by his successors.

In England, as well as on the Continent, the problem of the authority of the reason in religion was early recognized as fundamental. Circumstanced as the Anglican Church was, the development of its theology in the direction of rationalism was

---

[11] Trans. from *Methode nouvelle,* I, 504–506.

[12] Abbé P. Feret, *La Faculté de théologie de Paris, Époque moderne,* IV (Paris, 1906), 56–63.

natural and necessary. It had enemies on two sides and needed the assistance of reason against both. On the one side were the sects, the Puritans and Independents, against whose doctrine of the "inner spirit" Hooker had contended that "we therefore stand on a plainer ground, when we gather by reason from the quality of things believed or done, that the Spirit of God hath directed us in both, than if we settle ourselves to believe or to do any certain particular thing, as being moved thereto by the Spirit. . . . There is as yet no way known how to dispute, or to determine of things disputed, without the use of natural reason." [13] On the other side were the Catholics proclaiming the necessity of an authoritative and infallible church, against whom Chillingworth provided a classic defense in his *Religion of Protestants* (1638). Chillingworth, like Hooker, appealed unhesitatingly to reason. His Jesuit adversary, Edward Knott, had said, for instance, that if the infallibility of the Church "be once impeached, every man is given over to his own wit and discourse." Chillingworth took up the gage: ". . . if you mean by *discourse*, right reason grounded on Divine revelation, and common notions written by God in the hearts of all men, and deducing, according to the never-failing rules of logic, consequent deductions from them; if this be it which you mean by *discourse*, it is very meet and reasonable and necessary, that men, as in all their actions, so especially in that of greatest importance, the choice of their way to happiness, should be left to it; and he that follows this in all his opinions and actions, and does not only seem to do so, follows always God; whereas he that followeth a company of men, may oft-times follow a company of beasts." [14]

This advanced position of the new Anglican champion was frequently thereafter attacked by Catholics. "Since the publishing of Mr. *Chillingworth's* book," wrote Father Cressy, "there ha's appeared in England a *new Judge* of controversies, and much defer'd unto there, which is *every mans private reason interpreting Scripture.*" As for private reason being a judge, he replies: "I will shew the impossibility for it to attain the ends for which Christ appointed a government in his Church; (viz. unity of minds

[13] *Ecclesiastical Polity*, Book III, Chap. VIII, pars. 15 and 17.
[14] William Chillingworth, *Works* (Oxford, 1838), I, 14-15.

and wills among Christians) together with the unavoidable absurdities attending such a Judge." His own theory is a development of the statement of Augustine: "That we believe any thing, we owe it to authority; that we understand any thing, to reason (*de util. cred. c. 2.*)." He will admit that "*Discourse of Reason* may, and ordinarily does precede belief; but belief it self is not discourse; but a simple assent of the understanding. In beliefe we are to distinguish between the *causes*, and the *motives* of it: and when men speak of the *last resolution of faith*, they intend to consider the last *motive* or authority into which it is resolved, not the primary *efficient cause* of it. Therefore though faith be an act of reason, yet it is not said to be resolved into reason, though produced by it, but into authority."[15] Characteristic of the new Catholic apologetics is the warning of Rushworth: ". . . what a follie were it for a man to venture his soule and conscience upon a subtiltie or present flash of wit, whereof peradventure within an hower hee him selfe will see the falsitie, and condemne his owne errour. Wherefore a Catholike is not to venter the cause upon his owne head, not to confesse it weake because he cannot defende it, for both may he improue him selfe, and some others perhapps may goe farr beyond him."[16] Against such instability of the reason he contrasted the rock of authority of the infallible church.

It was therefore becoming more and more clear up to 1660 that the question of religious knowledge and authority was the great crux of the whole complicated controversy; and on this question both sides concentrated their efforts.[17] The Anglicans were coming frankly to recognize that their final appeal must be to the power of the individual reason to interpret Scripture, and the

[15] Hugh Cressy, *Exomologesis* (Paris, 1647), pp. 387, 415–419; 2d ed. (1653), pp. 283, 303–306. Father Cressy was a Benedictine of Douay who came to England after the Restoration as chaplain to Queen Catherine, and exercised great influence in Catholic circles. Dryden mentions him in his Preface to *Religio Laici*.

[16] William Rushworth, *Dialogues* (Paris, 1640), p. 342.

[17] A similar change was taking place from 1640 on in France; the principle of authority became the center of the controversy, and the Roman Catholics dwelt particularly on the multiplicity of Protestant sects as evidence that Protestantism possessed no effective inner principle of authority. The classic expression of this argument is of course Bossuet's *Histoire des variations des églises protestantes* (1688). See Alfred Rébelliau, *Bossuet, Historien du Protestantisme*, 3d ed. (Paris, 1909).

Roman Catholics devoted themselves particularly to a destructive criticism of this kind of religious authority. The controversial tactics of Gontery and Veron became the standard tactics of English Catholicism of the seventeenth century.

But although the issue was thus growing in definiteness in the first half of the century, it must not be supposed that these developments were universally approved within the respective parties to the controversy. Some Anglicans voiced the fear that the rationalism of Chillingworth was indistinguishable from Socinianism, and Catholic writers, of course, joined in the cry.[18] The charge was not true, and was later dropped, at least among Anglicans, when these new controversial developments became more universally understood. On the other hand, the Roman Catholic diatribes against reason also struck the age as in some degree novel, and did not escape censure even among the Catholics themselves. We have a significant comment on them from the famous Thomas White, who later crossed swords with Glanvill over skepticism and whose writings, says Dodd, "made a great noise in the world."[19] White was no critic of the reason; he was for certainty both in philosophy and in religion.[20] He criticized severely such Protestants as, with Chillingworth, admitted that they believed on evidence, not on authority, and would willingly change their religion should new evidence seem to tip the balance against it; who admitted that for historical facts, whether secular or religious, we can have at best a "moral certainty"; a new branch, says White, shoots out "from the old oak of reformation and boldly professes it enough to guess at Tenets of Religion, and that we

[18] John Tulloch, *Rational Theology and Christian Philosophy in England in the Seventeenth Century*, 2d ed. (Edinburgh, 1874), I, 296 ff.; Hugh Cressy, *Exomologesis* (ed. 1653), p. 283; Richard Baxter, *Saints' Everlasting Rest*, Preface to Part II.

[19] Dodd's *Church History of England* (Brussels, 1742), III, 285. Dodd quotes Wood's *Athenae Oxonienses* to the effect that Hobbes and White used to visit one another, "but seldom parted in cold blood. For they would wrangle, squabble, and scold about philosophical matters, like young sophisters, tho' either of them was eighty years old." This little vignette suggests vividly the ease with which Roman Catholic clergy operated in the London of Charles II.

[20] As in his *Religion and Reason Mutually corresponding and assisting each other* (Paris, 1660).

ought to be ready (if more reason should appear) to change the *Bible* for the *Alcoran;* . . . these delicate Believers content their easie and civil natures with a dow-bak't probability, as if they were little concern'd, whether the Religion they profest were true or false." Unfortunately, he must admit, there were similar errors current among the Catholics: "Yet I'le not do them the wrong," he continues, "to say, they had not some ground or rather occasion out of some of our Divines; who (raising more dust then they were able to keep out of their own eyes) seem to have unawares contributed to the hatching of this dangerous Cockatrice, *Incertitude*, which these bold Reformers have at last shewed to the world, like *the Abomination of Desolation standing in the Temple*, to be abhorr'd by all Christians hearts and true lovers of vertue." [21] But in spite of such criticism and opposition, both Anglican rationalism and Roman Catholic Pyrrhonism continued their development and dominated in the controversies after the Restoration.

Purely as an exigency of controversy, then, this fideistic and traditionalistic mode of thought arose and spread early in the seventeenth century, first in France and then in England. It is apparently unrelated to any secular movement, such as that of Montaigne's disciples; its exponents are innocent of Sextus Empiricus; it was but faintly tinged, if at all, with any old religious tradition such as Augustinianism. It was what Veron had called it, an "engine of war." No doubt it proved very successful in

---

[21] *Preface* to *Rushworth's Dialogues . . . Corrected and enlarg'd by Thomas White, Gent.* (Paris, 1654). The "dow-bak't probability" of which White accused the Protestants should not be confused with Pyrrhonism; it refers to the Protestant position regarding historical evidences in religion. The Catholics declared that the historical element in Christianity, like its doctrines, must be believed on the authority of the Church; the Protestants admitted that absolute demonstration is in such matters impossible, but that we may content ourselves with a "moral certainty" that the facts of history were as they are represented. The doctrine of "moral certainty" was therefore one of the alternatives to Roman infallibility of faith. For representative passages in this controversy see: Chillingworth, ed. cited, I, 114 ff.; II, 317 ff.; Edward Knott, *Infidelity Vnmasked or the Confutation of a Booke Published by Mr. William Chillingworth* (Ghent, 1652), pp. 102–103; E. Stillingfleet, *Origines Sacrae* (Oxford, 1836), I, 132 ff.; Edward Worsley's criticism of Stillingfleet in *Protestancy without Principles* (Antwerp, 1668), 49–62; and Johannes de la Placette, *The Incurable Scepticism of the Church of Rome,* translated by Tenison (1688), Chap. I.

proselytizing both in France and in England; for by 1660 it had become a major weapon, ready for the great campaigns waged by the Roman Catholics in England between the Restoration of Charles II and the flight of James II.

II

Theological controversy underwent some change with the Restoration, no less than the other aspects of the intellectual and moral life of the nation.   But the change in Roman Catholic apologetics was chiefly in the accentuation of elements already present, and their adaptation to the prevailing mode of thought in English society under Charles II.   All forms of sophistication flourished in the reign of the merry monarch as never before; among the teachings which then fell on fruitful soil and multiplied a hundredfold were those of philosophical skepticism in its ancient and modern forms, in Sextus Empiricus and the Academics, in Montaigne and Charron and Sir Thomas Browne.   Roman Catholic propagandists, who were sensitive to the new intellectual atmosphere and desired to conduct their controversies with intellectual as well as social finesse, put their emphasis on fideism and traditionalism as never before.

Throughout the period Anglicans voiced their sense of the scandal to religion in these tactics.   Gilbert Burnet has left a notice of this new phenomenon in controversy; he observes in his *History:*

And now that the main principles of religion were struck at by Hobbes and his followers, the papists acted upon this a very strange part.   They went in so far even into the argument for atheism, as to publish many books in which they affirmed, that there was no certain proof of the Christian religion, unless we took it from the authority of the church as infallible.   This was such a delivering up of the cause to them, that it raised in all good men a very high indignation at popery; that party shewing, that they chose to make men who would not turn papists become atheists, rather than believe Christianity upon other ground than infallibility.[22]

This statement by Burnet — and those of other Anglicans, like Tillotson, who used the same phrasing — may seem harsh and un-

<hr>

[22] *History of My Own Time*, ed. Osmund Airy (Oxford, 1897), Part I, I, 335.

intelligent; Pyrrhonism and atheism are not equivalent terms. And yet Burnet correctly interpreted the situation and the dilemma raised by the Roman Catholic tactics; for an Anglican who was convinced by the skeptical argument would naturally find it difficult to remain an Anglican; his choice must have been between atheism and submission to the authority of Rome. Skepticism became a highroad leading from Anglicanism to Rome; and any man who, like Dryden, betrayed the influence of Pyrrhonism in his religious ideas, was likely to be branded indiscriminately as a "papist" or a man of no religion.[23]

Among the most famous Roman Catholic books of the period was *Fiat Lux*,[24] by a Franciscan, John Vincent Canes. Appearing immediately after the Restoration, it struck the appropriate and popular note of genial tolerance. "There is no colour of reason or just title," this is the substance of the first chapter, "may move us to quarrell and judge one another with so much heat about religion." The second gives us the philosophical "motive to moderation": "All things are so obscure that no man in prudence can so far presume of his own knowledge as to set up himself a guide in Religion to his neighbour." From this point the reader is gently led through the succeeding chapters to the shelter of Catholic authority.

John Owen, the eminent Independent preacher, immediately published a voluminous answer.[25] Of first importance for our purposes is a passage in which he indicates how the style and argument of *Fiat Lux* was adapted to the new temper of the time.

---

[23] Likewise the Roman Catholic appeal to the infallible authority of the Church lent itself to confusion with the "atheistical" doctrine of state authority in religion promulgated by Hobbes. See, for instance, *A Brief and Impartial Account of the Nature of the Protestant Religion* (London, 1682), p. 28.

[24] *Fiat Lux, or, A general Conduct to a right understanding in the great Combustions and Broils about Religion here in England. Betwixt Paptist and Protestant, Presbyterian & Independent To the end That Moderation and Quietness may at length hapily ensue after so various Tumults in the Kingdom. By Mr. J. V. C. a friend To men of all Religions. . . .* 1661. It was dedicated to the Countess of Arundel and Surrey, mother of Philip Thomas Howard, later Cardinal of Norfolk. Reprinted in 1662 and 1665.

[25] *Animadversions on a Treatise Intituled Fiat Lux* (London, 1662), 440 pages.

Unto the ensuing whole Chapter [that is, the second], wherein our Author expatiates, with a most luxuriant Oratory, throughout; and oft times soars with Poeticall raptures, in setting forth the obscurity and darkness of all things, our ignorance and disability to attain a right and perfect knowledge of them, canting by the way, many of those pretty Notions, which the Philosophical discoursive men of our dayes do use to whet their wits upon, over a glass of Wine: I have not much to offer: Nor should I once reflect upon that discourse, were it not designed to another end, than that which it is ushered in by, as the thing aymed to be promoted by it. Forbearance of one another in our several perswasions, on a sense of our infirmity and weaknesse, and the obscurity of those things, about which our minds and contemplations are conversant, is flourished at the entrance of this Harangue: After a small progresse, the Snake begins to hiss in the grass, and in the Close openly to shew it selfe, in an enticement unto an imbracing of the Roman-Religion; which, it seems will disentangle our minds out of that maze about the things of God and Man, in which, without its guidance, we must wander for ever. As for his Philosophicall notions, I suppose they were only vented, to shew his skill in the Learned talks of this Age, and to toll on the Gallants, whom he hath most hope to enveagle; knowing them to be Candidates for the most part, unto that Scepticism which is grown the entertainment of Tables and Taverns. How a man that is conversant in his thoughts about Religion, and his choice of, or settlement therein, should come to have any concernment in this Discourse, I cannot imagine. That God, who is infinitely wise, holy, good, who perfectly knows all his own excellencies, hath revealed so much of Himself, his Mind, and Will, in reference to the Knowledg which he requires of himself, and Obedience unto him, as is sufficient to guide us whilst we are here below, to steer our Course in our subjection to him, and dependence on him, in a manner acceptable unto him, and to bring us to our utmost end and blessednesse in the enjoyment of him: This Protestants think sufficient for them, who as they need not, so they desire not to be wise above what is written; nor to know more of God, than he hath so revealed of himself, that they may know it. . . . Thus are poor unstable souls ventured to the Borders of Atheisme, under a pretence of leading them to the Church.[26]

The formula of objurgation became a commonplace in the Anglican apologetics in the seventeenth century. It is "the general unhappiness of most of the popish arguments," wrote Tillotson

[26] *Ibid.*, pp. 148–156.

in his *Rule of Faith* (1666), that they strike not only "at prot-estancy, but at Christian religion." [27]

In 1665 Edward Stillingfleet struck at the doctrine of papal infallibility in his *Rational Account of the Grounds of the Protestant Religion*. And in the same year appeared another famous Catholic book of controversy, *Sure-Footing in Christianity*, dedicated to the Queen, the work of the widely known John Sergeaunt. This book arrives at the same conclusion as *Fiat Lux*, but by a different path. Sergeaunt was a man of philosophical interests who devised a curious system of reasoning all his own. His quarrel with the Protestants, he wishes us first to believe, was not so much that they relied on reasoning as that not one of them had the happiness to understand the true principles of that science. His volume bore the subtitle, *Rational Discourses on the Rule of Faith*. He first defined the nature and properties of that rule: "namely, it must be plain and self-evident as to its Existence to all and Evidenceable as to its Ruling Power to enquirers even the ruder vulgar, apt to settle and justify undoubting persons, to satisfy fully the most Sceptical Dissenters and rational Doubters, and to convince the most obstinate and acute Adversaries, built upon unmoveable Grounds, that is: Certain in it self, and absolutely as-certainable to us." [28] No Protestant rule of faith could show that it possessed these necessary properties — or indeed pretended to possess them. But Roman Catholic authority constitutes such a rule for the believer who accepts it implicitly, who submits to it for the a priori reason that it is guaranteed by the "Divine Veracity"; such submission Sergeaunt called a "Rational Assent" and he said

[27] Part II, sec. iii, par. 4. In *Works* (ed. 1742), IV, 604. One might multiply quotations to this effect indefinitely. The following from the *Rule of Faith* will serve as illustrations:

"Is it not very pretty to see what pitiful shifts men that serve an hypothesis are put to? when, to maintain infallibility, they are forced to run to the extremities of scepticism. . . ." — Part II, sec. iii, par. 7 (ed. cited, IV, 609).

"Pyrrho himself never advanced any principle of scepticism beyond this, viz. that men ought to question the credit of all books, concerning which they cannot demonstrate as to every sentence in them, that the particle *not* was not inserted (if it be affirmative) or left out (if it be negative)." — Part II, sec. v, par. 1 (ed. cited, IV, 646).

[28] *Sure-Footing in Christianity* (London, 1665), pp. 11–12.

that it "establishes my Faith against the assaults of any doubts from Humane Reasons." [29]   After this leap from philosophy to authority there can therefore be no further appeal to the reason as judge in any matter of religious doubt or debate. Consequently, though Sergeaunt begins with a great show of reasoning, his conclusions are as inimical to rationalism as were those of *Fiat Lux*.

It was in reply to *Sure-Footing* that Tillotson wrote his *Rule of Faith*,[30] already noticed and quoted. Daniel Whitby, a Fellow of Trinity College, Oxford, published in the same year a pamphlet against both Sergeaunt and Canes, in which he set forth the Protestant doctrines in a systematic manner, with propositions and corollaries.[31] He asserted that "nothing can be judge in any case but Reason." Even in the decisions of the Church, "Reason must still become their Judge, for sure they must have motives to encline them either way." "Hence I infer, That Reason cannot be rejected, as unsure, and unsufficient to ground an Article of Faith upon; for the certainty of our whole Faith depending upon that of Reason, it must fall together with it. So that to quarrel with the use of Reason upon that account, (as Papists usually do) is in effect to quarrel with Religion and Christianity." [32]

How acute the situation was becoming is apparent from the rather remarkable change of mind of Joseph Glanvill, who in 1664 had been elected to the Royal Society as the champion of the *scepsis scientifica*. In 1670 he put forth a pamphlet in defense of reason against its detractors.[33] He addressed himself to those Protestants who with evangelical fervor had been declaiming from the pulpit against rationalism in religion. He warned them that

---

[29] *Ibid.*, p. 182.

[30] The *Rule of Faith*, published in 1666, was reprinted in 1676 and 1688.

[31] ΔῸΣ ΠΟῪ ΣΤΩ, or, *An Answer to Sure Footing, So far as Mr. Whitby is concerned in it. Wherein the Rule and Guide of Faith, the Interest of Reason, and the Authority of the Church in Matters of Faith, are fully handled and vindicated; From the Exceptions of Mr. Serjeant, and the Petty Flirts of Fiat Lux* . . . (Oxford, 1666).

[32] *Ibid.*, p. 5.

[33] ΛΟΓΟΎ ΘΡΗΣΚΕΙΑ: *Or, A Seasonable Recommendation, and Defence of Reason, In the Affairs of Religion; against Infidelity, Scepticism and Fanaticisms of all sorts* (London, 1670). 36 pages.

they were laboring to the advantage of the enemies of the Anglican Church:

And now give me leave to speak a word to *You*, my *Brethren* of the CLERGY, (*Those*, I mean of the *Younger* sort, for I shall not presume to teach my Elders). You have heard, no doubt, *frequent*, and *earnest* declamations against Reason, during the years of your *Education.* . . . And I shall not wonder if you have been possessed with very *hard thoughts* of this pretended *terrible* enemy of *Faith*, and *Religion.* . . . But yet, I shall beg leave to *refresh* your thoughts, with some CONSIDERATIONS of the DANGEROUS TENDENCIES and *issues* of such Preachments.

(1) *To disclaim Reason, as an Enemy to Religion, tends to the introduction of Atheism, Infidelity*, and *Scepticism; and hath already brought in a floud of these upon us.* . . . These are the Consequences of the *defamations of Reason*, on the pretended account of *Religion;* and we have seen, in multitudes of deplorable Instances, That they follow in *practice*, as well as *reasoning.* Men of *corrupt* inclinations, suspect that there is *No Reason* for our *Faith*, and Religion, and *so* are upon the borders of quitting it; And the *Enthusiast*, that pretends to know *Religion best*, tells them, that these *Suspicions* are *very true;* and thence the *Debauchee* gladly makes the *desperate* Conclusion. And when *others* also hear *Reason* disparaged as *uncertain, various*, and *fallacious*, they deny all credit to their *Faculties*, and become *confounded Scepticks*, that settle in nothing. This I take to have been one of the greatest, and most deadly occasion of the *Atheism* of our days; and he that hath rejected *Reason*, may be *one* when he *pleaseth*, and cannot reprehend, or reduce, any *one*, that is *so* already.

(2) *The Denial of Reason in Religion hath been the principal Engine, that Hereticks, and Enthusiasts have used against the Faith; and that which lays us open to infinite follies, and impostures.* . . .

(3) *By the same way great advantage is given to the Church of Rome;* which those of that Profession know very well; and therefore *Perronius, Gonterius, Arnoldus, Veronius*, and other Jesuites, have *loudly* declaimed against Reason; and the *last* mentioned, *Veronius*, presented the World with a *Method* to overthrow *Hereticks*, (meaning those of the *Protestant* Faith) which promised more than ordinary; And that was, to deny, and renounce all *Principles* of *Reason* in affairs of *Faith absolutely*, and *roundly;* and not to vouchsafe an *Answer* to any *Argument* against *Transubstantiation*, or any other *Article* of their *new Faith;* but point-blank to deny whatever *Reason* saith, in such matters. And he affirms that even these *Principles* of *Reason*, viz. *Non entis non sunt Attributa: at omne quod est, quando est, necesse est esse;* and such

like which are the *foundations* of all *reasoning*, are dangerous to the *Catholick Faith;* and therefore not to be heeded. This man speaks *out*, and affirms *directly*, and *boldly*, what the other enemies of Reason *imply;* but will not *own*. This is a *Method* to destroy *Hereticks* in *earnest;* but the mischief is, all *Christians*, and *all other* Religions, and *all other* reasonings are cut off by the same Sword. This *Book*, and *Method* of *Veronius* was kindly received by the Pope,[34] priviledged, by the *King* of *Spain*, approved by *Cardinals*, *Archbishops*, *Bishops*, and all the *Gallick Clergy*, as *solid*, and *for the advantage* of *Souls;* and the *Sorbone Doctors* gave it their *approbation*, and recommended it as the *only way* to confute Hereticks. Did *these* know *what* they recommended? And did they, think we, *understand* the *interests* of the *Roman* Church? If *so, we* kindly serve their ends, and promote their Designs in the *way*, which they account *best*, while we vilifie, and disparage *Reason*. If *This* be renounced in matters of *Religion*, with what face can we use it against the Doctrine of *Transubstantiation*, or any other Points of the *Roman Creed?* Would it not be *blameless*, and *irreprovable* for us to give up our understandings *implicitly* to the Dictates, and Declarations of *that Church?* May we not follow blindly whatever the *Infallible Man* at *Rome*, and his *Councils*, say? And would it not be vain *self-contradiction* to use *Arguments* against their *Decrees*, though they are never so *unreasonable?* Or to alledge *Consequences* from *Scripture* against any of their Articles, though never so *contrary* to the *Holy Oracles?* How easily may They rejoyn, when we dispute against them; You argue from *Reason*, and by *Consequences;* But *Reason* is *dull*, and *carnal*, and an *enemy* to the things of the *Spirit*, and not to be heard in the *high* matters of *Religion?* And what can we *say next*, if we consent to the Accusation? I say, by this way, we perfectly disable, or grossly contradict our selves in most of our disputes against the *Romanists:* And we are very *disingenious* in our dealings, while we use *Reason* against *them*, and deny *It*, when 'tis urged against our selves by *another* sort of Adversaries: which implies, that when we say, *Reason is not to be heard*, we mean, 'Tis not to be *heard against us;* But It *must*, against the *Church* of *Rome;* or *any others* we can *oppugn* by *It*. Thus, I say, our denying *Reason* in *Religion* is either very *humoursome*, and *partial;* or, 'tis a direct *yielding* up our selves to our *enemies*, and *doing that* our selves, which is the only thing *They desire*, to *undo* us, and to promote their own *interests* upon our *Ruines*.[35]

[34] The tradition to the effect that Veron's *Methode* received the approbation of Urban VIII is wrong, according to the Abbé Feret, *op. cit.*, IV, 62, n. 1.
[35] Glanvill, *op. cit.*, pp. 29–34.

Dangers to the English Church which could necessitate so much italicization must have been very serious; and certainly Glanvill's analysis makes it clear that there were other powerful forces besides the vague "spirit of the age" to explain the increasing rationalism of the Anglicans in the seventeenth century.

At the risk of some repetition it may be well also to comment on Glanvill's associating under one general tendency three such widely divergent parties as the "fanatic enthusiasts," the atheists, and the Catholics. Glanvill, who as a disciple had penetrated to a real understanding of skepticism, saw clearly what we have observed earlier, that a simple form of evangelical piety may on occasion have the same effect on religious thought as an outright philosophical skepticism; or, to put it in terms of historical traditions, the influence of Augustine sometimes parallels or interweaves with the influence of Montaigne or Sextus Empiricus. Consequently, in an age when Catholicism seemed about to prosper again in England, the anti-intellectual piety of the evangelicals, both in the Anglican Church and among the dissenters, became dangerous in an unexpected new way. And it was not pure fancifulness or malevolence in the Anglicans to accuse the sectaries, in religion as in politics, of aiding the party of Rome.

But there were dissenters of many kinds, and some of them, such as Baxter,[36] were as rationalistic as the leaders of the Church of England. In 1676 fifteen Non-conformist leaders, including Manton and Baxter, issued a manifesto [37] which bears interesting witness to the importance the subject had assumed in public discussion in the decade before Dryden's *Religio Laici*.

Among the other Church-troubling Controversies of these times [so they began], we find it is one, and not the least, *How far Mans Reason hath to do in matters of Religion:* And deep accusations we find brought against each other on this account; some suspecting others of Socinianisme, as overmagnifying Reason, and others in-

---

[36] See especially *Saints' Everlasting Rest*, Preface to Part II, as it was expanded in the later editions.

[37] *The Judgment of Non-conformists, of the Interest of Reason in matters of Religion. In which It is proved against Make-bates, that both Conformists, and Non-conformists, and all Parties of true Protestants are herein really agreed, though unskilful Speakers differ in Words* (London, 1676). 21 pages.

simulating such as they seem to differ from, as guilty of making Religion seem unreasonable; and some (who go over the Hedge where it is low) do lay this charge of unreasonableness, in special, on the *Non-conformists.*

They sought to avoid this "scandalous Contention" in the future by a series of careful definitions and statements of principle, to which they believed both dissenters and Anglicans would be able to subscribe; but they did not pretend to satisfy "Quakers, Seekers, Papists, Antinomians, or any such Sect which are more than *Meer Non-conformists.*" There had been in the past, they admitted, serious arguments and accusations: "We deny not but some Non-conformists, and Conformists did cast out their suspitions of two very Learned rational Men, Mr. *Hales,* and Mr. *Chillingworth,* as if they had favoured *Socinianisme,* because they so much used, and Ascribed to Reason, in Judging of matters of Religion; and *Knot* the Jesuite would have *Chillingworth* therefore taken to be a Socinian." [38] But those disputes, they said, were private disputes between particular men, and should not be regarded as the judgments of the churches. They now wished it understood that there was a Non-Conformity which was ready to unite with "all Parties of true Protestants" against those who would renounce the use of reason in religion.

The Roman Catholic controversialists were also ready with a reply to those who accused them of disseminating "atheism" in the interest of their own religion. Their answer was, of course, that they were misunderstood; their skepticism was merely a propaedeutic to faith, to be superseded by faith; it was only a method for showing, by beginning with a hypothetical assumption of Protestant principles, that these principles contained within themselves the seed of their own destruction. Thus Canes retorted rather superciliously to Owen, that in *Fiat Lux* he had treated

. . . a case of metaphysical concernment, which you apprehend not. . . . I speak wholly there, as in other parts of *Fiat Lux,* upon a supposition of the condition, the generality of people are now actually in, here in *England,* where every one lets himself loose at pleasure to frame opinions and religions of themselves. And so

[38] *Ibid.,* p. 6.

cannot be thought to speak of a settled belief, but only of a settling one, or one to be settled. . . . Perhaps it is hard for you to conceiv your self in a state you are not actually in at present: And if you cannot do this, you will be absolutely unfit to deal with such hypothetik discourses, as I see indeed you are. . . . And I cannot but tell you, whatsoever you think of your self, you are in truth, except you dissemble and mistake on purpose, but a weak man, to take that as spoken absolutely by me, and by way of positiv doctrine, which I only deliver upon an *hypothesis* apparent to all the world besides your self." [39]

That is, skepticism was a useful controversial weapon. But this argument assumes that further distinction between reason and faith which was held also by those Roman Catholics, such as Edward Worsley and John Sergeaunt, who admitted a rational evidence previous to faith: the distinction, namely, that reason appeals to evidence but faith accepts authority. By this distinction — which the Protestants refused to recognize as valid — the certainty of faith was supposed to be preserved even after the most devastating criticism of rational evidence. To this distinction Edward Worsley appealed in a reply to Glanvill's attack on Catholic "sceptics," already quoted:

Other Flawes I find in this Gentlemans Discourse, but haue not time to pursue halfe of them. Here is One, and of main Importance also. He neuer rightly distinguisheth, between that Obiect wherevpon Reason rest's, And the Obiect of Faith, Considered in it self. Reason euer precedes Faith, and is grounded vpon those rational Motiues which Induce to Belieue. Faith, *precisely Considered as Faith*, relies vpon a quite Different Obiect, *God's pure Reuelation*, and cannot Discourse, For the Reasons giuen aboue not here to be repeated. Only know thus Much in passing, That the wrong done by this Author to the Learned *Perron*, *Veron*, and Others, hath its Origin from this Ouersight, of not distinguishing between the Obiect of Reason, and Faith. These Saith He, *loudly declaim* against Reason, All know it very well. I Answer, they declaim against Reasoning or Arguing, in the very intrinsick Act or Tendency of Faith (For *Fides non quaerit cur, aut quomodo*) is most true, and So you and the whole world must do, if you Belieue.

[39] *Three Letters . . . Written by J. V. C.* (1671), pp. 34–35, and 45–46. The first letter, here quoted, is dated 1663 and was apparently first printed in that year.

They declaim against Reason, or all rational Discourse built vpon Manifest Motiues Inductiue to Faith, is a Calumny, and most vntrue.[40]

Whatever the logician may think of the tangle of logic, the historian will recognize here again Veron's "machine de guerre de nouvelle invention," playing its part in the theological warfare of the reign of Charles II.

Although England was inundated with controversial pamphlets in the short reign of James,[41] there was nothing new in Roman Catholic propaganda except the unprecedented quantity of it. It was now no longer necessary to print books in English on the French presses of Paris or Douai, sometimes with accents on the vowels, and smuggle them into England. Under the new monarch Catholics enjoyed the privilege of printing in London. And the press of Henry Hills, "Printer to the King's Most Excellent Majesty for His Household and Chappel," poured forth a stream of Catholic books and pamphlets "Publish'd with Allowance." The Anglicans countered vigorously with an even greater inundation and left nothing unanswered; every possible phase of the Protestant-Catholic controversy was debated over and over in the four years of the reign of James. With most of this we are not concerned. We are interested primarily in the problem of authority in religion, and this problem was recognized at this time by both sides to be the fundamental question of the whole controversy.[42] It became particularly acute with the publication of the posthumous papers of Charles II [43] and the answer to them by Stillingfleet. From this

---

[40] *Reason and Religion* (Antwerp, 1672), p. 605.

[41] See *Catalogue of the Collection of Tracts for and against Popery in the Manchester Library*, ed. Thomas Jones, in *Publications of the Chetham Society*, Vols. XLVIII (1859) and LXIV (1865). Further bibliographical information is given in Appendix A of this volume.

[42] See, for instance, John Williams, *A Short Discourse Concerning the Churches Authority in Matters of Faith* (London, 1687), Preface, and pp. 6 and 22; *Mr. Claude's Answer to Monsieur de Meaux's Book, Intituled, A Conference with Mr. Claude* (London, 1687), "An Advertisement from the Translator to the Reader," p. xxii.

[43] *Copies of Two Papers Written by the Late King Charles II. Together with a Copy of a Paper written by the late Dutchess of York. Published by His Majesties Command* (London, 1686); and *An Answer to some Papers Lately Printed, concerning the Authority of the Catholick Church in Matters of Faith* (London, 1686).

vast mass of repetitious controversy one or two illustrations must
suffice.

In 1687 Joshua Bassett, who had been made master of Sidney
College, Cambridge, by James II the preceding year, published
his *Reason and Authority: or the Motives of a late Protestants Reconciliation to the Catholic Church.* Thomas Bambridge, Fellow of
Trinity College, Cambridge, replied later in the same year with *An
Answer to a Book Entituled, Reason and Authority.* This is how he
summarized the apostate's autobiography:

I have just now read over a late *Book*, entituled *Reason and
Authority;* I read it with an excess of pleasure, being surprized
and amazed to find Reason so baffled, and a monstrous Authority
advanced against all reason. Non-sense, I perceive, is in fashion;
and if I and You have as little sense, and are as impertinent as
others, I may be a *Writer*, and You a *Reader*.

I perceive by that *Book*, that a certain Man has left our Church
without reason: He was advised to take reason, and make the
best use of it in the choice of his Religion, and the setling of his
life and practice in order to salvation; but he could find no reason
to serve him. He narrowly escaped being an *Atheist* with reason,
and had almost denyed the Being of a God, or at least his Providence, with reason; and something that looked like to a demonstration against the immortality of the Soul had so confounded
him, that he was up head and ears in the water all soused, and
plunged in the doubt, and whether he is yet out of it, we know not.

The Man goes on and considers the grounds of Religion, the
Jewish and the *Christian;* and finds little reason to think that the
five Books commonly ascribed to *Moses*, were ever written by him;
he finds so many mistakes, and so many errours in the beginning
of *Genesis*, that he gives you to guess his meaning, though he will
not speak it, to be, that the *Jewish* Religion is little else than a
forgery, and that it has but small evidence of a Revelation from
God Almighty.

Thus leaving the *Jewish* Religion, the Man in all haste goes to
the *Christian*, and considers the New Testament, as the Book which
all Christians in all Ages have owned, to be the Records of the
Christian Doctrine: He does not say by whom they were written,
but at the reading of the first *Chapter* of St. *Matthew* he was hair'd
out of his wits; He met with such difficulties, that his reason could
not answer, if he brought any with him to the reading of it; for
it is to be suspected that he used none, because a little reason in
such a case as this, would at this time have lead him to have con-

sulted his Authority. For if he, whom this Man calls God's *Vicegerent*, and the great *Elias*, that is supposed to solve all doubts, can say no more to this difficulty, than he himself could, he might have kept his Reason still, as bad as it was, and have been content to be ignorant with Reason, as well as under Authority....

But when *Reason*, and the *Holy Scriptures* are to be thrown down, it is no great wonder, if the *Bishops* of the Church of *England* fall with them.[44]

A more temperate and reasoned examination of the question is found in a very important preface "concerning the Nature of Certainty and Infallibility" in William Sherlock's *A Discourse Concerning a Judge of Controversies in Matters of Religion* (1686):

It is thought (and certainly it is so) the most compendious way to reduce Protestants to the Communion of the Church of *Rome*, to perswade them, that they can have no certainty of their Religion without an infallible Judge, and that there is no Infallibility but in the Church of *Rome:* Now could they prove that the Church of *Rome* is infallible, this indeed would be an irresistible Reason to return to her Communion; but this they say little of now-a-days, this they would gladly have us take for granted, especially if they can prove that we can have no certainty without an infallible Judge, and therefore this they apply themselves to, to run down Protestant certainty, and first to make men Scepticks in Religion, and then to settle them upon Infallibility.

Now the way they take to do this, is not by shewing that the Reasons on which Protestants build their Faith, either of Christianity in General, or of those particular Doctrines which they profess, are not sufficient to found a rational Certainty on; for this would engage them in particular Disputes, which is the thing they as industriously avoid, as if they were afraid of it; but instead of this, they declaim in general about the nature of Certainty; ask us, how we know we are Certain; if we rely upon Reason, other men do not reason as we do, and yet think their Reason as good as ours; if on Scripture, we see how many different and contrary Expositions there are of Scripture; and how can we be certain then that we only are in the right, when other men are as confident, and as fully perswaded as we?

Whereupon Sherlock restated in a succinct way the position of the Anglicans regarding the use of reason in religion.[45] In the *Biblio-*

---

[44] *An Answer to a Book Entituled, Reason and Authority* (London, 1687), pp. 1–2 and 10.

[45] Sherlock's pamphlet is reprinted in Edmund Gibson's *A Preservative against Popery*, ed. John Cumming (London, 1848), IV, 298–381.

thèque universelle et historique, August, 1687, Jean le Clerc reviewed Sherlock's volume and took occasion to signalize the trend of controversy:

Quelques Controversistes Catholiques Romains ont fait beaucoup valoir en Angleterre un raisonnement, qu'avoit fait auparavant beaucoup de bruit en France. C'est que les hommes étant d'eux mêmes sujets à se tromper, on ne pourroit avoir aucune certitude de la verité de sa Religion, si Dieu n'avoit donné à l'Eglise un esprit d'infallibilité, sur lequel on pût se réposer sans crainte d'être trompé. *M. Sherlock*, Docteur en Théologie, que l'on assure être Auteur de ce Livre, entreprend d'y répondre dans une Préface assez longue qui est au devant, & qui n'est pas sans doute le moindre endroit de cet ouvrage. . . .[46]

Such was the intellectual milieu of the skeptically inclined John Dryden when he submitted to the authority of the Roman Catholic Church and wrote *The Hind and the Panther*.

In casting a glance in retrospect over this survey it is evident that the ideas of John Dryden were not his peculiar property. They were representative ideas of the age, growing out of the dominant temper of the age, which happened also to be the temper of Dryden himself. But before we can proceed to a demonstration of this close interrelation between Dryden and his milieu, we must examine Father Simon's *Histoire critique du Vieux Testament* and its English translation, which furnished the occasion for *Religio Laici*.

III

Father Simon's great work, which marked an epoch in the history of Biblical criticism, was the result of a life of special opportunities and great concentration of scholarly effort. As a member of the Oratory of Paris, Simon had been permitted to devote his whole time to research in Biblical questions. He became one of the most erudite Biblical scholars of any age; he handled with the power and sureness of a master the enormous volume of learning on the Scriptural text, a learning which was of course complicated by intricate traditions of exegesis and controversy; in knowledge of the Oriental languages he was rivaled by few; he had studied closely

---

[46] *Bibliothèque universelle et historique*, VI, 295–296.

all types of Biblical manuscripts and representative manuscript sources of Jewish and Christian interpretation; and to his critical task he brought a clear and acute mind and a genuine historical sense. The result was a classic of scholarship, in which the firm organization of a multitude of details and the systematic criticism of a whole library of erudition affords a keen intellectual satisfaction even to a modern reader who is not a specialist in the field. It is an imposing achievement, the product of a capacious and masterful mind.

Simon does not appear to have been guided in his labors by any philosophical or theological "first principles"; he was always first a scientist, seeking carefully for the facts. And yet, rigidly scientific as he was, his work had a distinct controversial significance, of which he himself thoroughly approved. A brief indication of the contents of the *Critical History* will suffice to show its tendency.[47]

The First Book is a history of the Hebrew text from the time of Moses; we learn that Moses could not have written all the books attributed to him, that we sometimes have in the Old Testament only abridgments of longer works now lost, that the manuscripts are all imperfect and there is no wholly reliable tradition for their interpretation, that readings are often doubtful, and the whole matter full of difficulties and obscurities. The Second Book points out the faultiness of all translations, from the Septuagint down to those made by Protestants. The Third Book is a project for a new translation; we have "at present no exact Translation of the Holy Scripture: If we consider the difficulties which have already been observ'd, it seems impossible for us to succeed. We shall nevertheless, to the best of our power, chalk out the way which ought to be observ'd in the making of a Translation of the Bible, which may come nigher to a true one than any thing that has yet been made upon this Subject." [48]

What made his book so dangerous to the Protestants was the immense and impressive learning with which Simon demonstrated

[47] Simon's similar work on the New Testament came later and does not concern us. The most important studies of Simon are A. Bernus, *Richard Simon et son Histoire critique du Vieux Testament* (Lausanne, 1869), and Henri Margival, *Essai sur Richard Simon et la Critique biblique au XVIIᵉ Siècle* (Paris, 1900).

[48] English translation (1682), Book III, pp. 1-2.

his thesis of the unreliability of the Biblical text. The idea was not new. Not to mention anything so heterodox and suspect as Spinoza's *Tractatus Theologico-politicus* (1670), the Catholics themselves, as we have seen, had been very busy already in the sixteenth century pointing out the necessity of an oral tradition to supplement the obscurity of the Bible. All through the seventeenth century English Catholic propaganda is full of the same thing. William Richworth, or Rushworth, devoted the second of his *Dialogues* to a discussion of the errors in the Scripture text and the general uncertainty of its interpretation.[49] Thomas White, who, we remember, hated that "dangerous Cockatrice, *Incertitude*," whether hatched by his own party or by Glanvill, had no fault to find with Rushworth's criticism of the Biblical text.[50] John Sergeaunt, also, though not ordinarily approving of the argument from philosophical skepticism, stressed the great hazard in trusting matters of salvation to the care of copiers and printers and translators and grammarians.[51] It was primarily against White and Sergeaunt that Tillotson wrote his *Rule of Faith;*[52] they offended him by such remarks as Sergeaunt's query whether the sacred writings were anything but "ink variously figured in a book, unsensed characters, waxen-natured words, not yet sensed, nor having any certain interpreter, but fit to be play'd upon diversly by quirks of wit? that is, apt to blunder and confound, but to clear little or nothing."[53]

The obscurity and difficulty of the Scripture was therefore by Simon's time a definite and long-established issue in the controversy between Catholics and Protestants. Even the exception illustrates the rule. Simon's most important predecessor in textual criticism was the French Protestant scholar, Ludovicus Cappellus, whose *Critica Sacra* was first published in 1650, after his death, and then under Catholic auspices by his son, who had in the mean-

---

[49] *The Dialogues of William Richworth or The iudgmend of common sense in the choise of Religion* (Paris, 1640).

[50] *Rushworth's Dialogues . . . Corrected and enlarg'd by Thomas White, Gent* (Paris, 1654).

[51] *Sure-Footing* (1665).

[52] Published 1666.

[53] Tillotson's *Sermons* (London, 1742), IV, 558.

time gone over to that Church. Simon himself tells us the story in the Preface to his *Critical History*. The Protestants of Geneva, Sedan, and Leyden, he says,

... oppos'd the publishing of this Book for ten years together, being perswaded it destroy'd the principle of their Religion, and oblig'd them to have recourse to the Tradition of the Catholicks. Father *Petau*, a Jesuit, Father *Morin* of the Oratory and Father *Mersennus*, a Minimme, got the Kings Licence for the printing of it. This so alarm'd the Court of *Rome* that it had almost condemn'd it, it being a thing without precedent that heretical Books wherein matters of Divinity are treated of, should be printed in *France* with the King's Licence. But Father *Morin*, who had helped forward the printing of it, and perhaps had not foreseen all the consequences, writ to Cardinal *Francis Barberini*, that they at *Rome* did *Capellus* a kindness in condemning his Criticism which had created him the hatred of those of his Sect, and that at the same time they did the Catholicks injury, who made use of this Book to shew that the Protestants have no certain principle of their Religion, having rejected the Tradition of the Church; *Capellus* however never intended to draw this consequence from his Book.[54]

But this was the consequence which Father Simon drew from the work of Cappellus, and which he also thought made his own book acceptable to intelligent and far-seeing Catholics.

When Simon was ready to publish his own work, he found that there were Catholics nearer than Rome who were afraid of "higher criticism" as a controversial weapon. In spite of long-standing enmity in certain circles in Paris, he had brought his work to completion and an edition of thirteen hundred copies was printed early in 1678. While Simon was waiting for Père la Chaise and the duc de Montausier to secure for him the privilege of dedicating it to Louis XIV, who was away on a military campaign, the printer utilized the consequent delay in binding and publication and advertised the book by printed sheets giving the contents of the chapters. Their audacity caused scandal, and through the influence chiefly of Bossuet and the members of Port-Royal the whole edition remaining in the hands of the bookseller was destroyed.

The 1678 edition of the *Histoire critique* is therefore one of the

[54] Ed. cited, Preface.

rarest of books. Such copies as now exist were probably sent out secretly in loose sheets to a few learned friends, while Simon was anxiously awaiting developments. Two copies we know went under such circumstances to England, to Bishop Compton and Lord Clarendon, with whom Simon had become acquainted during their earlier visits to Paris.[55] These copies were dispatched by Henri Justel, librarian to Louis XIV, a man of learning who, though a Protestant, was a close friend of learned men of both churches. His letters to Bishop Compton written from Paris on the 12th of March and the 13th of April, 1678, breathe the excitement of the rescue of the copies from their impending fate in Paris as well as Justel's concern for the reception of Simon's labors among men of learning in England.[56] He is anxious that the tendencies of the book should not frighten competent men away from an admiration of the scholarship, to which he is deeply devoted. He endeavors to smooth the path for the author, to prepare the Bishop for the first disconcerting shock: "C'est un homme d'esprit hardi." Above all, he desires that the book should be examined by De Veil, who could render a really competent judgment on it.[57]

The reception in England was not quite what Justel had hoped

[55] Simon's own account in a letter dated February, 1679, in *Lettres choisies de M. Simon* (Amsterdam, 1730), IV, 85.

[56] Bodleian *Mss. Rawl.* C984. Fol. 16 and 27. See Appendix B. Justel came to England in the autumn of 1681 and was appointed keeper of the manuscripts in the Royal Library; on the accession of William and Mary he was appointed royal librarian. His biography in the *Dictionary of National Biography* must be supplemented by the calendars of state and treasury papers for that period. The article on Justel in the *Bulletin de la Société de l'histoire du Protestantisme français* (1930), by Ph. Dally, is entirely unsatisfactory on Justel's life in England, since it left the important sources of information untouched. Justel's interest in Simon's work continued unabated until his death in 1693. Two of his letters on the subject are in the British Museum, *Add. Mss.* 22, 910, fol. 426 and 428.

[57] Charles Marie De Veil's competence can be deduced from his record. He was a Jew from Metz who had been converted by Bossuet to Catholicism, but who later came to England and embraced Protestantism. In 1678 he held a living at Fulham and appears to have been peculiarly under Bishop Compton's protection. His brother also came to England and became a royal librarian. See Eugène and Émile Haag, *La France Protestante*, IX, 455–456. Concerning Charles Marie we are further told that he at last turned Anabaptist, whereupon Bayle remarked (*Nouv. de la Rép. des Lettres*, Dec., 1684, article 9): "Dieu veuille qu'il ne fasse pas comme le soleil tout le tour du zodiaque." Quoted by Bernus, *Richard Simon*, p. 99.

for, though De Veil certainly lost no time over his task. For although Justel had sent the copies from Paris as late as the 13th of
April, on the 14th of May De Veil had already examined the work
and completed a pamphlet letter to Robert Boyle, which he immediately printed in London.[58] He did not choose to devote his
critique to questions of pure erudition; instead he marked clearly
the large religious issue involved, as to the adequacy of the Scriptures as the basis of authority in the Church. His pamphlet was
nothing more than a warning that Father Simon's book would
undermine Protestant principles.

In the autumn of the same year Friedrich Spanheim, the
younger, was able to borrow one of the two copies in London and
make a more extended study of it. On the 10th of December he
completed a long review, which was published the following year
at Amsterdam.[59] Spanheim eulogized the masterful learning of
the book and discussed with thoroughness some of the erudite
questions raised. But he also recognized, as did De Veil, that
Simon's principles were frankly intended to ruin Protestantism;
and, he adds,[60] they at the same time ruin the very foundations of
the Greek and Roman Church of antiquity, and of the first councils,
as well as of the Jewish religion — sweeping consequences by no
means intended by Father Simon.[61]

---

[58] *Lettre de Mr. De Veil, Docteur en Theologie, & Ministre du Saint Evangile,
À Monsieur Boisle, De la Societe Royale des Sciences à Londres. Pour prouver
contre l'Autheur d'un Livre nouveau, Intitule,* Critique du Vieux Testament, *que La
seule Ecriture est la Regle de la Foy. À Londres, Imprimé par M. Clark, 1678.* The
imprimatur is dated May 16, 1678.

[59] *Lettre à un amy Ou l'on rend compte d'un livre, qui a pour titre, Histoire
Critique du Vieux Testament, Publié à Paris en 1678. À Amsterdam, Chez Daniel
Elsevir. 1679.* 214 pages. Dated at end, *Ce 10 Decembre 1678.*

[60] *Ibid.,* p. 20.

[61] As one might expect, there was gossip current that Simon was intentionally
undermining the whole Christian religion; Dryden (*Religio Laici,* 252–253) refers
to it:

> "Some, who have his secret meaning guessed,
> Have found our author not too much a priest."

This insinuation is, however, without foundation. The true explanation is simply
that Simon did not regard such sweeping conclusions as necessary consequences of
his work. His sincere loyalty to the Roman Catholic Church is evident enough in
his letters. See Henri Fréville, "Richard Simon et les Protestants d'après sa
correspondance," *Revue d'histoire moderne,* VI (1931), 30–55.

The only visible result of Justel's vigorous efforts on behalf of the *Histoire critique* was, therefore, the appearance of two Protestant replies, both emanating from England, before the book itself was available in print. However, in 1680 Elzevir printed an edition in Amsterdam, not from a printed copy, which he was unable to procure, but from a manuscript copy made for the Duchesse de Mazarin from one of the printed volumes sent to England. The edition of 1680, as Simon complained, was very faulty; but in 1685 a new edition was issued in Amsterdam, based on the Paris edition, of which somehow a copy had been procured; and this edition, which included also the criticisms of De Veil and Spanheim and Simon's replies, is standard.[62]

Such was the previous history of the work which appeared in an English translation early in 1682. On the 19th of March the worthy John Evelyn wrote an agitated appeal to Dr. Fell, Bishop of Oxford:

It cannot but be evident to your Reverend Lordship, to how great danger and fatal consequences the 'Histoire Critique,' not long since published in French by Père Simon, and now lately translated (though but ill translated) into English, exposes not only the Protestant and the whole Reformed Churches abroad, but (what ought to be dearer to us) the Church of England at home, which with them acknowledges the Holy Scriptures alone to be the canon and rule of faith; but which this bold man not only labours to unsettle, but destroy. From the operation I find it already begins to have amongst divers whom I converse with, especially the young men, and some not so young neither, I even tremble to consider what fatal mischief this piece is like to create, whilst they do not look upon the book as coming from some daring wit, or young Lord Rochester revived, but as the work of a learned author, who have the reputation also of a sober and judicious person. And it must be acknowledged that it is a masterpiece in its kind; that the man is well studied in the oriental tongues, and has carried on his project with a spirit and address not ordinary amongst critics; though, after all is done, whether he be really a Papist, Socinian, or merely a Theist, or something of all three, is not easy to discover; but this is evident — as for the Holy Scriptures, one may make what one will of them, for him. He tells the world he

---

[62] See Preface to edition of 1685, and *Lettres choisies de M. Simon*, I, 37-47.

can establish no doctrine or principles upon them; and then are not we of the Reformed Religion in a blessed condition! For the love of God, let our Universities, my Lord, no longer remain thus silent; it is the cause of God, and of our Church! Let it not be said, your Chairs take no notice of a more pernicious plot than any that yet has alarmed us. Whilst everybody lets it alone, men think there's nothing to be said against it; and it hugely prevails already, and you will be sensible of its progress when it is too late to take off the reproach. I most humbly therefore implore your Reverend Lordship to consider of it seriously; that the pens and the Chairs may openly and on all occasions assert and defend the common cause, and that Oxford may have the honour of appearing the first in the field. For from whom, my Lord, should we expect relief, if not from you the Fathers of the Church, and the Schools of the Prophets? It is worthy the public concern to ward the deadly blows which sap the roots, and should by no means be abandoned to hazard, or the feeble attempts of any single champion, who, if worsted, would but add to the triumph of our enemies, Papists and Atheists.[63]

Evelyn went on to lament that against such men as Simon and Spinoza nothing of importance had been published in England. Old books against the atheists were of no avail among men "of this curious and nicer age," and unless the heads of the hydra were constantly beaten down, the evil cause, he feared, was certain to triumph.

Oxford did not respond to the call. The English scholars and theologians did not meet Simon in controversy. There was very likely much preaching against him, but in print there appeared only a brief pamphlet on the authorship of the Books of Moses, written in the spring and published in the autumn of 1682.[64] And

---

[63] *Diary and Correspondence* (London, 1859), III, 264–267.

[64] *An Excellent Discourse Proving the Divine Original, and Authority of the Five Books of Moses. Written Originally in French by Monsieur Du Bois de la Cour, and Approved by six Doctors of the Sorbon. To which is added a Second Part, or an Examination of a considerable part of Pere Simon's Critical History of the Old Testament, wherein all his Objections, with the Weightiest of Spinoza's against Moses's being the Author of the first Five Books of the Bible, are Answered, and some difficult places of Holy Scripture are Explained. By W. L.* (London, 1682).
The preface, by "R. B.," dated April 7, 1682, speaks of "the two following Treatises, one written and the other translated by Mr. *W. L.* my greatly valued Friend, well known by me to be a man of Learning and Judgment and exemplary faithfulness to God and Conscience."

in the following year De Veil's letter to Boyle appeared in an English translation.[65]

Meanwhile the English version of the *Critical History* enjoyed a peculiar success; it received the public endorsement of the circle of Dryden. As Evelyn noted, it was not a good translation; it has many marks of haste and carelessness which become apparent upon comparison with the original text. Of the translator nothing further is known with certainty than that his name was Henry Dickinson, and that he was a friend of Richard Duke.[66] But his book had been in print only a short time when the stock seems to have been transferred from the original publisher, Walter Davis in Amen Corner, to the shop of Dryden's publisher, Jacob Tonson. The printed sheets, including the Walter Davis title-page, were bound up with a new Tonson title-page, a translation by Dickinson of Simon's reply to Spanheim, and three commendatory poems by Richard Duke, Nahum Tate, and "N. L.," possibly Nathaniel Lee.[67] These facts can be explained only by the assumption that, after Dickinson's book had appeared in print, it came under the patronage of Dryden's circle. At any rate, Dryden's acquaintance with it was perhaps the most critical event in his intellectual life. It stimulated a summer of thinking and writing, and in November appeared *Religio Laici*, verses "written for an ingenious young Gentleman, my Friend, upon his Translation of *The Critical*

---

[65] *A Letter to the Honourable Robert Boyle, Esq. Defending the Divine Authority of the Holy Scripture, And that it alone is the Rule of Faith. In answer to Father Simon's Critical History of the Old Testament. Written by C. M. Du Veil, D.D.* (London, 1683).

[66] Richard Duke, *Poems upon Several Occasions* (London, 1717), p. 418. Inasmuch as Duke was from Trinity College, Cambridge, where he received his B.A. degree in 1678, it is quite likely that the translator was the Henry Dickinson who was at Trinity at the same time; but as the Cambridge records yield nothing but the bare facts of his academic career, he remains only a name. See J. Venn and J. A. Venn, *Alumni Cantabrigienses*. For previous attempts at identification of the translator see Dryden, *Works*, X, 32, n.

[67] The poems are signed "R. D.," "N. T.," and "N. L." Duke's poem was acknowledged in the edition of his poems in 1717, *ut supra;* Nahum Tate reprinted his in *Poems written on several Occasions, by N. Tate. The Second Edition enlarged* (London, 1684), p. 157. The fact that Tate and Duke were both close to Dryden at this time lends strength to the supposition that the third man was Nathaniel Lee. For further description of the two issues of the *Critical History* see Appendix C.

History of the Old Testament, composed by the learned Father Simon." [68]

IV

Although Dryden may have felt the full impact of fideistic thought for the first time when he read Father Simon's book, it does not follow that he then made the acquaintance of an entirely new set of ideas, unrelated to his previous thought. There is evidence that he had already been considering the philosophical, as well as political, bearings of the religious problems of his time. The discussion of Dryden's conservatism in secular and ecclesiastical politics must be deferred to another chapter; for the present we must limit the investigation to the more philosophical aspects of the subject, to discover, if possible, whether Dryden had been turning over in his mind the problem of certainty and truth in religion before he wrote *Religio Laici*, or whether, as Christie would have it, "much of his learning and many of his opinions were probably acquired for the occasion." [69]

We may dismiss as libels the customary insinuations of Dryden's enemies that his conduct and conversation betrayed an indifference to religion. It was a charge which he particularly resented. In the Preface to *Tyrannic Love* (1670) he defends that play against the accusation of "no less crimes than profaneness and irreligion." When the tyrant Maximin scoffs against religion, Dryden pointed out, he speaks in character and his sentiments are not in justice to be imputed to the author.

This, reader, is what I owed to my just defence, and the due reverence of that religion which I profess, to which all men, who desire to be esteemed good, or honest, are obliged. I have neither leisure nor occasion to write more largely on this subject, because I am already justified by the sentence of the best and most discerning prince in the world, by the suffrage of all unbiassed judges, and above all, by the witness of my own conscience, which abhors the

---

[68] Dryden's Preface to the poem. *Religio Laici* was advertised in *The Observator* for November 30, 1682.

[69] "Memoir," *Poetical Works of John Dryden*, ed. W. D. Christie (Globe edition), p. liii.

thought of such a crime; to which I ask leave to add my outward conversation, which shall never be justly taxed with the note of atheism or profaneness.[70]

A dozen years later Thomas Hunt accused him of atheism and impiety on the basis of a speech in *The Duke of Guise*. To this foolish charge Dryden again answered that the passage was in character, and also that it was written, not by him, but by Lee. As for Mr. Hunt, "I am not malicious enough to return him the names which he has called me; but of all sins, I thank God, I have always abhorred atheism; and I had need be a better Christian than Mr. Hunt has shown himself, if I forgive him so infamous a slander." [71] Inasmuch as Dryden showed himself so tender on this point, any suspicions of overt atheism are entirely gratuitous.

Some modern students of Dryden have advanced the theory, more worthy of investigation, that Dryden was a Deist during his life in London up to his conversion to Catholicism. Some autobiographical lines in *The Hind and the Panther* tell us that he had not been uniformly orthodox:

> My thoughtless youth was winged with vain desires,
> My manhood, long misled by wandering fires,
> Followed false lights; and, when their glimpse was gone,
> My pride struck out new sparkles of her own.
> Such was I, such by nature still I am,
> Be Thine the glory, and be mine the shame.[72]

Scott ventured an explanation of these lines: the "vain desires" of Dryden's "thoughtless youth" refer merely to "that inattention to religious duties which the amusements of youth too frequently occasion." The "false lights" of his manhood, Scott thought, were his "puritanical tenets," which he would have derived from his family and have held up to his thirtieth year. The "sparkles" struck out by his pride were those ideas which he held from the Restoration to his conversion to Catholicism. Scott concluded

---

[70] *Works*, III, 377–378.   [71] *Ibid.*, VII, 171.

[72] *The Hind and the Panther*, I, ll. 72–77. In interpreting these lines, so far as they can definitely be interpreted, it should of course be borne in mind that they are written from the point of view of a Roman Catholic; it is therefore not impossible that Dryden was thinking of his profession of faith and his own individual speculations as a member of the Anglican Church.

that Dryden was "sceptical concerning revealed religion," and that "his conviction really hovered between natural religion and the faith of Rome"; [73] in other words, Dryden was really a Deist from 1660 to 1686. And this is also the opinion more recently expressed by Verrall in his lectures on Dryden.[74]

The most obvious and most serious objection to this theory is that Dryden in *Religio Laici*, both in the preface and in the poem, rejects Deism and contrasts its presumption with his own skeptical habits of thought. He declares that he is unable to believe that the reason of man, "without the benefit of Divine Illumination," can attain even to the few essential tenets of Deism; he ventures to suppose that these tenets are really "the faint remnants or dying flames of revealed Religion in the Posterity of Noah"; and he thinks "that our Modern Philosophers, nay and some of our Philosophising Divines have too much exalted the faculties of our Souls, when they have maintained that by their force, mankind has been able to find out that there is one Supream Agent or Intellectual Being which we call God." Dryden's disagreement with the central principle of religious rationalism is, therefore, so complete and conclusive in *Religio Laici* that it separates him not only from Deism, but from the rationalistic tendencies of such Anglican leaders as Chillingworth, Stillingfleet, Tillotson, and the Cambridge Platonists.

They who wou'd prove Religion by Reason, do but weaken the cause which they endeavour to support: 'tis to take away the Pillars from our Faith, and to prop it only with a twig: 'tis to design a Tower like that of *Babel*, which, if it were possible (as it is not) to reach heaven, would come to nothing by the confusion of the Workmen. For every man is Building a several way; impotently conceipted of his own Model, and his own Materials: Reason is always striving, and always at a loss; and of necessity it must so come to pass, while 'tis exercis'd about that which is not its proper object. Let us be content at last, to know God by his own methods; at least, so much of him, as he is pleas'd to reveal to us in the sacred Scriptures; to apprehend them to be the word

---

[73] *Works*, I, 256–262.
[74] A. W. Verrall, *Lectures on Dryden* (Cambridge, 1914), p. 150. Saintsbury, however, declared he could find no evidence of the supposed Deism of Dryden. See *Works*, XVIII, 321.

of God, is all our Reason has to do; for beyond it is the work of
Faith, which is the Seal of Heaven impress'd upon our humane
understanding.[75]

Obviously, the philosophical groundwork of *Religio Laici* was
Pyrrhonism, not rationalism; Dryden was not a Deist in 1682.

What he was before 1682 is not very easy to say; the evidence
is ambiguous and must be interpreted. We have, first of all, some
argumentative passages on questions of religious controversy in
a few of Dryden's rhymed plays. But where such a debate is a
part of a drama, its composition must perforce be guided also by
considerations of dramatic character and situation; the convictions
of the author may have nothing to do with it. All we can be sure
of is that such an episode has sprung from Dryden's intellectual
curiosity, from his delight in testing certain arguments by throw-
ing them into the arena with their opposites. Such a debate is
more than a mere rhetorical exercise; for the best rhetoric is always more than rhetoric, it is the vigorous play of the intelligence.
One of the most engaging characteristics of Dryden's mind is his
readiness to understand the other side of the question, even after
he has settled his own convictions. Being of a skeptical and diffident temper, he naturally hesitated about settling his convictions.
In the argumentative passages of the plays his ideas are still, in
greater or less degree, in solution; in his poems on politics and
religion they appear in precipitated and crystallized form.

A scene of this kind, below Dryden's best in both thought and
versification, but pertinent to the question of his supposed Deism,
appears in *The Indian Emperor* (acted 1665). The dialogue takes
place, astonishingly enough, between a fanatical Spanish priest
and his two Indian victims, the king Montezuma and the Indian
High Priest, who by his orders have been stretched on the rack.
The Spaniard applies the torture with the double purpose of ex-
tracting a confession regarding hidden gold and forcing the savages
to acknowledge the Christian religion. The scene obviously is an
early illustration of Dryden's lifelong hatred of priestly greed and
fanaticism; by the dramatic action he directs our sympathies to
the side of the two suffering representatives of "the noble savage":

[75] *Poems*, ed. John Sargeaunt, p. 95.

Christian Priest to Montezuma. Fond man, by heathen ignorance misled,
    Thy soul destroying when thy body's dead:
    Change yet thy faith, and buy eternal rest.

Indian High Priest to Montezuma. Die in your own, for our belief is best.

Montezuma. In seeking happiness you both agree;
    But in the search, the paths so different be,
    That all religions with each other fight,
    While only one can lead us in the right.
    But till that one hath some more certain mark,
    Poor human-kind must wander in the dark;
    And suffer pain eternally below,
    For that, which here we cannot come to know.

Chr. Pr. That, which we worship, and which you believe,
    From nature's common hand we both receive:
    All, under various names, adore and love
    One Power immense, which ever rules above.
    Vice to abhor, and virtue to pursue,
    Is both believed and taught by us and you:
    But here our worship takes another way —

Mont. Where both agree, 'tis there most safe to stay:
    For what's more vain than public light to shun,
    And set up tapers, while we see the sun?

Chr. Pr. Though nature teaches whom we should adore,
    By heavenly beams we still discover more.

Mont. Or this must be enough, or to mankind
    One equal way to bliss is not designed;
    For though some more may know, and some know less,
    Yet all must know enough for happiness.

Chr. Pr. If in this middle way you still pretend
    To stay, your journey never will have end.

Mont. Howe'er, 'tis better in the midst to stay,
    Than wander farther in uncertain way.

Chr. Pr. But we by martyrdom our faith avow.

Mont. You do no more than I for ours do now.
    To prove religion true —
    If either wit or sufferings would suffice,
    All faiths afford the constant and the wise:
    And yet even they, by education swayed,
    In age defend what infancy obeyed.

Chr. Pr. Since age by erring childhood is misled,
    Refer yourself to our unerring head.

Mont. Man, and not err! what reason can you give?

Chr. Pr. Renounce that carnal reason, and believe.

Mont.	The light of nature should I thus betray,
	'Twere to wink hard, that I might see the day.
Chr. Pr.	Condemn not yet the way you do not know;
	I'll make your reason judge what way to go.
Mont.	'Tis much too late for me new ways to take,
	Who have but one short step of life to make.
Pizarro.	Increase their pains, the cords are yet too slack.
Chr. Pr.	I must by force convert him on the rack.[76]

The argument of Montezuma certainly comes near to being Deism, and must have been familiar enough in certain London circles of the Restoration; but it would be unwarranted to affirm on the strength of this debate that Dryden, like Montezuma, rejected Christian revelation.

It might well be assumed that we are on surer ground in the discussions of religion in *Tyrannic Love* (1670). Dryden here represents Saint Catherine disputing among the pagans, and it may reasonably be supposed that he put in her mouth the most cogent arguments he was capable of, as her triumph was part of the dramatic action. The saint converts Apollonius, a heathen philosopher, by demonstrating the rational and ethical superiority of Christianity.

S. Cath.	Nor pride, nor frenzy, but a settled mind,
	Enlightened from above, my way does mark.

Maximin.	Though heaven be clear, the way to it is dark.

S. Cath.	But where our reason with our faith does go,
	We're both above enlightened, and below.
	But reason with your fond religion fights,
	For many gods are many infinites:
	This to the first philosophers was known,
	Who, under various names, adored but one;
	Though your vain poets, after, did mistake,
	Who every attribute a god did make;

[76] *The Indian Emperor*, V, ii (*Works*, II, 397–399). This passage attracted the attention of "R. F.," who in 1668 attacked Dryden in *A Letter from a Gentleman to the Honourable Ed. Howard Esq.; Occasioned by a Civiliz'd Epistle of Mr. Dryden's, before his Second Edition of his Indian Emperour.* "We may justly presume," he says (p. 7), "that when his *Indian Emperour* was first acted, he intended to instruct and reform all Churches in Polemical Divinity, by his admirable Dispute between a Christian and a Heathen Priest; which also shows how great a loss the Church had of him, when he was diverted from entering into Orders."

And so obscene their ceremonies be,
As good men loathe, and Cato blushed to see.

Max. War is my province! — Priest, why stand you mute?
You gain by heaven, and, therefore, should dispute.

Apollonius. In all religions, as in ours, there are
Some solid truths, and some things popular.
The popular in pleasing fables lie;
The truths, in precepts of morality.
And these to human life are of that use,
That no religion can such rules produce.

S. Cath. Then let the whole dispute concluded be
Betwixt these rules, and Christianity.

Apol. And what more noble can your doctrine preach,
Than virtue, which philosophy does teach?
To keep the passions in severest awe,
To live with reason, nature's greatest law;
To follow virtue, as its own reward;
And good and ill, as things without regard.

S. Cath. Yet few could follow those strict rules they gave
For human life will human frailties have;
And love of virtue is but barren praise,
Airy as fame; nor strong enough to raise
The actions of the soul above the sense.
Virtue grows cold without a recompence.
We virtuous acts as duty do regard;
Yet are permitted to expect reward.

Apol. By how much more your faith reward assures,
So much more frank our virtue is than yours.

S. Cath. Blind men! you seek e'en those rewards you blame:
But ours are solid; yours an empty name.
Either to open praise your acts you guide,
Or else reward yourselves with secret pride.

Apol. Yet still our moral virtues you obey;
Ours are the precepts, though applied your way.

S. Cath. 'Tis true, your virtues are the same we teach;
But in our practice they much higher reach.
You but forbid to take another's due,
But we forbid even to desire it too:
Revenge of injuries you virtue call;
But we forgiveness of our wrongs extol;
Immodest deeds you hinder to be wrought,
But we proscribe the least immodest thought.
So much your virtues are in ours refined,
That yours but reach the actions, ours the mind.

Max. Answer, in short, to what you heard her speak. [To Apol.]

Apol. Where truth prevails, all arguments are weak.
To that convincing power I must give place;
And with that truth that faith I will embrace.[77]

The saint is obviously so rationalistic in her presentation of the Christian religion that she hardly goes beyond the principles of natural religion; Apollonius announces his conversion without hearing a word about Christ or the sacraments. Nevertheless we must beware of regarding Saint Catherine's arguments as an exact reflection of Dryden's thought; we must remember the exigencies, not to say the proprieties, of the theater, which certainly forbade a disquisition on every part of the Catechism; the scene could not be indefinitely prolonged. Furthermore, Apollonius was a philosopher, to be appealed to first in that character; and possibly Dryden also meant us to understand that he was not unacquainted with the tenets of the Christians when he entered into this critical debate.[78]

In spite of these reservations, however, readers will probably agree that rationalism made a strong appeal to Dryden's mind. That it was not an evanescent appeal is clear from his discussion of the religion of Plutarch, a passage written in 1683, when his animadversions upon Deism in *Religio Laici* were still warm in his memory:

I have ever thought, that the wise men in all ages have not much differed in their opinions of religion; I mean, as it is grounded on human reason: for reason, as far as it is right, must be the same in all men; and truth being but one, they must consequently think in the same train. Thus it is not to be doubted but the religion of Socrates, Plato, and Plutarch was not different in the main; who doubtless believed the identity of one Supreme Intellectual Being, which we call God.[79]

At first glance, this statement of what he had "ever thought" seems closer to *Tyrannic Love* than to *Religio Laici;* but it is really

---

[77] *Tyrannic Love*, II, iii (*Works*, III, 403–405). Compare other rather rationalistic arguments and remarks, pp. 391, 435, and 441.

[78] Notice might also be made of Raphael's instruction to Adam in *The State of Innocence*, II, i (*Works*, V, 134). But as Raphael was speaking before the Fall, it was impossible for him to present to Adam the Christianity of the New Testament. There is no inconsistency between this passage and Dryden's position in *Religio Laici.*

[79] *Works*, XVII, 33. Cf. Saintsbury's note, XVIII, 321.

inconsistent with neither. The application of the passage is definitely limited: "I mean, as it is grounded on human reason"; Dryden is emphasizing in the context the probability that Plutarch was too enlightened to have been a polytheist.

That he was no Christian [he continues] is manifest. . . . But we need not wonder that a philosopher was not easy to embrace the divine mysteries of our faith. A modern God, as our Saviour was to him, was of hard digestion to a man, who probably despised the vanities and fabulous relations of all the old. Besides, a crucified Saviour of mankind; a doctrine attested by illiterate disciples; the author of it a Jew, whose nation at that time was despicable, and his doctrine but an innovation among that despised people, to which the learned of his own country gave no credit, and which the magistrates of his nation punished with an ignominious death; the scene of his miracles acted in an obscure corner of the world; his being from eternity, yet born in time; his resurrection and ascension; these, and many more particulars, might easily choke the faith of a philosopher, who believed no more than what he could deduce from the principles of nature; and that too with a doubtful academical assent, or rather an inclination to assent to probability, which he judged was wanting in this new religion. These circumstances considered, though they plead not an absolute invincible ignorance in his behalf, yet they amount at least to a degree of it; for either he thought them not worth weighing, or rejected them when weighed; and in both cases he must of necessity be ignorant, because he could not know without revelation, and the revelation was not to him.[80]

Those principles on which Dryden thought the wise men of all ages agree, turn out therefore to be but a very small part of essential Christianity and indeed reach to but half of the few tenets of Deism.

The rationalistic tendency in Dryden evidently did not develop very freely or very far; it must inevitably have been inhibited by that Pyrrhonistic turn of his mind, indications of which are scattered throughout his writings. Again and again he recognized that he was a skeptic living in an age predominantly skeptical. His *Essay of Dramatic Poesy* he described in 1668 as "sceptical, according to that way of reasoning which was used by Socrates, Plato, and all the Academics of old, which Tully and the best of

[80] *Ibid.*, pp. 34–35.

the Ancients followed, and which is imitated by the modest inquisitions of the Royal Society." [81]   Three years later he asked why
there should "be any *ipse dixit* in our poetry, any more than there
is in our philosophy." [82]   In the *Defence of the Epilogue* (1672) he
noted that "we live in an age so sceptical, that as it determines
little, so it takes nothing from antiquity on trust." [83]   Discuss-
ing the two Catos in his dedication of *Don Sebastian* (1690), he
expressed that dislike for the presumption and dogmatism of
the Stoics which characterized the skeptics from antiquity down
through the ages:

> The eldest of them, I will suppose, for his honour, to have been
> of the academic sect, neither dogmatist nor stoic; if he were not, I
> am sure he ought, in common justice, to yield the precedency to
> his younger brother.   For stiffness of opinion is the effect of pride,
> and not of philosophy; it is a miserable presumption of that knowl-
> edge which human nature is too narrow to contain; and the rugged-
> ness of a stoic is only a silly affectation of being a god, — to wind
> himself up by pulleys to an insensibility of suffering, and, at the
> same time, to give the lie to his own experience, by saying he suffers
> not what he knows he feels.[84]

And in the *Life of Lucian*, written about 1696, he said that "all
knowing ages" are "naturally sceptic, and not at all bigotted;
which, if I am not much deceived, is the proper character of our
own." [85]

Dryden never showed himself out of sympathy with this aspect
of his age.   His skeptical temperament and diffidence of opinion,
we have seen in an earlier chapter, alienated him from the philosophy of Hobbes; it must also have halted whatever inclination he
felt toward Deism or religious rationalism.   The criticism of Deism
which he propounded in *Religio Laici* in 1682 was not a new opinion
"acquired for the occasion."   In the *Defence of an Essay of Dramatic Poesy* (1668) he noted that "our divines, when they have
proved a Deity, because there is order, and have inferred that this
Deity ought to be worshipped, differ afterwards in the manner of
the worship"; [86] in other words, he had observed that religious

[81] *Essays*, ed. W. P. Ker, I, 124.   [82] *Ibid.*, p. 138.
[83] *Ibid.*, p. 163.   [84] *Works*, VII, 302–303.
[85] *Ibid.*, XVIII, 70.   [86] *Essays*, ed. W. P. Ker, I, 123.

rationalism is of very limited application. In 1672 he loaned this thought to Almanzor, in *The Conquest of Granada:*

> By reason, man a godhead may discern,
> But how he would be worshipped cannot learn.[87]

In his old age he penned a retrospective statement of his thought which has great biographical importance: "We have indeed the highest probabilities for our revealed religion; arguments which will preponderate with a reasonable man, upon a long and careful disquisition; but I have always been of opinion, that we can demonstrate nothing, because the subject-matter is not capable of demonstration. It is the particular grace of God, that any man believes the mysteries of our faith; which I think a conclusive argument against the doctrine of persecution in any Church." [88] Such was Dryden's characteristic temper of mind from the beginning to the end of his literary career; and his confession lends authority to the belief that *Religio Laici* was the expression of a mode of thought with which he had long been familiar, and that many of the ideas of the poem came to him as the result of reading and study extending over many years.

v

Though Dryden confessed it to his shame that he never read anything but for pleasure,[89] his tastes and pleasures were varied and extensive and certainly included philosophical and theological subjects. His work abounds with allusions that have not been identified, and no one as yet has been able to track him through all his studies. But enough is known to warrant the statement that Dryden was not unacquainted with the problems of religious and philosophical certitude. We know that he cultivated Montaigne, the "wise Montaigne" and "honest Montaigne" mentioned in the prefaces.[90] In the dedication of the *Aeneis* Dryden states he is "of Montaigne's principles, that an honest man ought to be contented with that form of government, and with those

---

[87] Part II, IV, iii (*Works*, IV, 190).
[88] *Works*, XVIII, 66.   [89] *Ibid.*, XVII, 56.
[90] *Ibid.*, VII, 314, and V, 328. In the latter passage Dryden quotes in French from the essay *De la presumption.*

fundamental constitutions of it, which he received from his an-
cestors, and under which himself was born." [91]   And in his Preface
to the *Fables* he confesses that he had "learned from the practice
of honest Montaigne" that "the nature of a preface is rambling,
never wholly out of the way, nor in it." [92] Montaigne's *Essays* were
therefore very much to Dryden's taste, among his favorite books;
they were at the very height of their popularity in England, the
delight of all sophisticated readers. Dryden was exactly of the
temperament to catch their drift; in the dedication to *Aureng-Zebe*
(1676) he alludes to Montaigne's depreciation of the human reason:

> As I am a man, I must be changeable: and sometimes the
> gravest of us all are so, even upon ridiculous accidents. Our minds
> are perpetually wrought on by the temperament of our bodies;
> which makes me suspect, they are nearer allied, than either our
> philosophers or school-divines will allow them to be. I have ob-
> served, says Montaigne, that when the body is out of order, its
> companion is seldom at his ease. An ill dream, or a cloudy day,
> has power to change this wretched creature, who is so proud of a
> reasonable soul, and make him think what he thought not yes-
> terday.[93]

Dryden had found these reflections in the *Apology for Raymond
Sebond:*

> This many-headed, divers-armed, and furiously-raging monster,
> is man; wretched weake and miserable man: whom if you consider
> well, what is he, but a crawling, and ever-moving Ants-neast?. . .
> A gust of contrarie winds, the croking of a flight of Ravens, the
> false pase of a Horse, the casual flight of an Eagle, a dreame, a
> sodaine voyce, a false signe, a mornings mist, an evening fogge,
> are enough to overthrow, sufficient to overwhelme and able to
> pull him to the ground.[94]

[91] *Essays*, ed. W. P. Ker, II, 171. The inclination of the skeptical temperament toward political conservatism, so apparent in both Montaigne and Dryden,
will be discussed in the succeeding chapter.

[92] *Ibid.*, p. 255. In *The Censure of the Rota. On Mr. Driden's Conquest of
Granada* (Oxford, 1673), pp. 18-19, Richard Leigh gave the following satirical
recipe for composing plays in Dryden's style: ". . . the descriptions may be
borrowed from *Statius*, and *Montaigns* Essays, the Reason and Politicall Orna-
ments from Mr. *Hobs*, and the Astrologicall (and if need be, the Language too)
from *Ibrahim*, or the *Illustrious Bassa*."   [93] *Works*, V, 199.

[94] *Essays*, trans. Florio, Tudor Translations (London, 1893), II, 172. Dryden's further quotation from the *Essays*, Book II, Chap. XVII, in the Preface to

This is from the heart of the *Apology;* it is part of that skeptical dialectic, that humiliation of the reason, which Montaigne took over from Greek skepticism and passed on to his disciples of later generations. Dryden's contemptuous reference to the "wretched creature, who is so proud of a reasonable soul," shows that he had been assimilating this dialectic; at least as early as 1676 he had made the acquaintance of the fideistic thought of Montaigne.

It goes without saying that Dryden knew Sir Thomas Browne's *Religio Medici;* the great vogue of the book and the title of Dryden's poem would be presumptive evidence, even had Dryden not paraphrased *Religio Medici* from memory in a note to his *Persius.*[95] It may probably be assumed that the man who described himself and his age, as well as the method of the Royal Society, as "sceptical," had not overlooked the interest of Glanvill's *Scepsis scientifica.* Pascal's *Pensées,* though published twelve years before *Religio Laici,* probably remained unknown to Dryden as to most other English readers until the first translation of them in 1688;[96] they reached him too late in his life to influence the direction of his thought. But that he had read Hooker and other Anglican "philosophizing divines" may be inferred from his Preface to *Religio Laici;* and as we have seen in the preceding chapter, Dryden's interest in the philosophical problems raised by Hobbes is apparent throughout his work.[97] Perhaps no evidence is more suggestive of the range of his reading than Congreve's statement that "I have heard him frequently own with Pleasure, that if he had any Talent

All for Love (1678), only two years after the publication of *Aureng-Zebe,* may indicate that he had been reading Montaigne with some diligence and digesting those ideas which he set forth in *Religio Laici.*

[95] *Works,* XIII, 229–230, and Saintsbury's note, XVIII, 315.

[96] Louis Charlanne, *L'Influence française en Angleterre au XVIIᵉ siècle* (Paris 1906), p. 341, attributes to Dryden the remark that "the *Pensées* of the incomparable M. Pascal, and perhaps of M. Bruyère, are two of the most entertaining books which the modern French can boast of." The opinion comes from Dryden's circle, but is not from Dryden. It is found in the Preface to the *Pastorals* contributed by William Walsh to Dryden's translation of Vergil, 1697.

[97] Dryden's careful study of the literature of controversy in the reign of James II can be appreciated only after one has compared representative pamphlets with *The Hind and the Panther.* But as Dryden had special reasons for reading such literature at that time, nothing can be safely argued from it regarding his habits of study before 1682.

for *English* Prose, it was owing to his having often read the writings of the great Archbishop *Tillotson.*" [98]   Just how literally we are to understand this extraordinary explanation of Dryden's prose style is a problem that does not come within this study; but it is authoritative and illuminating information regarding his intellectual interests.   For if Dryden was early in his literary career an assiduous reader of Tillotson — and we cannot infer anything less — he could hardly have avoided that divine's most important early work, *The Rule of Faith* (1666), written in reply to Sergeaunt's *Sure-Footing;* and thus he would have been introduced to that controversy between Anglicans and Catholics over the principle of authority in religion which was described in the first part of this chapter.

Such information as is available regarding Dryden's reading up to his composition of *Religio Laici* tends, therefore, to discredit Christie's thrust: "As was often the case with Dryden, much of his learning and many of his convictions were probably acquired for the occasion."   Dryden had meditated on the strength and weakness of Deism as well as of Hobbism, had recognized that his own skepticism and that of his age were out of harmony with both, had read in the rational divinity of the Anglican Church, had very probably some knowledge of Catholic controversy through Tillotson, and had met with fideistic thought in such classic expositions of it as *Religio Medici* and *The Apology for Raymond Sebond;* what else he read on this particular subject we do not know, but a man of Dryden's intellectual zest is not likely to drop quickly a subject which has aroused his interest.   Congreve says, in the Dedication already quoted, that "as his Reading had been extensive, so was he very happy in a Memory tenacious of every thing that he had read."   No one who reads Dryden extensively can fail to receive the impression that his intellectual contacts with his age were many and fruitful.   But like all vigorous and independent minds, he gradually selected out of the mass of his knowledge a set of convictions in harmony with his own nature.

[98] Congreve's Dedication to *The Dramatic Works of John Dryden* (1717).

VI

This assimilation was complete by 1682 and thenceforth no fundamental intellectual change is observable in his nature. *Religio Laici* and *The Hind and the Panther* are so closely allied in their philosophy that the earlier poem might be regarded as a sort of prelude or introduction to the later; both are basically skeptical and fideistic. And when the modern scholar has placed both poems in their context in the history of seventeenth-century thought, it becomes clear — much clearer than it could have been to Dryden himself — that he was already in 1682 far along on the road to the Roman communion; he had already accepted the essential principles on which the Roman Catholics of the time based their apologetics. If the question of his sincerity is to be raised, it would therefore seem more discerning to raise it in connection with his Anglicanism in the earlier poem, rather than with his conversion a few years later.[99] But even an ambiguous position may, of course, be held with both moral and intellectual sincerity, with no real expectation of those later developments which by the illusion of history appear to us to have been inevitable. That Dryden regarded *Religio Laici* as conformable to Anglicanism is clear from his Preface; and this opinion was shared by his friends, Roscommon and Richard Duke, good Anglicans both, who contributed commendatory poems for the occasion; though Roscommon does seem to imply that some of the "Reverend Levis" of the English Church were far from pleased with Dryden's theology.

Since both poems are woven on the same warp of Pyrrhonism and fideism, they may conveniently be treated together in our analysis. In their similarities, more than in their divergencies, we shall find what is characteristic of Dryden's mind.

[99] Scott thought that Dryden, when he wrote *Religio Laici*, "was sceptical concerning revealed religion." Scott's whole discussion of this stage of Dryden's life is vitiated by his failure to distinguish between philosophical skepticism and religious skepticism or "free-thinking." Knowing nothing of the fideism of the seventeenth century, Scott confused Dryden's avowed skepticism with irreligion. With characteristic insight, however, even where his information was inadequate, he corrected himself with a phrase: Dryden, he said, "was converted to the Catholic faith from a state of infidelity, or rather of Pyrrhonism." See Dryden, *Works*, I, 258–263.

The fideistic argument may take two distinguishable, though related, forms — the one theological or philosophical, and the other ecclesiastical. The first emphasizes the importance in the inner life of the individual of that faith which unsympathetic critics have described as "the continuous suicide of reason"; and therefore in the interest of this faith either submits the reason to a destructive philosophical analysis, as in Montaigne and Pascal, or proceeds by assuming the darkening and enfeebling of man's intellect by the fall, as in the Augustinian tradition; according to this way of thinking, rationalism is one of the greatest menaces to religion. This argument therefore proceeds by a direct attack upon the authority of the reason. The other, the ecclesiastical, argument, arrives at the same conclusion by an indirect course; it demonstrates by an appeal to experience and history that we must of necessity submit to some authoritative tradition and organization in the Church; it attempts to show that there is in all purely human institutions an inherent tendency to disintegration and anarchy; as a practical fact, therefore, the unity and perpetuity of the Church can be preserved only by the sacrifice of the independence of the individual reason in the final decision of controversies. The great classic of this argument, which was one of the commonplaces of seventeenth-century apologetics, is Bossuet's *Histoire des variations des églises protestantes* (1688). Both forms of argument aim at the subjection of the reason to faith. They are so closely interrelated that, more often than not, they are found together, as they are in Dryden.

The Pyrrhonistic defense of faith supports the whole logical structure, and inspires the loftiest poetical flights, of both of Dryden's poems on religion. It prompts the slow and solemn rhythms of the opening lines of *Religio Laici*, which so pleased Landor: [100]

> Dim as the borrow'd beams of Moon and Stars
> To *lonely, weary, wandring* Travellers
> Is *Reason* to the *Soul:* And as on high
> Those rowling Fires *discover* but the Sky

---

[100] "Nothing," said Landor, "was ever written in hymn equal to the beginning of the *Religio Laici*, — the first eleven lines." — H. Crabb Robinson's *Diary*, III, 194. Quoted by G. Birkbeck Hill in his edition of Johnson's *Lives of the Poets* (Oxford, 1905), I, 442, n. 6.

> Not light us *here;* So *Reason's* glimmering Ray
> Was lent, not to *assure* our *doubtfull* way,
> But *guide* us upward to a *better* Day.
> And as those nightly Tapers disappear
> When Day's bright Lord ascends our Hemisphere;
> So pale grows *Reason* at *Religions* sight;
> So dyes, and so dissolves in Supernatural Light.[101]

In *The Hind and the Panther* the argument is extended, in defense
of transubstantiation, to a questioning of sense as well as of reason:

> Can I believe eternal God could lye
> Disguis'd in mortal mold and infancy?
> That the great Maker of the world could dye?
> And after that, trust my imperfect sense
> Which calls in question his omnipotence?
> Can I my reason to my faith compell,
> And shall my sight, and touch, and taste rebell? [102]

The identity of thought in the two poems is so close that the
second, almost unavoidably, repeats some of the first. In *Religio
Laici* (ll. 39–40) Dryden asked:

> How can the *less* the *Greater* comprehend?
> Or *finite Reason* reach *Infinity?*

And in *The Hind and the Panther* (I, ll. 104–105):

> Let reason then at Her own quarry fly,
> But how can finite grasp Infinity?

The fact that Dryden's polemics in the second poem are directed at the church to which he adhered when he wrote the first,
should not be permitted to obscure the consistency of the purely
philosophical content of both. In *Religio Laici* he was defending
Christian revelation against Deism. The greatest pagan philosophers, he said, have not been able to find the true source of human
happiness; the Deist is presumptuous in asserting that there is a
universal religion of prayer and praise discoverable by the reason
of man:

> Those Gyant Wits, in happyer Ages born,
> (When *Arms*, and *Arts* did *Greece* and *Rome* adorn,)
> Knew no such *Systeme:* no such Piles cou'd raise
> Of *Natural Worship*, built on *Pray'r* and *Praise,*
> *To One sole* GOD:
> Nor did Remorse, to Expiate Sin, prescribe:
> But slew their fellow Creatures for a Bribe.[103]

---

[101] *Poems*, ed. John Sargeaunt, p. 99.   [102] *Ibid.*, p. 119.   [103] *Ibid.*, p. 100.

But in *The Hind and the Panther* the polemic is Roman Catholic, and directed against the rationalistic principle inherent in Protestantism. It is true that the long discourse on reason is, in appearance, aimed at Socinianism; but Dryden, like the other Catholic controversialists of his time, believed that Protestantism inevitably tended toward this heresy:

> With greater guile
> False *Reynard* fed on consecrated spoil;
> The graceless beast by *Athanasius* first
> Was chased from *Nice;* then by *Socinus* nurs'd.
> His impious race their blasphemy renew'd,
> And natures King through nature's opticks view'd.
> Revers'd they view'd him lessen'd to their eye,
> Nor in an Infant could a God descry:
> New swarming Sects to this obliquely tend,
> Hence they began, and here they all will end.[104]

For if the reason is yielded the right to examine and regulate faith, even the cherished doctrines and sacraments of the Protestants will soon go; and therefore, said Dryden and the Catholic disputants, the Protestant denunciation of the irrationalities of transubstantiation plays directly into the hands of the Socinians. The doctrine of transubstantiation became, indeed, one of the centers of the controversy over reason in religion; Dryden's discussion of the question is conducted throughout with reference to this doctrine.[105]   And he is thinking, not so much of the Socinians as of the Anglicans, with their semi-rationalistic interpretation of the Communion, when he writes:

> To take up half on trust, and half to try,
> Name it not faith, but bungling biggottry.
> Both knave and fool the Merchant we may call
> To pay great summs and to compound the small.
> For who wou'd break with heav'n, and wou'd not break for all?
> Rest then, my soul, from endless anguish freed;
> Nor sciences thy guide, nor sense thy creed.

---

[104] *Poems*, ed. cited, p. 118. It was a favorite argument with the Catholics that Socinianism was the logical outcome of Protestantism. See, for instance, Abraham Woodhead's pamphlet with the ironical title: *The Protestants Plea for a Socinian: Justifying His Doctrine from being opposite to Scripture or Church-Authority; And Him from being Guilty of Heresie, or Schism* (London, 1686).

[105] *The Hind and the Panther*, Part I, ll. 63–149.

Faith is the best ensurer of thy bliss;
The Bank above must fail before the venture miss.[106]

The second poem is imbued with the same anti-rationalism as the earlier; though Dryden had changed his church allegiance, he had not changed his fundamental philosophical convictions. His criticism of Protestant principles in 1687 is only a more extended application of his animadversions against Deism in 1682.

As we examine Dryden's use of the other fideistic argument, the argument for some final and unassailable authority, we arrive at the same result; there is no change of mind observable on this question in the interval between the two poems. *Religio Laici*, as well as its Preface, is imbued with bitter feeling against the individualism of the English sectaries, who, since the Bible had been translated into English, "have used it so as if their business was not to be saved, but to be damned by its contents."

> The Book thus put in every vulgar hand,
> Which each presum'd he best cou'd understand,
> The *Common Rule* was made the *common Prey;*
> And at the mercy of the *Rabble* lay.
> The tender Page with horney Fists was gaul'd;
> And he was gifted most that loudest baul'd;
> The *Spirit* gave the *Doctoral Degree,*
> And every member of a *Company*
> Was of *his Trade* and of the *Bible free.* . . .
> While Crouds unlearn'd, with rude Devotion warm,
> About the Sacred Viands buz and swarm,
> The *Fly-blown Text* creates a *crawling Brood;*
> And turns to *Maggots* what was meant for *Food.*[107]

Such chaos, Dryden thought in 1682, can be averted by respecting the authority of the old Church Fathers, and by realizing that the truths necessary to salvation are so plain in Scripture that dispute about them is unnecessary. The solution was the usual one of the Anglican divines and was not invented by Dryden. Its weak-

---

[106] *Poems*, ed. cited, p. 119. Though the breaking bank, as a religious metaphor, is not to modern taste, it carried an idea home in Dryden's day. John Owen said with reference to the Roman Catholic Church: "For notwithstanding all their pleas of a sure and safe *bank* for the consciences of men, there are great presumptions that they will *break at last*, and leave them who have entrusted them unto eternal beggary." — *The Church of Rome no Safe Guide* (London, 1679), p. 17.

[107] *Poems*, ed. cited, pp. 97, 104–105.

ness, theoretically at least, was that it provided no real ultimate authority for the settlement of disputes; it merely substituted a judicious and learned individualism for the extravagant individualism of the Private Spirit. And Dryden shows himself even in *Religio Laici* not entirely satisfied with this Anglican compromise; his arguments, as Scott has observed, "carried him too far." The famous lines,[108]

> Such an *Omniscient* Church we wish indeed;
> 'Twere worth *Both Testaments*, and cast in the *Creed*,

reveal how strong a hold the notion of authority already had on his mind, despite his vigorous rejection of the doctrine of infallibility. And in the conclusion of the poem he yields an obedience to the Church of England as by law established, more strict than it theoretically could claim, and more blind than that Church, in its fear of being identified with Popery, would want to claim:

> And after hearing what our Church can say,
> If still our Reason runs another way,
> That private Reason 'tis more Just to curb,
> Than by Disputes the publick Peace disturb.
> For points obscure are of small use to learn:
> But *Common quiet* is *Mankind's concern*.[109]

If it is objected that this is only base compromise for the sake of an external quiet, one can only answer that Dryden probably recognized this weakness of his position, and therefore abandoned it for what he considered the stronger position of the Catholic Church. Authority he was looking for; and in *The Hind and the Panther* he speaks with scorn of a state church without any inner principle of authority on the basis of which it can *demand* obedience:

> How answ'ring to its end a church is made,
> Whose pow'r is but to counsel and perswade?

---

108 *Works*, I, 261.

109 *Poems*, ed. cited, p. 105. This argument from "common quiet" might perhaps be described as pure Hobbism. But, as the Anglican divines often pointed out, Hobbes's conception of absolute obedience to a state church was not so very different from the submission to an infallible church demanded by the Roman Catholics. In either case private reason would be curbed in the interest of public peace, though Hobbes would not have insisted that the submission be accompanied by such thorough searching of the heart.

> O solid rock, on which secure she stands!
> Eternal house, not built with mortal hands!
> Oh sure defence against th'infernal gate,
> A patent during pleasure of the state! [110]

He subjects Anglicanism to scrutiny, pointing out what great difficulties any seceded body must encounter in attempting to suppress further secession from itself. The Panther is therefore in an embarrassing situation:

> Fierce to her foes, yet fears her force to try,
> Because she wants innate auctority;
> For how can she constrain them to obey
> Who has her self cast off the lawful sway?
> Rebellion equals all, and those who toil
> In common theft, will share the common spoil.
> Let her produce the title and the right
> Against her old superiors first to fight;
> If she reform by Text, ev'n that's as plain
> For her own Rebels to reform again.
> As long as words a diff'rent sense will bear,
> And each may be his own Interpreter,
> Our ai'ry faith will no foundation find:
> The word's a weathercock for ev'ry wind:
> The *Bear*, the *Fox*, the *Wolfe* by turns prevail,
> The most in pow'r supplies the present gale. [111]

In the second part of the poem, when the Hind argues that the Anglican Church does not possess any satisfactory principle of authority, the Panther is represented as being unable to

> . . . enlarge
> With weak defence against so strong a charge.

It was an argument to which Dryden had quite evidently found no sufficient answer, and which had played an important part in his submission to the Catholic Church.

Such fundamental identity of thought in two poems which superficially appear to be of opposite tendencies is obviously not an insignificant accident. Both poems are thoroughly characteristic of Dryden, both spring from the same temper of mind, the same attitude toward philosophical and ecclesiastical problems. And the study of Dryden's thought is important and profitable for this reason, if for no other, that it minimizes, and possibly solves

[110] *Ibid.*, p. 124.   [111] *Ibid.*, p. 123.

entirely, the biographical problem of his conversion, which has proved such a stumblingblock to some of his critics. The continuity and consistency of his philosophical convictions, and their close relationship on the one hand to Dryden's native temperament, and on the other to notable tendencies in his immediate intellectual milieu, all these considerations make it appear quite improbable that his ideas were merely borrowed for the needs of the occasion. His shifts of allegiance were all changes in the same direction, toward greater conservatism. He feared the crowd, the "dregs of democracy," and believed that the weaknesses of human nature must be offset by some compelling and supreme authority in church and state. When he finally confessed to himself that the Anglican Church had renounced the necessary principle of authority, he went over to the church which seemed to him still to possess it. There is a type of conversion to Roman Catholicism which appears to the external observer to be mere timidity; the desire above all for inner peace and external quiet seems to rugged individualists to be only sluggishness of mind and spirit. Dryden did not advance upon Catholic doctrines, like a victorious army upon enemy fortifications, and subdue them by sheer intellectual conquest; Dryden was subdued by them. His assent to Catholicism was more in the nature of a retreat to an impregnable fortification when the more forward position had been proved untenable. The Catholic controversialists of the seventeenth century well understood the psychology of this process when they so persistently disseminated their fideistic propaganda, choosing, as the Anglican divines continually complained, to make people skeptics in order that they might the more easily reduce them to the authority of Rome. Dryden, being naturally inclined to skepticism, was all the more susceptible to this argument, because this tendency of his temperament had been sustained, clarified, and developed by his contacts with Montaigne and Browne, with the Royal Society, with the tradition of Catholic apologetics in England, and with Simon's *Critical History*. And the same temperament reveals itself, in an equally characteristic manner, in his poems on politics, which are indeed an essential part of its complete expression. Assuming the preconceptions of the seventeenth century, the problem of religious knowledge was never far removed from the problem of authority in church and state. Dryden's views on religion are full of political implications, and lose some of their cogency when isolated from those political and ethical questions with which they were, in his own mind, intimately associated.

CHAPTER V

TORYISM

i Skepticism and conservatism   ii Hobbes and Filmer   iii Dryden's
view of Whiggism   iv Dryden's formulation of Toryism

I

THE organic relation between Dryden's Toryism and his other
ideas has been repeatedly alluded to in the course of this
study.   For not only were the issues of politics and religion involved with one another, but Dryden was predisposed, by his diffidence of temperament and his philosophical skepticism, toward
the conservative wing in political theory.   Pyrrhonism, though
it often lent itself to disruptive and libertine tendencies, has by
and large since the time of its founder been the doctrine of tradi-
tionalists and conformists rather than of reformers.   It stimulated
fear of change and distrust of novelty far more than dissatisfaction
with things as they are.   Such a connection between skepticism
and conservative politics was almost a commonplace of thought
in the seventeenth century, when every man who pretended to
reading was familiar with his Montaigne.   For this arch-skeptic
was skeptical of nothing more than of reform:

A wise man of our times, saith, that where our Almanakes say
warme, should a man say cold, and in lieu of drie, moyst; And
ever set downe the contrarie of what they foretell; were he to lay
a wager of one or others successe, he would not care what side he
tooke, except in such things as admit no uncertaintie; as to promise
extreame heat at Christmas, and exceeding cold at Midsomer.
The like I think of these politike discourses.   What part soever
you are put unto, you have as good a game as your fellow: Provided you affront not the apparant and plaine principles.   And
therefore (according to my humor) in publike affaires, there is no
course so bad (so age and constancie be joyned unto it) that is not
better then change and alteration.   Our manners are exceedingly
corrupted, and with a marveilous inclination bend toward worse

and worse; Of our lawes and customes many are barbarous, and
divers monstrous; notwithstanding, by reason of the difficultie to
reduce us to a better estate, and of the danger of this subversion, if
I could fixe a pegge into our wheele, and stay it where it now is, I
would willingly doe it. . . . Instabilitie is the worst I find in our
state, and that our lawes, no more then our garments, can take
no settled forme. It is an easie matter to accuse a state of imper-
fection, since all mortall things are full of it. As easie is it to beget
in a people a contempt of his ancient observances: No man ever
undertooke it, but came to an end: But to establish a better state
in place of that which is condemned and raced out, divers who
have attempted it, have shronk under the burthen.[1]

Although Dryden was not so timorous as Montaigne, he was willing to put his conservative convictions under the protection of
Montaigne's authority. In his dedication of the *Aeneis* he declared
that he was "of Montaigne's principles, that an honest man ought
to be contented with that form of government, and with those
fundamental constitutions of it, which he received from his an-
cestors, and under which himself was born." [2]

As has often been pointed out by those who have written on
these subjects, skepticism and conservatism have in common a dis-
illusioned, even cynical, view of human nature. The typical revolutionist has a sublime confidence that when human nature is
emancipated from traditions, both intellectual and political, and
is at liberty to assert its own reasonableness and competence, the
terrible evils of society will quickly be done away with. The enlightened conservative, such as Montaigne, admits the existence
of the evils: ". . . Our manners are exceedingly corrupted, and
with a marveilous inclination bend toward worse and worse; Of
our lawes and customes many are barbarous, and divers monstrous."
But at the same time he is convinced that human nature cannot
meet the high expectations of the revolutionist. Montaigne joins
in a eulogy of Pyrrhonism both the political argument for submission to the state and the fideistic argument for humiliating the
reason to faith: for Pyrrhonism, he says,

[1] *Essays*, trans. Florio, Tudor Translations (London, 1893), II, 390–391.
This passage is from the essay *Of Presumption*, with which Dryden was certainly
familiar, as he quoted from it in his preface to *Aureng-Zebe* in 1676. See *Works*,
V, 328.   [2] *Essays*, ed. W. P. Ker, II, 171.

... representeth man bare and naked, acknowledging his naturall weaknesse, apt to receive from above some strange power, disfurnished of all humane knowledge, and so much the more fitte to harbour divine understanding, disannulling his judgment, that so he may give more place unto faith: Neither misbeleeving nor establishing any doctrine or opinion repugnant unto common lawes and observances, humble, obedient disciplinable and studious; a sworne enemy to Heresie, and by consequence exempting himselfe from all vaine and irreligious opinions, invented and brought up by false Sects. It is a white sheet prepared to take from the finger of God what form soever it shall please him to print therein.[3]

Such intellectual humility is a necessary condition to our genuine obedience to the state as well as to our inner tranquillity:

It is better for us to suffer the order of the world to manage us without further inquisition. A mind warranted from prejudice, hath a marvellous preferment to tranquillity. Men that censure and controule their judges, doe never duly submit themselves unto them. How much more docile and tractable are simple and uncurious mindes found both towards the lawes of religion and Politike decrees, than these over-vigilant and nice wits, teachers of divine and humane causes?[4]

That Dryden, true to the traditions of skepticism, shared this distrust of human nature, is obvious to the most cursory reader of his political poems. Nor was this conviction any late discovery, after the Popish Plot; for there is no evidence that Dryden ever held democratic principles. It is a somewhat extraordinary fact that the poet whose family was on the Parliamentary side during the Civil War and whose uncle held high office under the Protectorate, should have avoided eulogizing Commonwealth principles in his *Heroic Stanzas to the Memory of Oliver Cromwell*.[5] That poem has praise only for the strong leader, the heaven-sent great man who saved his country from chaos. Scott long ago pointed out the "caution and moderation" of Dryden's treatment of the political situation, in honorable contrast to Sprat's poem on the same occasion.[6] Again, Dryden's praise of the returned Charles, in *Astræa*

---

[3] *Essays*, ed. cit., II, 211–212.   [4] *Ibid.*, p. 211.

[5] On the contrary, as Saintsbury has noted, the twenty-seventh stanza of that poem "does not look as if Dryden's anti-democratic ideas were due to the Restoration merely." — *Works*, IX, 22, n.   [6] *Ibid.*, p. 7.

Redux and the *Panegyric on his Coronation,* similarly avoids extravagance in political opinion. That Dryden, in Johnson's phrase, had "changed with the nation" is evident enough. But the change offers no more difficulty than the account of any modern patriotic English historian who, after doing justice to the greatness of Cromwell, proceeds to describe the jubilant welcome to Charles in 1660, without implying that the latter event is a cause for national humiliation. Dryden's mind moved with the march of events, just as Milton's did in the opposite direction from 1641 to 1650; but we need not impugn the sincerity of either for that reason. On Dryden's behalf it should be noted that, as he nowhere in his early poem expressed any approval of a republican political establishment, so neither did he in his congratulatory poems to the king make any disparaging reference to Cromwell. It is indeed just possible that the sudden changes in political events did not modify his fundamental convictions. It is a curious fact that the phrase, "drawn to the dregs of a democracy," which Dryden later twice incorporated into his own work,[7] had lingered in his mind since *Lacrymæ Musarum,* the volume in memory of Lord Hastings to which he had contributed in 1650, in which one of his fellow contributors had thus expressed himself:

> It is decreed we must be drained, I see,
> Down to the dregs of a democracy.[8]

To appreciate how carefully Dryden phrased the *Heroic Stanzas* one has only to read them through with this expression in mind.

But if Dryden, early and late, was naturally inclined to doubt the stability of a democratic government, if he took a low estimate of the political capacity of mankind, he was also among those in whom the turbulence of contemporary English politics inspired profound misgivings. In no century since the Wars of the Roses had England been the scene of such violent and such long-continued tumult. We can now easily appreciate that the great constitutional change which was in progress was a blessing to England and to mankind; but this happy issue was not then so easily perceived, especially with the swarm of extreme and revolutionary doctrines

---

[7] See *Absalom and Achitophel,* 227, and *The Hind and the Panther,* i, 211.

[8] Dryden, *Poetical Works,* ed. W. D. Christie, p. 229, n.

which were everywhere agitated and expounded. It was possible, then, to denounce the political instability of the Anglo-Saxon race. Dryden could describe the English as

> . . . a Headstrong, Moody, Murm'ring race
> As ever tri'd th'extent and stretch of grace;
> God's pamper'd People, whom, debauch'd with ease,
> No King could govern nor no God could please.[9]

The frequency of rebellion was humiliating to contemplate:

> For, govern'd by the *Moon*, the giddy *Jews*
> Tread the same Track when she the Prime renews:
> And once in twenty years, their Scribes record,
> By natural Instinct they change their Lord.[10]

From such a state of mind springs absolutist political theory, which in this period received its most extreme and uncompromising statement and enjoyed its widest popularity. Such theorists as Hobbes and Filmer could never have had any practical political influence in England during a period of calm and security; they belong peculiarly to the turbulence of the seventeenth century.

Dryden's Tory allegiance is, therefore, not difficult to account for, notwithstanding his upbringing in a family of Parliamentary sympathies. In view of the traditions of thought of his century, he was quite naturally, one might say inevitably, of the conservative party. His convictions were intensified when, after the Popish Plot, another period of demagoguery and rebellion threatened, as he believed, the stability and the honor of the nation. Moreover, he had fortified himself by extensive study of history, his favorite reading, whence he drew parallels to illuminate the situation in his own day. The fact that he was ever the student raises his political pronouncements above the level of the mere pamphleteer. And if we can define his thought and follow him in some of his studies, we shall come perceptibly nearer to an understanding of his mind and character.

II

Dryden must have been forcibly tempted by absolutist political theory. His friend Hobbes was the most notorious exponent of it, and the political as well as philosophical tenets of Hobbes flourished

---

[9] *Absalom and Achitophel*, ll. 45–48.   [10] *Ibid.*, ll. 216–219.

among fashionable and courtly circles after the Restoration. "Mr. John Dreyden, Poet Laureat," records Aubrey about 1679–80, "is his great admirer, and oftentimes makes use of his doctrine in his plays," adding that this information came "from Mr. Dreyden himself." [11] In an earlier chapter I have illustrated Dryden's very frequent use in his plays of Hobbes's doctrine of necessitarianism; it is less easy to find characteristic Hobbesian political theory in his dramas. Perhaps there is an echo of it in the speech of Boabdelin, king of Granada:

> 'Tis true from force the noblest title springs;
> I therefore hold from that, which first made kings.[12]

But it can hardly be said that the dramatist used the argument sympathetically; for Don Arcos, the ambassador of the king of Spain, immediately retorts:

> Since then by force you prove your title true,
> Ours must be just, because we claim from you.

The audience was left to form its own conclusions after this typical dramatic passage at arms.

In the second part of *The Conquest of Granada*, however, we find a discussion of less equivocal import:

Boabdelin. See what the many-headed beast [the people] demands. — [Exit Abdelin.]
Cursed is that king, whose honour's in their hands.
In senates, either they too slowly grant,
Or saucily refuse to aid my want;
And, when their thrift has ruined me in war,
They call their insolence my want of care.

Abenamar. Cursed be their leaders, who that rage foment,
And veil, with public good, their discontent:
They keep the people's purses in their hands,
And hector kings to grant their wild demands;
But to each lure, a court throws out, descend,
And prey on those they promised to defend.

Zulema. Those kings, who to their wild demands consent,
Teach others the same way to discontent.
Freedom in subjects is not, nor can be;
But still, to please them, we must call them free.

---

[11] *Brief Lives*, ed. A. Clark (Oxford, 1898), I, 372.
[12] *The Conquest of Granada*, Part I, Act I, sc. i (*Works*, IV, 47).

> Propriety, which they their idol make,
> Or, law, or law's interpreters, can shake.

Abenamar.   The name of commonwealth is popular;
>   But there the people their own tyrants are.

Boabdelin.   But kings who rule with limited command,
>   Have players' sceptres put into their hand.
>   Power has no balance, one side still weighs down,
>   And either hoists the commonwealth or crown;
>   And those, who think to set the scale more right,
>   By various turnings but disturb the weight.

Abenamar.   While people tug for freedom, kings for power,
>   Both sink beneath some foreign conqueror:
>   Then subjects find too late they were unjust,
>   And want that power of kings, they durst not trust.[13]

So far as this is Hobbesian, Dryden may be said to have reflected the political ideas of that philosopher in his plays. Similar passages might be culled from *The Indian Emperor* and some of his other heroic plays.[14]

But it may be fairly questioned whether this strained political declamation in Dryden's heroic drama is anything more than plastered decoration. In was found appropriate for that theatrical genre not only by Dryden, but by Orrery, and earlier than either by Davenant, of whom it has been said that "his monarchic sentiment and scorn of the crowd are typical of the heroic play, which was, in its origin, the expression of an aristocratic ideal." [15] These stupendous spectacles required large and exaggerated effects; the ideas and sentiments conformed in tone to the general sensational nature of the characters and plot. In an earlier chapter we have hesitated to impute to Dryden an adherence to the philosophical conception of determinism which is so frequently debated in his plays. It is likewise neither necessary nor advisable to take his characters literally as his mouthpieces on political theory.

For when Dryden began to express his ideas in his own person, he carefully avoided all such forms of absolutist politics as were

---

[13] *The Conquest of Granada*, Part II, Act I, sc. ii (*Works*, IV, 130).

[14] See, for instance, the following, with references to the edition of Scott and Saintsbury:

The Indian Emperor, Act I, sc. ii (II, 339); Act II, sc. ii (II, 346); Act IV, sc. ii (II, 377); *Tyrannic Love*, Act II, sc. iii (III, 402).

[15] B. J. Pendlebury, *Dryden's Heroic Plays* (London, 1923), p. 78.

then current. There is no trace of Hobbes in *Absalom and Achitophel* and *The Medal;* and what is of greater import, no trace of Filmer.

Sir Robert Filmer is known to fame chiefly through Locke's ridicule in his *Discourses on Government* (1691) of the *Patriarcha*, Filmer's "thinnest and most confused" [16] work, and the only one which he himself did not give to the press. Filmer died in 1653, leaving an incomplete manuscript, which was first published in 1680. The *Patriarcha* does not fairly represent Filmer as a political thinker; but what is more important for our immediate purpose, it is not representative of Tory thought in 1680. Filmer maintained that royal authority is an inheritance, by the principle of primogeniture, from the patriarchal authority first bestowed by God on Adam. This was Filmer's way of avoiding the theory of a contract between king and people, which, with its corollary principle of repudiation, seemed to open too wide the door to rebellion. With this patriarchal theory, which "was not in the least essential" [17] to the general system of Filmer, Locke succeeded in making merry; Locke was able to show that under this theory no reigning family in Europe could produce its credentials; he established beyond doubt that under this theory the authority of monarchical government would be dissipated in genealogical obscurity. The triumph of Locke over Filmer's posthumous book was complete. But it is not so clear that Locke thereby triumphed over the principles seriously held by the Tories from 1679 to 1685. From Charles down they were far too shrewd politicians to stake their cause, in a moment of threatened civil war, on an unverifiable and obviously fictitious pedigree. It appears from a contemporary pamphlet that "this notion of the Divine and Patriarchal Right of absolute Monarchy" obtained especially "among some modern Churchmen, who cry it up as their *Diana*, and consequently hath . . . much infected our Universities." [18] Possibly, therefore, the more

---

[16] So described in the admirable essay on Filmer by J. W. Allen, *The Social and Political Ideas of Some English Thinkers of the Augustan Age*, ed. F. J. C. Hearnshaw (London, 1928), p. 28.   [17] Allen, *op. cit.*, p. 46.

[18] *Patriarcha non Monarcha* [by James Tyrrell], (London, 1681), *Preface.* Cf. also *Absalom Senior: or, Achitophel Transpros'd. A Poem* (London, 1682), p. 20.

"high-flying" divines were disseminating Patriarchy in the pulpits and universities as their version of Toryism; but, in general,
Tory theory was more respectable intellectually than this, and
dealt with less fanciful topics. And Dryden, who represents the
higher levels of Tory thought, never once leans his case on the
Patriarchal theory.

III

It is not easy for the modern reader of Dryden to do justice
to the intellectual merits of his political poems; from our point
of view he was on the wrong side. The Revolution establishment
settled the constitutional conflict of the seventeenth century, and
thereafter many of the old Tory arguments disappeared from
English political life. We are, accordingly, too likely to forget that
the Toryism represented by Dryden had in it some elements of
political wisdom of more than mere historical interest, that it contributed, in fact, toward a settlement in 1688 on less revolutionary
principles than might otherwise have been adopted. Only by an
effort of the historical imagination can we realize the dreaded
possibilities before England in 1680, the threats of catastrophe
which, in the light of later events, appear to us as mere chimeras.
We must realize that Dryden's poems were written while the whole
nation was in a state of panic: the Whiggish element in a furor
over the supposed revelations of the Popish Plot and the danger
of a Roman Catholic monarch; the Tory element fearing another
civil war, another social and economic upheaval, and another disastrous experiment in constitutional subversion. And the fears of
each party determined its political measures. However, on this
point also we find it easier to understand the Whigs; their fears
appear to have been amply justified by the succeeding reign of
James II, whereas the Tories seem to have been only perverse ob-
structionists to the inevitable course of constitutional development. In short, the Tories of 1680 appear to us as mere obstinate
victims of a delusion.

But all this was less clear in 1680. If it is true that some Tory
principles became extinct after 1688, the same may also be said
for some very forward Whig doctrines. The Whiggism of 1680 is as
different from the Whiggism of Sir Robert Walpole and the later

eighteenth century as the Toryism of 1680 is from the principles of Swift or Bolingbroke. The poems of Dryden deal with the situation as it existed from 1679 to 1682; and only as we consent to move back to this point in history and peer into the, as yet, uncertain future, can we have much sympathy with the motives back of the Toryism which Dryden represented.

The immediate occasion of the division of England into the Whig and Tory camps was of course the Exclusion Bill, intended to prevent the succession of the Roman Catholic Duke of York to the throne. But the roots of both parties reached deep into the past. The Exclusion Bill merely served to make the public more aware of political divergences that had been developing for a century or longer, and to combine and organize the many shades of radical and conservative opinion into two well-defined hostile groups. As this fact was plainly perceived and taken for granted at the time, much of the controversy consisted of each party reading to the other the lessons of history; though perhaps the Tories excelled somewhat in this art, lingering over the disastrous results of earlier rebellions, whereas the Whig argument was more likely to turn into a prophecy of the dire effects to come should a Papist king sit on the throne of England. Dryden, at any rate, made significant and pointed use of this appeal to history in his examination and judgment of Whiggism.

The close connection between Whiggism and Dissent did not escape anyone; Tory pamphleteers were never weary of proclaiming that the new Saints of '79 were intent on repeating the history of '42. Dryden went much further than this facile parallel; he made up his mind about the fundamental political tendency of the Sects — among which he included the Presbyterians of England and Scotland and the Huguenots of France — from their very origin. He read extensively in modern history, and this reading confirmed in him a conviction that these Sects were factious and rebellious by nature and in principle.

Among the most revealing chapters of modern history, as Dryden read it, was the account of the French League in the sixteenth century. His interest in it seems to anticipate the Restoration; for when he began a play on the Duke of Guise, as early as 1660, he must already have read Davila's history, which is the main source of that play.[19] This work had been translated into English at Oxford while Charles I had his headquarters there, and the king "read it there, with such eagerness, that no Diligence could Write it out faire, so fast as he daily called for it; wishing he had had it some years sooner, out of a Beliefe, that being forewarned thereby, He might have prevented many of the mischiefs we then groaned under." [20] The parallel of the Holy League of France and the Covenanters of England, which struck the unhappy Charles so forcibly, was not lost on later readers; the League, despite the difference in religion, came to be used as a commentary on the political principles and practices of English Dissenters and Whigs.[21] "Any one who reads Davila," said Dryden, in his *Epistle to the Whigs* prefixed to *The Medal* (1682), "may trace your practices all along." The Ligueurs held that, as Catholics, they were not bound to submit to Henry of Navarre, Huguenot heir to the French throne; in justification of this attitude they asserted, against the sacredness of the legal succession, the sovereign rights of the people. There was irony in the fact that the Whigs, who professed such hatred for papistry in England, should have been so startlingly anticipated by the Catholic Guisards of France, and Dryden, in his *Epistle to the Whigs*, drove the parallel home: "There were the same pretences for reformation and loyalty, the same aspersions of the king, and the same grounds of a rebellion." When Dryden wrote these lines in 1682 he had probably already turned again to the play he first projected in 1660; within a few months he had completed, with the assistance of Lee, his indictment of Whiggism drawn in the form of a historical drama, *The Duke of Guise*. The subject had then been on his mind for more than twenty years.

But the Ligueurs had no monopoly on the theories of popular

[19] See *Works*, VII, 146. In 1683 Dryden still had the first edition of the English translation by him (*ibid.*, VII, 161), though the second impression had been issued in 1678.

[20] H. C. Davila, *The History of the Civil Wars in France*, Second Impression (London, 1678), Preface to the Reader.

[21] The fact that Dryden drew this parallel in *Astræa Redux*, 101–102, confirms the natural supposition that his political purpose in taking up the story of the Duke of Guise was the same in 1660 as when he actually completed the play in 1682.

rights; their contemporaries, the Huguenots, also reserved a theoretical right to resist the authority of an heretical monarch. This doctrine was proclaimed by at least three eminent French disciples of Calvin: Theodore Beza, in a number of his publications, François Hotman, in *Franco-Gallia* (1573), and Philippe de Duplessis-Mornay, whose *Vindiciæ contra Tyrannos* (1579) was published under the pseudonym of "Junius Brutus." The great Scotch humanist, George Buchanan, who in political thought was of the school of Calvin and Mornay, expounded similar ideas in his work *De Jure Regni apud Scotos* (1579). Dryden was informed about these developments among the Calvinists of the sixteenth century. In his *Epistle to the Whigs*, after comparing them to the Guisards, he turns to the political traditions of Calvinism itself:

I know not whether you will take the historian's word, who says it was reported that Poltrot, a Hugonot, murdered Francis, duke of Guise, by the instigations of Theodore Beza, or that it was a Hugonot minister, otherwise called a Presbyterian (for our Church abhors so devilish a tenet), who first writ a treatise of the lawfulness of deposing and murdering kings of a different persuasion in religion: but I am able to prove from the doctrine of Calvin and the principles of Buchanan, that they set the people above the magistrate; which, if I mistake not, is your own fundamental, and which carries your loyalty no farther than your liking.[22]

And thus, Dryden believed, the nature of the new Whiggism — closely allied to English Presbyterianism — could be elucidated by the double parallel of Huguenot and Roman Catholic political thought.[23] For the politics of the extinct Ligueurs was in a sense

[22] A recent student of this subject, the Reverend R. H. Murray, says that Beza did not condemn Poltrot's assassination of the Guise, believing that tyrannicide was under some circumstances justifiable. Beza therefore carried the rights of the subject further than either Calvin, Hotman, or Duplessis-Mornay, who all stopped short of tyrannicide. See R. H. Murray, *The Political Consequences of the Reformation* (London, 1926), p. 188.

[23] Dryden's special interest in French history of the sixteenth century led him to read widely on the subject. In addition to Davila, he refers in his *Vindication* to the memoirs of Villeroy and the journals of Henry III [by L'Estoile], both of which he seems to have used as sources for some incidents also in *The Duke of Guise*. In the postscript to his translation of Maimbourg's *History of the League*, he also mentions Mezeray, and refers the reader to Sleidan for further information on the Münster Anabaptists. Dryden was doing more than collect material for a play.

continued by the Jesuits, to whom Dryden paid his respects in the Preface to *Religio Laici*, and again in the postscript to the *History of the League:*

> But some of the Jesuits are the shame of the Roman church, as the sectaries are of ours. Their tenets in politics are the same; both of them hate monarchy, and love democracy; both of them are superlatively violent; they are inveterate haters of each other in religion, and yet agree in the principles of government. And if, after so many advices to a painter, I might advise a Dutch maker of emblems, he should draw a Presbyterian in arms on one side, a Jesuit on the other, and a crowned head betwixt them; for it is perfectly a battle-royal. Each of them is endeavouring the destruction of his adversary; but the monarch is sure to get blows on both sides.[24]

Tory pamphleteers frequently made a point of this similarity in anti-monarchic thought between the Jesuits and the English Dissenters. Dryden regarded it as one more proof of the essentially rebellious spirit of Sectarianism.

So far we have been following Dryden's studies in Continental politics. But in his reading of English history, also, he observed how the individualism of the "Schismatics" had tended toward heresy in the Church and insubordination in both Church and State. "Since the Bible has been translated into our tongue," he said, in his Preface to *Religio Laici*, these Sectaries "have used it so as if their business was not to be saved, but to be damned by its contents. . . . How many heresies the first translation of Tyndal produced in a few years, let my Lord Herbert's *History of Henry the Eighth* inform you." He points out that the influence of Calvinism in England was of a disruptive nature, referring the reader to "the works of our venerable Hooker, or the account of his life [by Walton], or more particularly the letter written to him on this subject by George Cranmer." [25] The spirit of Dissent being

---

[24] *Works*, XVII, 167.

[25] Henry Care charged Dryden with having stolen his whole preface from Cranmer's letter. See *The Weekly Pacquet of Advice from Rome*, V, 165–166 (January 12, 1682–83). Evidently Care thought that Dryden expressed himself entirely in the spirit of Cranmer. Cranmer's letter to Hooker, written in 1598, was printed as appropriate to the times, in February, 1642. See *Thomason Catalogue*, I, 84.

in principle wayward and factious, it was impossible, Dryden believed, to reconcile it with a settled and authoritative order in Church and State. This is the interpretation of the Sects which runs through *Absalom and Achitophel*, *The Medal*, *Religio Laici*, and *The Hind and the Panther*, and it was one of Dryden's most deep-seated convictions. As Dissent was such an important contributory element in Whiggism, this conviction carried over into his judgment of the whole Whig party.[26]

For the Whigs, however conservative some of them may have been, inherited a good many Commonwealth tendencies. The Exclusion Bill raised all the sleeping dogs of political theory; its constitutional implications were many and far-reaching. It could not be passed without establishing a new precedent which would in effect make England an elective monarchy. Inasmuch as Charles resolutely refused to countenance the Bill, to continue to press it in Parliament was nothing less than threatening to seize the law-making power for Parliament alone, with the alternative of civil war if the royal party resisted. The grooming of the illegitimate Duke of Monmouth for the succession to the throne was, of course, a challenge to established constitutional principles. It is not surprising, therefore, that the old political doctrines of the French Huguenots, of Buchanan, of Milton and Harrington, as well as of a host of other pamphleteers of the Commonwealth period and later, now enjoyed a new life in the propaganda of the Whigs. They provided much of the current philosophy of the rights of the subject: government exists, not for the governors, but for the benefit of the governed, and its legitimacy is to be judged accordingly; government can exercise no authority against the will of the people; government is established by a contract between ruler and ruled, and when the ruler breaks this contract it becomes void. Dryden condensed the mass of this argument in the speeches of Achitophel, which could easily be illustrated at length from the pamphlets of the Whigs. At times he even tones down Whig extravagance. Thus, in a very violent Whig pamphlet of 1679, *An Appeal from the Country to the City*, we read:

[26] See especially *Absalom and Achitophel*, ll. 511–532.

The greatest danger accruing to your Persons, as well as to the whole Kingdom, upon the King's untimely death, will proceed from a confusion and want of some eminent and interested person, whom you may trust to lead you up against a *French* and *Popish* Army: for which purpose no person is Fitter than his Grace the Duke of *Monmouth*, as well for quality, courage and conduct, as for that his Life and Fortune depends upon the same bottom with yours: he will stand by you, and therefore ought you to stand by him.   And remember, the old Rule is, *He who hath the worst Title, ever makes the best King;* as being constrain'd by a gracious Government, to supply what he wants in Title; that instead of *God and my Right*, his Motto may be, *God and my People.*[27]

Achitophel says the same thing in a much milder way to Absalom:

> And Nobler is a limited Command,
> Giv'n by the Love of all your Native Land,
> Than a Successive Title, Long, and Dark,
> Drawn from the Mouldy Rolls of *Noah's* ark.[28]

But the essence of Whig doctrine is condensed into a few lines in *The Medal:*

> He preaches to the Crowd that Pow'r is lent,
> But not convey'd to Kingly Government;
> That Claimes successive bear no binding force;
> That Coronation Oaths are things of course;
> Maintains the Multitude can never err;
> And sets the People in the Papal Chair.
> The reason's obvious: *Int'rest never lyes;*
> The most have still their Int'rest in their eyes;
> The pow'r is always theirs, and pow'r is ever wise.
> Almighty crowd, thou shorten'st all dispute;
> Power is thy Essence; Wit thy Attribute!
> Nor Faith nor Reason make thee at a stay,
> Thou leapst o'er all Eternal truths in thy *Pindarique* way![29]

Whiggism involved the belief, not only in the *right* of the people to the ultimate authority in government, without any check, but also in the wisdom of their having it.   As Dryden saw it, to be a good Whig one must have, or pretend to have, unbounded confidence in human nature in the mass.

[27] *An Appeal from the Country to the City; For the Preservation of His Majesties Person, Liberty, Property, and the Protestant Religion.   Salus Populi, Suprema Lex.* (London, 1679).   The pamphlet is significantly signed "Junius Brutus," the pseudonym of the author of *Vindiciæ contra Tyrannos.*
[28] *Absalom and Achitophel,* ll. 299–302.   [29] *The Medal,* ll. 82–94.

Such was Dryden's conception of the Whig party, its principles, its antecedents, and its ultimate goal. The analysis might be extended to greater length and profusely documented from Whig pamphlets, books, and newspapers. But our only purpose here is to show how Dryden envisaged the political problems of his time, and how he sought in them for fundamental and leading principles — how he reduced the chaos to order in his own mind. If it was truly said by Dr. Johnson that Dryden found the English language brick and left it marble, the remark is even more appropriate to the political and religious controversies which he handled with intellectual as well as artistic distinction. It is evident enough that he wrote these controversial poems only after wide reading and laborious study. He was not a methodical research scholar — such as John Selden —, he was not an impartial student of history; but neither was he an irresponsible pamphleteer. His estimate of the Whigs may appear to us to be mistaken; but given Dryden's native temperament and cast of mind, as well as the historical knowledge at his disposal, and his dread of a Whig triumph becomes easily understandable. For his Toryism may almost be defined as a fear of Whig control over the destinies of England.

IV

If the Whigs, as Dryden conceived the matter, were demagogic flatterers of human nature, the Tories safely avoided that error. Dryden's whole statement of Tory belief is a series of variations on the theme that government must save human nature from itself. Of no Tory tenet is this more true than of that much-misunderstood doctrine of the divine right of kings.

This theory, which sought to give a religious sanction to government, was not of ecclesiastical origin. On the contrary, it arose only because it was necessary in the Middle Ages to assert the independent right of secular authority as against the imperialistic claims of the papacy. When the advocates of papal supremacy maintained that the pope, as holding his authority from God alone, could interfere with the conduct of secular governments, it was natural to reply that kings, also, hold their authority from God. The theory of the divine right of kings was therefore at first of a liberal and popular nature, and in its time served a very important and useful purpose.[30]

In the sixteenth and seventeenth centuries it seems to have been accepted or rejected by the various parties according as expediency dictated. Those Protestant churches which were state churches, and which therefore leaned for support on the authority of the king or prince, adhered to the theory. Outcast sects without legal status, threatened every moment with persecution by the secular authorities, were inclined to deny that these authorities governed by any divine sanction; they welcomed another theory, the theory of *salus populi suprema lex*, which, interpreted, could mean that the people had a right to judge and cashier kings. Then there were the Jesuits, who loved no kings but Spanish ones; a whole group of famous Jesuit political writers, passionately devoted to the spread of Catholicism and the extermination of heresy, developed such doctrines as the right of orthodox subjects to rebel against heretic princes; and in the pursuit of this end they particularly sought to degrade secular authority by relegating it to the level of a mere human convenience. The Jesuits were, therefore, as we have seen Dryden pointing out, at one with the English Whigs and Dissenters in political theory. They were at one in denying the sacredness of secular authority.

It was these dangers, real or imagined, to the stability of the state that gave the theory of divine right such a remarkable renewal of vitality in seventeenth-century England. Conservative-minded men counted upon it more than upon any other doctrine to impress the duty of obedience upon the consciences of subjects. The fact that it was challenged, not only in theoretical discussion, but in practical politics, the fact that a civil war had ravaged the country and a king had been put to death by his subjects, only lent the theory all the greater importance, as demonstrating that it was absolutely necessary to the preservation of law and order. The Anglican Church, of course, championed it against the Sects. It became the informing principle of that remarkable loyalist sentiment which, in the face of the political stupidity and misconduct

[30] See the classic treatise by John Neville Figgis, *The Divine Right of Kings*, 2d ed. (Cambridge, 1914).

of the Stuart monarchs, distinguished in succession the Cavaliers, the Tories of the reigns of Charles II and James II, and the Jacobites after 1688. The strength and vitality of the theory of divine right in England cannot be explained as theological pedantry; it was a statement in the best terminology then available of a vital political truth.

What the doctrine really meant in the time of Dryden was that there must be in government an ultimate authority beyond which there can be no appeal. When that authority has spoken, it cannot be impugned or brought to trial for its decision without crumbling the fabric of government. As Dryden put it, if the people

> . . . may Give and Take when e'er they please,
> Not Kings alone, (the Godheads Images,)
> But Government it self at length must fall
> To Natures state, where all have Right to all.[31]

Dryden proceeds in the next lines to a thoroughly pragmatic justification of the theory:

> Yet, grant our Lords the People, Kings can make,
> What prudent man a setled Throne woud shake?
> For whatsoe'r their Sufferings were before,
> That Change they Covet makes them suffer more.
> All other Errors but disturb a State;
> But Innovation is the Blow of Fate.
> If ancient Fabricks nod, and threat to fall,
> To Patch the Flaws, and Buttress up the Wall,
> Thus far 'tis Duty; but here fix the Mark:
> For all beyond it is to touch our Ark.
> To Change Foundations, cast the Frame anew,
> Is work for Rebels who base Ends pursue:
> At once Divine and Humane Laws controul,
> And mend the Parts by ruine of the Whole.
> The tamp'ring World is subject to this Curse,
> To Physick their Disease into a Worse.

Men did not adhere to the doctrine of divine right because of any blind admiration for supposed virtues or saintliness in the Stuart monarchs; the real explanation must be sought in an entirely different direction, in a vivid consciousness of the dangers of "innovation." Dryden even says that the doctrine was for this reason established as part of the English constitution by "our fathers,"

---

[31] *Absalom and Achitophel*, ll. 791–794.

> Who, to destroy the seeds of Civil War,
> Inherent right in Monarchs did declare:
> And, that a lawfull Pow'r might never cease,
> Secur'd Succession, to secure our Peace.[32]

A theory of divine right conceived in such an historical and utilitarian spirit is well on the way to becoming a modern doctrine of the sovereignty of the state.

The Whigs of course believed that the theory meant nothing but absolutism and "arbitrary" government; they accused the Tories of an intention — or at least a willingness — to sacrifice the ancient English rights of the subject in order to enlarge the royal prerogative. Whether there were many such Tories might be questioned; this much is certain, Dryden was not one of them. He expressed himself on this subject repeatedly and emphatically. Toward the close of his life he made a noble testament of his principles in his epistle to his kinsman John Driden, in which, as he stated in his letter to Montague, he gives his "opinion of what an Englishman in Parliament ought to be, and deliver it as a memorial of my own principles to all posterity.[33] He referred proudly to his grandfather's imprisonment for refusing to meet an irregular levy of money under Charles I. But Dryden was not retracting his principles in his old age; he was only confirming what he had frequently said before. As early as 1678, in the dedication of *All for Love* to Danby, then Lord Treasurer, he thus defined the problem of an English statesman: "Moderation is doubtless an establishment of greatness; but there is a steadiness of temper which is likewise requisite in a minister of state; so equal a mixture of both virtues, that he may stand like an isthmus betwixt the two encroaching seas of arbitrary power, and lawless anarchy. . . . For no Christian monarchy is so absolute, but it is circumscribed with laws. . . . The nature of our government, above all others, is exactly suited to both the situation of our country, and the temper of the natives. . . . And, therefore, neither the arbitrary power of One, in a monarchy, nor of Many, in a commonwealth, could make us greater than we are." [34]

This thoroughly English conception of constitutional mon-

---

[32] *The Medal*, ll. 113-116.   [33] *Works*, XI, 70, n.   [34] *Ibid.*, V, 320-321.

archy, with checks and balances to insure the freedom of the subject as well as the stability of the state, Dryden recurs to again and again. In *Absalom and Achitophel* (ll. 977–978) David sarcastically remarks that

> A king's at least a part of Government,
> And mine as requisite as their Consent.

In *The Medal* (ll. 117–118), after the passage on how "our fathers" declared inherent rights in monarchs and established a secure succession, Dryden continues:

> Thus Property and Sovereign Sway, at last
> In equal Balances were justly cast.[35]

In the same poem (ll. 247–251) the Englishman in him speaks again:

> Our Temp'rate Isle will no extremes sustain
> Of pop'lar Sway or Arbitrary Reign:
> But slides between them both into the best;
> Secure in freedom, in a Monarch blest.

From the *Vindication of the Duke of Guise* one might quote somewhat profusely to the same effect, but the following passage must suffice: "Neither does it follow, as our authors urge, that an unalterable succession supposes England to be the king's estate, and the people his goods and chattels on it. For the preservation of his right destroys not our propriety, but maintains us in it." [36] Dryden's Toryism was eminently reasonable and constitutional. And if some modern admirer of Burke were to search in the political literature of the late seventeenth century for some faint anticipations of the temper and principles of Burke, he would not find much to his taste in the Whig pamphleteers, but a great deal in John Dryden. Dryden deserves that high praise. For if he seems at first glance to be the champion of theories and loyalties

---

[35] On the political significance of "property" see also *The Medal*, ll. 311–312, and *Absalom and Achitophel*, ll. 499–500:

> By these the Springs of Property were bent,
> And wound so high, they Crack'd the Government.

These passages do not refer to Harrington's theory that power follows property, but to the current Whig propaganda that those who have the property *should* have the political power.   [36] *Works*, VII, 215.

of mere historic interest, extinct with a phase of English history, on closer examination he turns out to be more than that; he was definitely and consciously an Englishman in his political thought and feeling, and he cherished his national traditions of freedom. The perpetual problem of politics is to preserve both the freedom of the individual and the continuity of the national traditions. The terminology and formulae of this problem vary from age to age; but the insights and realities behind these transient formulae continue from age to age and reappear in new guises. Dryden's political poems, if read in this spirit, are still of vital interest to us. They speak the fundamental convictions of the conservative temperament, but also of the Englishman. There was in Dryden something even of the spirit of that Revolution which he never could bring himself to accept.[37]

[37] Some aspects of Dryden's politics under James II are discussed in Appendix D.

CHAPTER VI

CONCLUSION

THIS study has not attempted to trace the "growth of a poet's mind." Occasionally it has been possible to establish points of chronology in Dryden's reading, in his intellectual interests, and in the settlement of his convictions; but most of our data remain too vague chronologically to establish any definite stages in the development of his thought. On the whole, it seems most likely that his ideas underwent no very violent change, but merely a clarification, as he added gradually to his stock of ideas in philosophy, religion, and politics, and as one after another the problems of his time pressed for a solution. Thus we do not know whether he made the acquaintance of philosophical skepticism before or after he became a Royalist in politics; it is entirely possible that he had been both skeptical and conservative for some time before he became aware of any connection in principle between the two tendencies. The growth of his thought to maturity appears to have been slow and uncertain, but on the whole, from his point of view at least, sound. Though he tarried to examine everything and try everything, yet from a sufficient distance and with perspective, his somewhat erratic and zigzag course does move with consistency toward a goal; he was a robust individuality, with strong instincts. If, from one point of view, the history of his mind is a clarification of his ideas and a reduction of them to some sort of order, from another it appears to be the triumph of his instincts and his temperament over the multitude of intellectual distractions, such as Hobbism, materialism, Deism, and other temptations of the time, each of which for a season exercised its fascination upon his intelligence. Dryden was not a philosopher in the strict sense of the word; the organizing force in his nature, which gives unity to his work, is as much his temperament as his reason.

He was not a discoverer of new ideas; his whole intellectual biography consists of his ardent and curious examination and testing of those ideas which were current in his age. He is consequently easily misunderstood if detached from his intellectual milieu. And both his temperament and his intellectual character must be defined in terms of what he rejected as well as of what he appropriated. For, although it may be admitted that he was fortunate to live in an age that provided him with precisely those ideas which he could make peculiarly his own, nevertheless the offerings of his age were no simpler than those of any other; and his success in achieving something like centrality and consistency in his intellectual life testifies to both the seriousness and the strength of his mind. His intellectual reactions are as thoroughly characteristic of him as his style, and manifest the same qualities of the man.

The final value of a study of Dryden's adventures among ideas lies, no doubt, in what it contributes to an understanding of the poet's personality. His versatility has long been recognized, usually with the qualifying suspicion or assumption that it precludes his having had any high purpose. But Dryden tried very seriously to find himself, and he eventually succeeded, even though at a mature age. Only a mind thus vigorously exercised could have produced prose and poetry of such solid and enduring value as he has left. The weft of his style crossed a strong warp of thought, skillfully laid to form the base of the completed pattern.

When Dryden said that he laid by his "natural diffidence and scepticism for a while" to take up the dogmatical way of Lucretius for the purpose of translating him, he indicated his own essential quality both of mind and temperament. His philosophical skepticism has been discussed at large in this study. His native diffidence of manner has been attested to by Congreve, who knew him in his old age:

He was of very easy, I may say, of very pleasing access; but something slow, and as it were diffident in his advances to others. He had something in his nature that abhorred intrusion into any society whatsoever. Indeed it is to be regretted that he was rather blamable in the other extreme; for, by that means, he was personally less known, and consequently his character might become liable both to misapprehensions and misrepresentations.

To the best of my knowledge and observation, he was, of all the men that ever I knew, one of the most modest, and the most easily to be discountenanced in his approaches, either to his superiors or equals.[1]

It is apparent how deeply the skeptical way of thinking was rooted in his whole nature, what an admirably fitted philosophical medium it was for the expression of his inborn temperament. A man whose intellectual possessions are so obviously his birthright should not be hastily set down as insincere.

As Dryden's sincerity may be discovered in his appropriation of exactly those ideas of his age which fitted him, so his consistency is to be understood from the historical development of those ideas. Some of the extensive ramifications of Pyrrhonism in the thought of the seventeenth century have been traced in the preceding pages of this study. It is obvious that the man who in that century found himself inclined to philosophical skepticism was likely to find his views to some extent determined thereby in such distantly related subjects as religion and politics. For if Pyrrhonism has made many "libertines" and "free-thinkers," it has had a far more distinguished following among serious-minded men of conservative tendencies in Church and State. Among the many great names representative of this comprehensive and important tradition of the century Dryden's is not the least. A survey of the history of the whole tradition reveals, therefore, as no mere analysis or commentary can, the fundamental and intimate relationship between Dryden's philosophical skepticism and his conservatism and traditionalism in religion and politics. The consistency of his thought is perhaps better not regarded as entirely a matter of logic; it is the consistency of a man who came to understand one of the profound impulsions of his age, through which also he could define and express his own temperament and convictions.

If such considerations as these are sound, Dryden is even on the intellectual side a significant and an imposing figure. He represents an important aspect of the seventeenth century. His poems

---

[1] Dedication to Dryden's *Dramatic Works* (1717).

on religion should be studied along with Montaigne, Charron, Pascal, Bishop Huet; his poems on politics would profit the historian of political thought as much as the writings of Hobbes — certainly more than the treatises of Filmer. But any work of first-rate historical importance has also some intrinsic value as an enrichment of the experience of later generations. Conservatives and liberals we shall always, fortunately, have with us. Those who belong to the same camp recognize and salute one another, however widely they may differ on particular doctrines in economics, politics, or theology; they are somehow like-minded and understand one another. Dryden has always had, and probably for a long time to come will have, some small following of those who delight not only in relishing his phrases, but also in thinking his thoughts. For such readers his work is one of the classic expressions of the conservative temperament.

APPENDIX A

THE BIBLIOGRAPHY OF ROMAN CATHOLIC CONTROVERSY IN ENGLAND IN THE SEVENTEENTH CENTURY

THE earliest guide to the controversial writings of both sides from the Reformation to the end of the reign of James II is Charles Dodd, *Certamen Utriusque Ecclesiae: or A List of all the Eminent Writers of Controversy, Catholicks and Protestants, since the Reformation*, published in 1724. It has been reprinted in the *Publications of the Chetham Society*, Vol. LXIV (1865). It is still the best point of departure for a bibliographical study of the subject, but its skeletonized outlines must be supplemented by the lists of publications of each Roman Catholic writer in Charles Dodd's *Church History of England*, 3 vols. (Brussels, 1737-42), and in J. Gillow's *Literary and Biographical History or Bibliographical Dictionary of the English Catholics*, 5 vols. (London and New York, 1885-1902).

The earliest bibliography of the Protestant publications during the reign of James II is *The Catalogue of all the Discourses published against Popery during the Reign of King James II.*, by Edward Gee, 34 pp. (London, 1689). In 1735 Francis Peck published *A complete Catalogue of all the Discourses written, both for and against Popery, in the Time of King James II.*, which, according to the title-page, contained four hundred and fifty-seven titles of books and pamphlets. Peck's work was made the basis of *A Catalogue of the Collection of Tracts for and against Popery (Published in or about the Reign of James II.) in the Manchester Library founded by Humphrey Chetham*, edited by Thomas Jones, *Publications of the Chetham Society*, Vols. XLVIII (1859) and LXIV (1865).

The more important Anglican pamphlets of the reign of James

II were collected under the title *A Preservative against Popery*, 3
volumes folio (London, 1738), by Bishop Edmund Gibson; this
collection was reprinted in 18 volumes, edited by the Reverend
John Cumming (London, 1848–49).

APPENDIX B

JUSTEL'S LETTERS TO HENRY COMPTON, BISHOP OF LONDON

From Bodleian Ms. Rawlinson C. 984.

fol. 16.   A Paris le 12 Mars 1678

Monseigneur

La Personne que vous voulez bien honorer de Votre
protection se prepare pour Vous aller rendre ses deuoirs et
Vous remercier de toutes les bontez que Vous auez eües
pour elle. La peur quelle a eue de Vous estre incommode
la obligee de retarder son uoyage. Nous ne pouuons nous
lasser dadmirer uostre generosite et linclination que Vous
auez a faire du bien a tout le monde, cependant ie croy quil
est a propos dexaminer le merite et la vie des gens deuant
que de les employer parce que la pluspart sont ignorans ou
libertins. Quand lAngleterre seroit deliuree dune partie des
personnes ramassees a Londre elle nen seroit pas plus mal.
On continue a parler auec estime de Monsieur de Veil, ses
ennemis mesme en disent du bien. l'Histoire Critique de la
Bible sera bien tost acheuee. Il nya plus que la Table et la

f. 17.   preface a imprimer des aussi tost quelle sera acheuee ie ne
manquerai pas de uous lenuoyer. Lautheur est un Pere de
loratoire nommé Simon que Vous auez veu autrefois a Paris.
Mons. de Veil pourra examiner ce traitte la et Vous en
rendre compte. Ce pere Simon est Scauant, qui a de les-

prit du bon Sens et qui Scait les langues orientales. Son ouurage est attendu parce quil est hardi.

Ie suis auec respect

Monseigneur

Votre tres Humble et tres obeissant seruiteur

JUSTEL

f. 27.   A PARIS le 13 Auril 1678

MONSEIGNEUR

   Ie vous suis infiniment obligé de l'honneur que uous mauez faict de mecrire et de la bonté que uous auez de me donner auis de ce que se faict de nouueau dans vostre Isle qui ne produit que de bonnes choses et des ouurages considerables. Vne dem^le. qui retourne en Angleterre laquelle est ma parente uous donnera l'Histoire du texte Sacree dont ie vous ai parlé. elle est imparfaite et point reliée parce qu'on veut la deffendre y ayant des propositions hardies et contraires au respect et a la veneration que nous deuons auoir pour la bible. La peur que iay eue de nen pouuoir auoir ma constraint a Vous loffrir dans un miserable estat dont i'ay bien de la confusion. Sans cette facheuse conjointure et le depart de Mad.^le delorme ma parente ie naurais pas osé uous offrir un ouurage si imparfait. Comme ie n'ai
f. 28. eu pour but que de contenter votre curiosité, iespere que Vous m'excuserez et que vous aurez assez de bonte pour croire que ien aurois usé dune autre maniere si ie nauois pas este contraint. Iay bien de la ioye de ce que la personne dont uous me parlez dans uotre lettre se porte au bien et quelle responde a lesperance quon a eue delle, ce qui luy faict esperer que Vous luy continuerez l'honneur de Votre protection et que Vous luy donnerez le moyen de seruir un iour lEglise Anglicane et Vous donner des marques de sa reconnoissance. Comme Vous auez quantite d'habiles gens ie ne doute point quon n'examine auec soin et exactitude le liure que ie Vous enuoye dont des esprits foibles peuuent abuser. M^r. Walton y est critique et Monsieur Vossius

aussi, ce qui me faict croire que quil [*sic!*] nen entreprendra la deffense du premier. M^r. de V. est propre pour lexaminer et pour marquer les endroits qui ne seront pas bien prouuez ny appuyez. Ie serai bien aise de scauoir le iugement quen auront faict uos docteurs. Lautheur a pour Vous beaucoup destime et de respect et Vous honore infiniment. Cest un homme desprit mais hardi. Ie Vous demande pardon de Vous estre importun et Vous supplie de croire que ie suis veritablement et auec respect

Monseigneur

Votre tres humble et tres obeissant Seruiteur

J<small>USTEL</small>

APPENDIX C

THE TWO ISSUES OF THE ENGLISH TRANSLATION OF FATHER SIMON'S *CRITICAL HISTORY OF THE OLD TESTAMENT*

I. THE WALTER DAVIS ISSUE

A / Critical / History / of the / Old Testament. / Written originally in French, / By Father Simon, Priest of the Con- / gregation of the Oratory; / And since translated into English, / By a Person of Quality. / London, / Printed, and are to be sold by Walter Davis in Amen-Corner. / MDCLXXXII.

Collation:

1. Title-page and *To the Reader*, A and A2.
2. *The Author's Preface Translated out of French*, a–b⁴.
3. *A Table of the Chapters*, c³.
4. Book I., B–Z⁴, Aa–Dd⁴.
5. Book II., A–Y⁴, Z².
6. Book III., Aaa–Yyy⁴, Zzz³.
7. *A Catalogue of the chief Editions of the Bible*, and *A Catalogue of Jewish and other Authours*, ¶–5¶⁴.

II. THE TONSON ISSUE

A / Critical History / of the / Old Testament, / In Three Books: / The First treating at large concerning the / several Authours of the Bible. / The Second containing the History of the chief / Translations of the Bible, made either by / Jews or Christians. / The Third laying down Rules whereby a more / exact Translation may be made of the Scripture / than hitherto has been. / Written Originally by Father Simon of the Oratory. / With a Supplement, being a Defence of / The Critical History, in Answer to / Mr. Spanheim's Treatise against it. / Both Translated into English by H. D. / London. / Printed for Jacob Tonson, at the Judge's Head in Chancery- / lane, near Fleetstreet. 1682.

Collation:

1. Title-page and two leaves of commendatory poems.
2. *A Catalogue of the chief Editions of the Bible*, and *A Catalogue of Jewish and other Authours*, with the same signatures as in the other issue.
3. *An Answer to Mr. Spanheim's Letter*, 6¶–11¶⁴, 12¶².
4. The Davis title-page, the author's preface, table of chapters, and the three Books, exactly as in the first issue.

APPENDIX D

ENGLISH CATHOLIC OPINION IN THE REIGN OF JAMES II

THE state of mind of the English Catholics in the reign of James II is a subject which has a very direct bearing on our understanding and judgment of Dryden. His conversion after the accession of James has brought upon him a very general suspicion of acting upon merely prudential and worldly-wise motives, of having decided that a pension was worth a mass. Thus Christie, who never forgave Dryden anything, says that "it is hard to believe that in this great change, coming so soon after James's accession, . . . visions of greater worldly advantage did not influence Dryden." [1] Christie's opinion on Dryden's character would hardly be worth quoting, except that on this point his judgment is supported by many more temperate critics. Thus Mr. Allardyce Nicoll has recently written: "The actual conversion, I have not the slightest doubt, was the result of not purely disinterested resolves. The Poet Laureate of a Catholic king was more likely to succeed if he himself were a Catholic." [2] The assumption is, of course, that English Catholics were enjoying a springtime of peace and prosperity under the blessing of a monarch of their own persuasion. Mr. Nicoll indeed observes on his own account that there were dangers ahead: "With Charles' decease," he says, "the temper of the age began to change. James was a Catholic, and Catholicism was hated and feared in England. It was inevitable that after his reign a Protestant should come to the throne. Apparently few contemporaries realized this, and Dryden at first may have rejoiced at the change." [3] "Apparently few contemporaries realized this." One could not have hazarded a wilder guess. The heir to the throne — since James had no son — was his daughter

---

[1] *Poetical Works of John Dryden*, Globe edition, *Memoir*, p. lviii.
[2] *Dryden and His Poetry* (London, 1923), pp. 95–96.　　　[3] *Ibid.*, p. 95.

Mary, wife to William of Orange, the courageous and determined leader of the Protestant interest in Europe. All the politics of the reign of James revolved about this prospect of an inevitable Protestant successor to the Catholic incumbent. Every man in England was thinking about it. Those embittered English who never reconciled themselves to the idea of a Catholic monarch were looking toward Holland, whence their deliverance was sure to come in time. The moderates, who believed that James was the constitutional and rightful king, even though his Catholicism was awkward and possibly dangerous, aimed chiefly to keep him to a trimming course until his death and the coming of William and Mary would put an end to the anomaly. The Catholics themselves were divided into two factions: those who wanted James to confine himself to moderate courses and keep up a good understanding with William; and those who thought that the king must act swiftly and decisively to liberate English Catholics from all their legal penalties and to make the Catholic Church in England absolutely secure from legal oppression forever; because, said these latter, when James in the not distant future dies, and William comes over, all hope of deliverance from these oppressive laws will be gone. James followed the advice of this second faction. Throughout the four years of his reign he was working against time. His attempts to coerce the English Parliament, his policy with the army and in Ireland, his appointments of Catholics to military and civil posts, were all desperate measures to do *something* for the liberation of the Catholics before it should be too late. English Catholics were so apprehensive of the inevitable coming over of William and Mary that when in 1686 the queen was in ill health, they were, in fact, cheered by the news; if she should die, they reasoned, the king might promptly marry again and possibly have a male heir, who would of course be brought up a Catholic, to exclude William and Mary.[4] The queen however lived on, and in 1688 actually presented the king with a son and the country with an heir to the throne. The Catholics were happy, but the rest of the country was in consternation; the more violent Whigs of the time even de-

[4] Terriesi's dispatches, 16/26 April, 26 April/6 May, 31 May/10 June, and 26 August, 1686. Add. Mss. 25, 372, fol. 33, 44, 105–106 and 206.

clared that the birth was a pretence to cheat William and Mary of
the succession, and that the pretended heir had been smuggled in
in a warming pan. By this time, however, the career of James was
nearly over; William fitted out six hundred ships in Holland and
descended upon the coast of England as her deliverer; in December James gave up, threw the Great Seal into the Thames and fled
in disguise to France. Such are the essential and elementary facts
about the reign of James II.

First, a word as to the sources of the information we are in
search of. Aside from some hints and anecdotes in the memoirs,
letters, and pamphlets of the time, we have to rely on the diplomatic correspondence of the reign, particularly that of ambassadors of the Catholic powers. The Dutch envoy either did not know
much about what the Catholics thought, or he was not given to
emphasizing that kind of information. But Barillon, the French
ambassador, and Terriesi, the Florentine minister, were in close
touch with English Catholics, and their dispatches are full of references to Catholic opinion; their testimony is the more valuable
because they represent both the English factions; Barillon was
intriguing with the extreme or Court party, and Terriesi was working with the moderate Catholics. The papal nuncio, D'Adda, who
was by nature reserved and circumspect, does not give very much
information on our subject, but what he does give is of the highest
authority. On the dispatches of these three representatives of
Catholic powers I have chiefly relied in the following account.[5]

From these sources one may gather abundant evidence that the
moderate English Catholics regarded the policies of James as precipitating their ruin. And I think it is worthy of note that this
evidence, first available to historians in the nineteenth century,
corroborates an oral tradition recorded in 1781 by an English priest,

---

[5] Barillon's dispatches have been partly published in Charles James Fox,
James the Second (1808), *Appendix;* in Mazure, *Hist. Rev.* (1825); in Marquise
Campana di Cavelli, *Les Derniers Stuarts à Saint-Germain en Laye* (1871); I have
made some transcripts of my own from the original correspondence in the French
office of Foreign Affairs.

For Terriesi I have used the transcription in the British Museum, *Add. Mss.*
25, 371—25, 375.

For D'Adda I have used the British Museum transcription *Add. Mss.* 15395
and 15396.

the Rev. Jos. Berington. "Bigoted, headstrong, and imprudent," he says of James II, "he had long before his accession, it seems, formed the design of new-modelling the religion of his country. Had the exclusion-bill passed, and James never reigned, it would have been well for Catholics." [6] Berington also records that the Catholics were divided as to policy.

> The Catholics, as a body [he says] merit not the reprehension, I give to Petre and his associates. They saw the wretched folly and the weak views of those bad advisers; and they condemned the precipitancy of measures which, they knew, could only terminate in their ruin. As must ever be the case with all men, in a similar situation, they wished to be relieved from oppression; but the undisturbed practice of their religion, with the enjoyment of some few civil liberties, would have satisfied their most sanguine desires. This I know from certain information: But unhappily for them and for their descendants, the voice of prudence and of cool religion was not attended to, whilst wild zeal and romantic piety were called in to suggest schemes of folly, and to precipitate their execution.[7]

Ironically enough, the very people whom James endeavored to liberate preserved his memory with detestation. The explanation of course lies in the events of his reign.

The policy of James through his four turbulent years on the throne was marked by consistent obstinacy and constantly increasing recklessness. But he began rather well; his accession was unexpectedly peaceful, and he declared in Council that he would maintain the laws of England and do nothing against the safety and preservation of the Protestant religion. The king was known to be a man of his word, and the country accepted his speech with joy. Moreover, he immediately called a meeting of Parliament for April, which seemed to imply that the new king recognized the right of his loyal subjects to parliamentary government; for, ever since the stormy session of March, 1681, Charles had made shift

[6] *The State and Behaviour of English Catholics from the Reformation to the Year 1781,* 2d ed. (1781), p. 71.

[7] *Ibid.,* pp. 75–76. Dodd's *Church History* (1742), which expressed Catholic resentment against Father Petres and Sunderland, was, says Berington in his Preface, "of use to me. It contains many things, regarding Catholics, during that period, extremely curious and well authenticated." But Dodd, whose language was cautious, must have been supplemented by oral tradition.

to get along without calling that ungovernable body together. On the surface prospects seemed bright for a happy understanding between the Catholic king and his Protestant subjects.

But the king had not taken his subjects fully into his confidence. In spite of his declaration in Council, he was from the very moment of his accession determined that his great aim should be to secure liberty of conscience for the Catholics. He said so to Barillon on February 19.[8] This policy he intended to unfold gradually and discreetly, and to pursue with firmness. He expected support for it from the Anglican Church, which had steadily remained loyal to him throughout the period since the Popish Plot of 1678. But when the king and queen attended mass in state, the pulpits of London immediately resounded with denunciations of Papistry, and the king called the Archbishop and the Bishop of London before him and sternly demanded that they control and discipline their clergy. The incident revealed clearly enough that the Anglican Church would regard toleration of Catholics as a deadly blow aimed at itself; and that James would find his plan impracticable. Already the Catholics began to fear the king's policy; on March 12, hardly five weeks after the accession of James, Barillon reported to Louis XIV that the English Catholics were divided and that rich and old established families, who called themselves "good English," urged a very moderate policy.[9] But James did not listen to this prudent counsel.

We must be careful, however, to state the king's aims with precision and fairness. It is often said or implied that James intended to force Catholicism upon unwilling Protestants, at the point of the sword if necessary. I find no evidence of this. He must, of course, have hoped that Catholicism, once it was no longer obstructed by penal laws, would flourish, but he could hardly have expected in his own lifetime to see it outnumber the Anglican

[8] Fox, *App.*, p. xix. For the next two sentences see Barillon, 26 February, in Fox, *App.*, p. xxxiii.

[9] "Il est certain qu'il y a de la division parmi les Catholiques; les uns sont même assez dangereux, car ils affectent une grande modération; ils craignent les désordres, étant pour la plupart riches et bien établis; ils prétendent être *bons Anglais*, c'est-à-dire, ne pas désirer que le Roi d'Angleterre ôte à la nation ses privilèges et ses libertés." — Mazure, I, 403-404. Onno Klopp, *Der Fall des Hauses Stuart*, III, 27, gives the date March 12 for this dispatch.

Church. What James really wanted was a complete *toleration* of Catholics and a removal of all disqualifications upon them; authoritative contemporary accounts are decisive on this point; [10] what James wanted to establish by law in England was — not the Catholic religion — but the *security* of the Catholic religion. If he could accomplish this, conversions, he believed, would be plentiful. The observation was frequently made during his reign that few people, and those not of any consequence, came over to the Catholic Church; James was convinced that this was due to fear of the ruinous penalties laid by the laws on such action. His first aim was, therefore, to abolish the penal laws, repeal the Test Act, and allow English Catholics equal opportunity with Protestants in the military or civil service of the king.

The second point of his policy was to secure this liberation of the Catholics by act of Parliament; the tenacity with which he pursued this aim, the devious and questionable conduct which it led him into, attest the importance of it in his mind. He could easily have chosen a more direct policy; he could have exercised that dispensing power over the laws which he, as well as Charles before him, always believed that the constitution of England gave to the sovereign. But the exercise of this power would not have served James's purpose, precisely because such a solution could last only

[10] "Ce Prince m'expliqua à fonds son dessein à l'égard des Catholiques, qui est de les établir dans une entière liberté de conscience et d'exercice de la Religion." — Barillon, 26 February, 1685. Fox, *App.*, p. xxxiii.

D'Adda, 19 July 1686, relates a conversation with the king: "Passò di poi a parlare delle cose d'Inghilterra, e disse, che riconoscendo che il maggior vantaggio della Religione sarebbe risultato dal togliere le leggi penali, l'apprensione delle quali tratteneva infiniti dal convertir si, mentre facevano timorosi il conto sopra l'avenire, e sopra la mutatione dello stato presente, e la successione presuntiva del Principe d'Oranges, volendo un si gran male spirituale presente sul dubbio di un possibile danno temporale futuro, onde le sue applicationi erano rivolte onninamente a prendere le misure più proprie ad ottenere questo fine, e levar di mezzo un si grand' ostacolo."

In a dispatch of 1 November 1686, D'Adda reports that the king said "che riuscendo felicemente il disegno di porre li Cattolici in un piede equale agl' altri suditi suoi, e che la religione Cattolica non fosse ostacolo alcuno per essere considerati equalmente capaci delle cariche, e di tutto quello che cade in un Suddito Inglese sperava in poco tempo di veder fiorire in questo Regno la vera Religione cessando li timori che ora regnano in quelli, che sono il maggior numero di perdere li loro beni e che riguardano la successione del Principe d'Oranges troppo da vicino."

as long as his own life; the real problem was to provide protection for the Catholics on that evil day when William should succeed him, and therefore only an act of Parliament would suffice.[11]   I stress this point, because it indicates with what obvious risk conversion to the Catholic Church at that time was attended.

But, as has been said, James knew what difficulties his policies would raise.   He determined to proceed cautiously, and step by step.[12]   He appeared publicly at mass; he relaxed the laws against Catholics and Quakers; he gave an Irish regiment to Colonel Talbot, a Catholic, in defiance of the Test Act.   But when Parliament met in May he did not judge the time ripe for the full expo-

[11] "A quanto poi Vostra Altezza Serenissima m'onora di scrivere in cifra replicherò: Che se con il consenso del Parlamento non riesce a Sua Maestà di fare qualche passo solido e legale a favore de' Cattolici; che converrà ne faccia per assicurarli a quale prezzo che sia qualcheduno de' violenti a meno di non volerli tutti sacrificare alla perfidia de' Protestanti doppo la sua morte." — Terriesi, 13 December, 1686.

"Vedendo bene che per rendere effetuale questa sua volontà per doppo la sua morte, o in fin a tanto almeno che non siano fatte leggi nuove in contrario, e che siano dal popolo ben ricevute, che e necessario che siano tali cose fatte da un Parlamento, e che fatte di violenza non serviranno che ad inasprire il generale, et a fare che non vivessero temp più lungo di quello che viverà la Maestà Sua." — Terriesi, 20/30 December, 1686.

"È dubbio ancora se anco ad Aprile lascerà sedere la Maestà del Re il Parlamento, perché quando Sua Maestà lo lascerà sedere, vuole in materia di religione che rimetta li Cattolici in Inghilterra nello stato libero e franco che sono tutti li altri sudditi della Maestà Sua, e che possino godere (essenti da ogni persequtione) delli avvantaggi istessi in temporale et in spirituale, che godano adesso li Protestanti, e che non vi siano più leggi contro di essi, perchè quando non lo volesse fare, dicano assolutamente che Sua Maestà lo dissolverià, e ne chiamerià un nuovo. Di sorte che se e vero, come chi puol saperlo assevera, che è verissimo, che Sua Maestà vuole avanzare il servitio delli Cattolici per la strada della quiete, che è quella del 'arlamento, non vi è probabilità alcuna che voglia servirsi di quella della violenza, che fanno temere al popolo li seditiosi . . . ." — Terriesi, 17/27 January, 1686/7.

[12] "Ce Prince m'expliqua à fonds son dessein à l'égard des Catholiques, qui est de les établir dans une entière liberté de conscience et d'exercice de la Religion; c'est ce qui ne se peut qu'avec du temps, et en conduisant peu-à-peu les affaires à ce but. Le plan de sa Majesté Britannique est d'y parvenir par le secours et l'assistance du parti épiscopal, qu'il regarde comme le parti royal, et je ne vois pas que son dessein puisse aller à favoriser les Nonconformistes et les Presbitériens, qu'il regarde comme de vrais républicains.

"Ce projet doit être accompagné de beaucoup de prudence, et recevra de grandes oppositions dans la suite." — Barillon, 26 February, 1685.   In Fox, *App.*, p. xxxiii.

sure of his plans. He first asked for money, which he received. But the House of Commons anticipated the king by raising the religious question; after some outspoken debate it was voted "that an address should be made to the king, purporting that the house did entirely rely on his royal declaration, that he would defend and secure the reformed religion of the church of England, as by law established, by far dearer and nearer to them than their lives." [13] This last phrase could only mean that the king's plans for establishing the Catholic Church would be resisted even to civil war. The conduct of the House amply justified the apprehensions which had been felt before the session opened.[14]

For the moment, however, the rebellions led by Monmouth and Argyle excited the country to the exclusion of other matters, and solidified sentiment on the king's side. But James, who understood military matters better than politics, seized this occasion for increasing the size of the standing army and for giving commissions to a considerable number of Catholics. He intended that these appointments should later be confirmed by Parliament, and that the Test Act, which prevented Catholics from holding any civil or military office, should be repealed.[15] But again the king miscalculated. The House of Commons in November again took the first step, and before the king was ready to propose his full program, the House complained about the large standing army and about the illegal army commissions, and drew up an address to his Majesty, stating that such dispensing of the law without act of Parliament "is of the greatest concern to the rights of all your Majesty's subjects and to all the laws made for the security of their religion,"

[13] *Memoirs of Sir John Reresby* (1904), p. 263.

[14] "Il n'y a point eu de Parlement depuis longtemps qui ait esté si important que la sera celuycy, et dont les suites deussent estre d'un plus grand poids à l'avenir." — Barillon, 9 April, 1685.

James expects to receive the revenues that Charles enjoyed, and to all appearances he will be granted them. "Mais cela ne met pas le Roi d'Angleterre en repos, et à son aise; car il ne peut avec réputation et avec sûreté abandonner la protection des Catholiques; cependant, il est fort apparent qu'il trouvera de grandes difficultés à établir une liberté d'exercice pour la religion Catholique. . . . V. M. peut donc tenir pour un fondement assuré, que le Roi d'Angleterre trouvera d'extrêmes difficultés à ce qu'il veut faire en faveur de la religion Catholique." — Barillon, 30 April, 1685. Fox, *App.*, p. lxix.

[15] Barillon, 5 November, 1685. Fox, *App.*, p. cxxxii.

and "we therefore . . . do most humbly beseech your Majesty that you would be graciously pleased to give such directions therein that no apprehensions or jealousies may remain in the hearts of your Majesty's good and faithful subjects." [16]   The king replied tartly, and in a few days prorogued Parliament until February — although the subsidies had not yet been voted — to prevent Parliament from proceeding to a formal declaration against him.   So far as his program of liberating the Catholics is concerned, the second session was an even more dismal omen than the first.

The first year of the reign was, therefore, discouraging enough to James and to those who sympathized with his aims.   But the English Catholics of established family entirely condemned his policies.   Lord Ailesbury tells us in his *Memoirs* that at the time when the Commons addressed the king regarding the army commissions, Lord Sunderland and Father Petres

. . . began to lay the axe to the tree, by framing the king's speech so contrary to the sense of the old and landed Roman Catholics. Perhaps I may not repeat the very words, but refer you to the annals.   "Let no man take exceptions at what I have done and I will stand by it."   The two Houses were in a deep melancholy.   That very evening, according to custom, I went to visit my worthy friend and kinsman the Lord Bellasis, who seldom stirred out, being so infirm in his limbs.   There were some lords and gentlemen of great substance of the same persuasion.   My Lord Bellasis, who was in a great chair, took me by the hand saying, "My dear Lord, who could be the framer of this speech?   I date my ruin and that of all my persuasion from this day."   This is true on my honour; and from that time downwards he expressed all grief and sorrow.[17]

Such moderate Catholics were remembering the Popish Plot of 1678 and expecting a return of a rigorous enforcement of penal laws upon the accession of William and Mary.   They knew well the temper of England, and saw from the beginning that the policies of James were impracticable and ruinous.   They insisted that their welfare demanded a mutual understanding and harmony between the king and Parliament;   they feared the domination of Louis XIV in English politics;   they counseled such a domestic

---

[16] Leopold von Ranke, *History of England*, IV, 274.
[17] *Memoirs of Thomas, Earl of Ailesbury* (1890), p. 126.

policy as would find favor with William of Orange; and in foreign affairs they preferred an alliance with Holland, the Empire, and Spain against France.[18] This policy was, of course, supported by the Spanish ambassador in London; and all the advice from Rome, where Cardinal Howard was the pope's trusted advisor on English affairs, was also for moderate courses.[19] The pope at this time had his own quarrels with Louis XIV and the Gallicanism of the French Church, as well as with the Jesuits, and was therefore drawn into a sort of *rapprochement*, not only with Spain and the Empire, but even with Holland and William of Orange. The desire of the Papal Curia to prevent an alliance between James and Louis XIV, therefore, naturally threw the influence of Rome on the side of the moderate English Catholics. When Bishop Burnet, an English exile and a friend of William, was in Rome in November and Decem-

---

[18] "Les Catholiques ne sont pas tout-à-fait d'accord entre eux. Les plus habiles et ceux qui ont plus de part à la confiance du Roy d'Angleterre connoissent bien que la conjoncture est la plus favorable qu'on puisse espérer, et que si on la laisse échapper, elle pourra bien n'estre de longtemps si avantageuse. Les Jésuits sont de ce sentiment qui sans doute est le plus raisonable; mais les Catholiques riches et établis craignent l'avenir et appréhendent un retour qui les ruineroit; ainsy ils voudroient admettre tous les tempéramens possibles et se contenteroient des plus médiocres avantages qu'on leur voudroit accorder, comme seroit la révocation des loix pénales, sans s'attacher à la revocation du Test qui rend les Catholiques incapables des charges et des emplois. Ce party est soustenu de tous les gens qui favorisent secrettement le Prince d'Orange, et leur avis prévandroit si les autres ne prennoient tous les soins possibles pour faire comprendre au Roy d'Angleterre que s'il ne se sert de l'occasion, et qu'il n'établisse presentement ce qu'il a dessein de faire pour les Catholiques et pour luy mesme, il verra tous les jours naistre de plus grands obstacles à ses desseins. Le naturel du Roy d'Angleterre le porte à tenir une conduite ferme et vigoureuse. Ceux de ses ministres qui sont dans les mesmes sentimens paroissent augmenter de crédit." — Barillon, 12 November, 1685. Fox, *App.*, p. cxxxv.

"Les Catholiques mesmes sont partagez entre eux; Car les uns voudroient qu'on se servist de l'occasion présente qui ne peut estre plus favorable. Les autres craignent l'avenir et qu'ils ne se trouvent entierement ruinez dans un changement qu'on ne scauroit envisager comme fort eloigné, et dans cette veue ils se contenteroient de la tolerance ou ils sont et de l'inexecution des loix sans en prétendre une révocation expresse. Ce dernier avis est fort dangereux, et laisse les Catholiques également exposez à l'avenir sans tirer aucuns avantages de la conjoncture présente. Le Roy d'Angleterre paroist à ses plus confidens determiné à ne se pas relascher, mais on n'obmet aucun soin ny artifice pour l'engager à tenir une conduite moins ferme et à ne vouloir pas tout emporter d'abord." — Barillon, 22 November, 1685.

[19] Gilbert Burnet, *History of His Own Times* (Oxford, 1833), III, 84.

ber of this year, 1685, Cardinal Howard freely expressed to him his despair regarding the situation in England. "He saw," the bishop relates, that "violent courses were more acceptable, and would probably be followed. And he added, that these were the production of England, far different from the counsels of Rome."

But James, who was secretly receiving subsidies from Louis XIV, leaned also by personal preference to a French policy, and at Court the French influence was supported by Lord Sunderland — probably the most changeable and least principled statesman in English history — , by three or four Catholic peers of no great ability, and particularly by the Jesuit, Father Petres, an Englishman of noble family. By December, 1685, this Jesuit appears to have achieved a dominating influence over James, and to have been supported especially by the Jesuit order in London.[20] His importance in the king's councils could not have been a secret. In October of this year James wrote the pope asking for a bishopric for

[20] "Les Catholiques sont divisés sur les moyens dont il se faut servir. Ceux qui sont les plus riches et les mieux establis apprehendent fort l'avenir, et voudroient conserver leurs biens par une conduite moderée qu'on ne leur pûst reprocher. Les gens qui ont le plus de relation à la Cour de Rome sont de ce sentiment, et tous ceux qui favorisent l'Espagne travaillent pour concilier les avis differens, et pretendent que pourvuque le Roy d'Angleterre soit dans des interests opposés à la France il aura les coeurs du peuple et de grands secours du Parlement. Le danger des Catholiques de cet avis est connu des Catholiques qui ont du sens et de ceux qui ont le plus de part à la confiance du Roy d'Angleterre, comme les Milords Arondel, Pues, Castelmene et Dovres. Les Jesuits sont joints à eux, et l'apparence est que leurs conseils estant les plus sages et les plus seurs seront suivis; mais les autres feront encore des tentatives, et tascheront de faire connoistre au Roy d'Angleterre que le pis qui luy puisse arriver est de se passer de Parlement, qu'il peut encore essayer une fois si les esprits seront plus traittables, et pour les mieux disposer on essayera de faire que sa Majesté Brittanique temoigne de n'estre pas dans les interests de V. M. C'est sur quoy on attend un grand secours des ministres du Pape. Je ne scais pourtant point que Mr. d'Adda se sont encore expliqué sur cela. Il paroist fort circonspect et retenu. Il ecoute ce qu'on luy dit, et ne paroist pas ouvertement declaré pour aucun party. — Barillon, 13 December, 1685.

"Milord Sunderland m'a confié depuis peu des choses fort secrettes qui le regardent. Il m'a dit que le Roy d'Angleterre luy a promis positivement de la faire Président du Conseil après l'assemblée du Parlement. . . . Sa Majesté Britannique a esté determinée à luy promettre cette charge par un Jésuite nommé le Père Piters qui a beaucoup de part en sa confiance. C'est un homme de condition et frère de feu Milord Piters. Il luy a représenté fortement combien il importoit d'acréditer et de récompenser un ministre qui le sert plus courageusement et plus fidellement que les autres." — Barillon, 26 November, 1685. Fox, *App.*, p. cxliv.

Petres.[21] But the pope refused for several reasons: Innocent XI was an enemy of the Jesuits; he would do nothing to encourage James in his rash domestic policies; he was unwilling to bestow ecclesiastical prestige on a man whose friendly policy towards France ran counter to the policy of the papal court; and finally, he had the sound reason, which was the only one he expressed in his replies to James, that Jesuits were by their vows excluded from elevation to offices in the Church hierarchy. But the disapprobation of the pope was no check on so obstinate a man as James; and after the pope had repeatedly refused a bishopric for Petres, James in 1687 began to ask a cardinal's cap for him; in which request, needless to say, he was no more successful than in the former. At home the influence of Petres over James augmented steadily, and to the consternation of both Protestants and Catholics the *London Gazette* on November 11, 1687, announced that this Jesuit had been appointed to the Privy Council.[22] Father Petres must share with Sunderland and James himself the responsibility for the downfall of the king in 1688.

To return to James and Parliament, James had hoped that the prorogation to February, 1686, might give him time and opportunity to manage more members and thus to be sure of a working majority. Few shared these hopes, and in January James himself acknowledged their futility. On the 10th of January was announced a further prorogation to the 20th of May.[23] But although James was thus facing defeat in his program for the emancipation of the Catholics, he and his cabal were nevertheless determined to

[21] The most extensive collection of the documents on Father Petres is in an article by Bernard Duhr, S.J., "Die Anklagen gegen P. Edward Petre, S.J., Staatsrath Jacobs II.," *Zeitschrift für katholische Theologie*, Vol. X (1886) and XI (1887). The articles are otherwise an unconvincing exculpation of Petres.

[22] Terriesi, 14/24 November, 24 November/4 December, and 28 November/8 December, 1687.

[23] "Cette prorogation a surpris beaucoup de gens; quoy qu'il y ait eu lieu de la prévoir, on s'imaginoit que Sa Majesté Britannique voudroit encore essayer si le Parlement ne seroit pas plus traittable, et s'il ne se trouveroit pas quelques expediens pour accomoder les affaires, mais ces sortes de tentatives sont toujours sujettes à beaucoup d'inconveniens. . . . Ce Prince veut attendre que la faction soit affoiblie et que les esprits soient moins agitez. C'est ce qui n'arrivera peutestre de longtemps. Cependant son intention n'est pas de se relascher de ses resolutions. . . ." — Barillon, 10 January, 1686.

pursue their extreme measures with firmness. The Catholics of substance were discouraged and alarmed; in March Terriesi reported that many of them were contemplating selling their property and taking refuge abroad.[24] About this time, apparently in January, Dryden went over to the Catholic Church.[25]

The conduct of James during the three following years was distressing to the Catholics for so many reasons that only two or three important aspects of them can be mentioned here.

James continued to try coercion and influence on the members of Parliament. He tried closetings, threats, dismissals from office; all would not do. He never got a House of Commons that he dared to call in session.

In regard to Ireland James appointed a rather irresponsible Catholic peer, the Duke of Tyrconnel, to the command of the army, and later made him Lord Lieutenant. Tyrconnel's mission was to organize the Irish government and man the army so that Ireland, when the worst should eventually happen, might be an asylum for the Catholics of England and separate itself from the British crown.[26] But this appointment raised a storm of indignation

[24] "Procurasi per altro, come s'e detto, di procurare per tutte le strade possibili la propalatione della Cattolica Religione, ma come non è possibile di farlo, che per quelle che danno da temere alli Cattolici di qualche futuro malore, senza prima vedersi assicurate alla successione della Corona d'un altro Re Cattolico, vi sono di quelli che procurano di già di mettersi in sicuro dal turbine, che prevedano, coll' alienatione delle loro sustanze; vedendo bene che senza una coperta tale, possano le procedure che si fanno a lor favore produre effetti non lasciati comprendere a chi li promuove dal zelo e dalla buona volontá che per essi tiene." — Terriesi, 1/11 March, 1685/6.

[25] "Dryden, the famous play-writer, and his two sons, and Mrs. Nelly (miss to the late —), were said to go to mass; such proselytes were no great loss to the Church." — Evelyn, *Diary*, January 19, 1686.

[26] "Si tiene per certo Serenissima Altezza che Sua Maestà sia per richiamare d'Irlanda ben presto Mylord Clarendon e mettere in quel governo Mylord Treconel Cattolico Irlandese; cosa che autentica il rapporto che corre che voglia Sua Maestà metter totalmente l'Irlandà in autorità e dominio nel potere dei Cattolici, e quello che viene più considerato de' Cattolici d'Irlanda, ch' è un affare che fa esclamare al cielo l'Inghilterra, che vede bene essere un mezzo per far perdere alla di lei monarchia quel Regno, subito dopo che haverà serrato gli occhi Sua Maestà; e tutto ciò dicesi che faccia alla rimostranza de' Cattolici, chi figurano a Sua Maestà con la successione imminente d'un Re Protestante loro acerrimo nemico la total distrutione di essi e de la loro Religione, a meno che non habbino una ritirata dove fortificarsi, come quella d'Irlanda, affatto in lor potere, dove potranno

among the English Protestants; and among the Catholics it was opposed even in the Council;[27] only Father Petres and those of his faction approved.

In 1686 James decided to have the bench pronounce on the disputed question whether the royal prerogative included the dispensing power over acts of Parliament. But since James did not intend to receive a decision except in his favor, he took pains first to see that the judges held orthodox opinions. When he sounded them out, he found that they were by no means unanimous. Those who had legal or conscientious objections to his doctrine were dismissed, and more pliable men were appointed to their places. Among these appointees was Christopher Milton, brother of the late poet, who was made baron of the exchequer. This renovated bench pronounced that James possessed the dispensing power.

The Earl of Ailesbury, who was inclined to blame Sunderland and Petres more than James, has recorded Catholic opinion of this procedure:

In order to ruin the King more and more by degrees they obliged him to make Romish Judges, and one of them — Milton — that had not common sense, and such to go on the benches throughout the kingdom. And to add, many Deputy Lieutenants and Justices of the Peace were put into commission, and in my hearing, the worthy Sir William Goring, of Sussex, reproached his friends of the same religion for their folly and vanity, adding, "You will

---

con le proprie forze e quelle del Re, mettendosi sotto la di lui protezione o dominio, discendere, se non la libertà, la religione almeno." — Terriesi, 22 October/1 November, 1686.

[27] John Lingard (1849), XIII, 97. Cf. the following from a contemporary Protestant pamphlet: "The Queen was altogether for their Counsells, but the King was not so forwardly inclined, being every day set upon by all his *Popish Lords*, not to proceed too far, in the revolution of *Ireland*, for that would spoil the general interest of the *Catholicks:* and upon the Lord *Bellasis, Powis*, and some others of that *Faction* understanding that *Neagle* was come over, they were so transported with Rage, that they would have him immediately sent out of *London.* . . . *Tyrconnel* having compleated his design in modelling the Army, goes for *England*, and there consults with his party to obtain the Government of *Ireland.* The King, Queen and Father *Petres* were for him; but the whole Council of *Papists* oppos'd it, still urging how unacceptable he was to the *English.* . . ." — *A Full and Impartial Account of all the Secret Consults . . . of the Romish Party in Ireland* (London, 1690), pp. 54 and 59. The pamphleteer was misinformed on some details, but knew the facts about the general situation among the English Catholics.

ruin us all by it." There were others of his opinion whose names
are not in my memory. This Sir William went with the king as a
volunteer to Salisbury, and afterwards retired, lived, and died in
his native country beloved and esteemed by both religions generally, and I knew many lords and great number of gentlemen of the
Roman Catholics that lamented, crying out, "These measures will
ruin us all." The Pope's Nuncio Dada (afterwards Cardinal) my
very good friend, discoursed with me as often as he saw me on the
same subject, and above all Don Pedro de Ronquillo, the Spanish
Ambassador, my most intimate friend, and we frequented each
other so often, and mutually greatly lamented these pernicious
counsels given to the king by a cunning dissembler, and by a hot-
headed, ignorant Churchman.[28]

In April, 1687, the king, by virtue of his dispensing power, issued
the Declaration of Indulgence, and thus liberated Catholics and
all other dissenting sects from the penal laws. The joy was of
course great, but it was by no means universal, among either Dissenters or Catholics. The Dissenters scrutinized the political motives behind the Declaration. The Catholics reflected that the
Declaration could have force only during the life of James, and that
their brief period of freedom would be paid for by a more relentless
persecution under William. The moderate Catholics therefore re-
doubled their efforts to have James come to an understanding with
William, and we are even told by Bonrepaus, the agent in England
of Louis XIV, that some of the English Catholics were secretly in
communication with William on their own account.[29]

[28] *Memoirs of Thomas, Earl of Ailesbury* (1890), p. 152.
[29] "Les Catholiques sont ceux qui sont le plus effrayés des menaces du prince
d'Orange. Il en est qui prennent avec lui des mesures secrètes." — Dispatch by
Bonrepaus in 1687, quoted by Mazure, II, 280.

Towards the end of 1687 Barillon relates that Dykvelt's attempts at moderat-
ing the feeling between James and William were seconded (but futilely) by the
"Catholiques modérés, qui, effrayés de l'irritation publique, voyoient surtout
l'avenir. 'Il suffit,' disoient-ils au Roi, 'de nous avoir mis à couvert de la rigueur
des lois. Avec un peu de condescendance, Sa Majesté peut rassurer l'esprit de ses
sujets, et dissiper les soupçons dont ils sont prévenus qu'elle aspire à changer leur
gouvernement. Si le Roi veut guérir leurs craintes, il peut obtenir beaucoup du
Parlement. Il faut surtout éviter des troubles dont on ne prévoit jamais les suites
dans une nation agitée. Il seroit trop périlleux de précipiter le prince d'Orange dans
des mesures déclarés, et de lui donner une occasion d'autoriser de son nom, de ses
droits et de son crédit, une révolte qui auroit pour prétexte la defense des lois et de
la Religion du pays.' Mais le Rois connoit le piège qu'on lui tend, et le danger de

There is ample material available for expanding this sketch, if one so desires. But from what has been said it must be evident that whenever James frightened or exasperated English Protestants, the English Catholics for reasons of their own were also frightened and embittered. Terriesi records that this attitude of the Catholics was particularly discouraging to the king and that he expressed himself feelingly about it.[30] As for Father Petres, in-

---

ces conseils. Il paroît fort résolu de ne pas se relâcher. Il prétend poursuivre ses desseins comme il a fait jusqu' à present." — Quoted by Mazure, II, 255–256.

The moderate Catholics had been laying this "snare" for some time, at least as early as January, 1687; on January 10 the Count d'Avaux wrote as follows: "A friend of mine brought me an account, that the Prince of Orange had desired Sir William Pen, the famous chief of the sect of quakers in England, when he was some months ago in Holland, to replace him on a good footing with the King of England: that Pen had endeavoured it since that time, and that matters were very far advanced; that Pen had sent advice to the Prince of Orange some time ago, that the King of England having debated in a council, in what manner it would be most for his service to behave to the Prince of Orange, some of the catholic members of it remonstrated to the King of England, that he could not hope to abolish the protestant religion in England as long as he sat on the throne; that consequently every step towards it would only serve to render the catholic religion odious: besides, that the hopes which the protestants entertained of having a Prince of their own for a sovereign (and one who, the worse he was treated now, would be the more in their interests) would render them much more disobedient to the King of England's will; that his Britanic Majesty had no better course to take for the advantage of the catholic religion, and for preventing the English professors of it from being hereafter sacrificed, than to shew a perfect union betwixt him and the Prince of Orange, who would be thereby engaged to treat them well when he was the Sovereign of England: that they were therefore of opinion, that the King of England should send some person of quality to the Prince of Orange, to assure him of his friendship, and of his desire to live in a perfect union with him; and at the same time to remit the pension which the Princess of Orange was to have, as presumptive heiress of the crown. The other English members on the contrary declared, that the King of England had no measure to pursue that was honourable and safe, but to proceed with an unshaken constancy against those of the church of England, and much more against the protestant dissenters." — *The Negotiations of Count d'Avaux* (London, 1754–55), IV, 100–102.

[30] "E li Cattolici secolari con il ritirarsi tutti, per paura d'un successore protestante dal volere havere parte nella condotta della Maestà Sua, di quello che puole fabbricare Sua Maestà in un anno. Nè potrei esprimere il discoraggiamento e la passione che ne riceve la Maestà Sua, che espone tutto con tanta vigilanza per essi." — Terriesi, 29 April, 1687.

"L'affare intrapreso qui Sua Maestà a favore della Religione Cattolica prende sempre aspetto peggiore, mostrandovi ogni giorno più avversi li Cattolici stessi." — Terriesi, 24 November/4 December, 1687.

dignation and hatred focused on him more and more, until in the end he was more hated by the Catholics than by the Protestants.[31]

Returning then to Dryden, we may, I think, safely assume that he was aware of what was going on; and that he was not neutral or indifferent to developments which concerned English Catholics so vitally. The question is to which side his sympathies leaned, whether to James and Sunderland and Petres, or to the moderate Catholics.

The important evidence is in *The Hind and the Panther*, published in April, 1687, and written, according to his own statement, during the winter and spring of that year. In the course of this theological fable the Panther, or Anglican Church, told a story of the swallows and the martin, which alluded to the situation of the English Catholics. The swallows were gathered for their autumn migration to avoid the rigors of the approaching winter. They were finally advised by a martin,

> A church-begot and church-believing bird;
> Of little body, but of lofty mind,
> And much a dunce, as Martins are by kind; [32]

they were induced by this martin to postpone their departure inasmuch as he had special and prophetic knowledge of easy and happy times for them where they were. A period of miraculous springtime seemed to verify his prophecies; but suddenly the snow and frost and winter winds caught them and they all died of exposure; except the martins, who hid in a hollow tree, where the "rabble of a town" found them and put them to an ignominious death; the great Martin was separately executed for treason, and his dead body suspended in the air to serve as a weather-vane.

The important Martin was of course Father Petres; the other martins were the Jesuits; the swallows, the English Catholics. But what is the significance of this projected *migration* of the swallows?

Sir Walter Scott is the only editor of Dryden who has attempted any comment on this fable, and his explanation has been repeated

---

[31] "Ma credami V. A. S. che detto Padre ha molti inimici e specialmente tra li Cattolici." — Terriesi, 28 June 1688. Quoted by Duhr, *op. cit.*, XI, 46, n. 3.

[32] Part III, 463–465.

by all later editors. Scott believed that the whole episode referred to a consultation of the Catholics at the Savoy in the autumn of 1686. He derived his knowledge of this consultation from Ralph's history, which in turn borrowed the story from a pamphlet, *A Full and Impartial Account of all the Secret Consults, Negotiations, Stratagems & Intriegues of the Romish Party in Ireland, From 1660, to this present Year 1689* (London, 1690), where the passage in question reads as follows:

About this time there was a general meeting at the *Savoy* before Father *Petres*, of the chief *Roman Catholics* of *England*, in order to consult what Methods were fittest to be pursued for the promotion of the *Catholick* Cause. The *Papists* were universally afraid of the King's Incapacity, or else unwillingness of exposing himself to the hazard of securing it in his Reign. They were sensible that he advanced considerably in Age; besides, they were not ignorant of what almost insuperable difficulties they had to contend with, before they could bring it to any ripeness: Wherefore upon these Considerations (carefully weighing and ballancing every Circumstance) some were for moving the King to procure an Act of Parliament for the security of their Estates, and only liberty for Priests in their own private Houses, and to be exempted from all Employments. This *Father Petres* Anathematized as Terrestrial, and founded upon too anxious a Sollicitude for the preservation of their Secular Interests; but if they would pursue his measures, he doubted not to see the Holy Church triumphant in England. . . . Others of the *Papists* were for addressing the King to have liberty (now that they might do it) to sell their Estates, and that his Majesty would intercede with the *French* King to provide for them in his Dominions. After several Debates, it was at last agreed upon to lay both Proposals before the King, and some of the number to attend his Majesty with them, which was accordingly done; to which the King's return was, *That he had before their Desires came to him, often thought of them, and had* (as he believed) *provided a sure* Sanctuary *and* Retreat *for them in* Ireland, *if all those endeavours should be blasted in* England, *which he had made for their security, and of whose success he had not yet reason to despair.* This Encouragement to the *Papists* in *England*, was attended with the most zealous Expressions, and *Catholick* Assurances of his Ardent Love to the Holy Church, which he said he had been a Martyr for. Thus we see how the Bigotry of this unhappy Prince, transported him beyond all bounds, and carry'd him to such Extravagancies in Government, as the moderate of the *English Papists* themselves thought to be extream hazardous and insecure; and would all of them have been content with a private exercise of their Religion, as thinking it abundantly more safe, rather than endanger the losing their Estates and Fortunes, (which they almost look'd upon as inevitable) if such violent extream courses were followed.[33]

This passage seemed to Scott to settle the matter. "It will hardly, I think, be disputed," he says, "that the fable of the Swallows about to cross the seas refers to this consultation at the Savoy." This conclusion, I believe, will have to be modified. Anyone reading the *Secret Consults* must be struck by the remarkable information of the author; but his information is hearsay and not trustworthy on details. This consultation at the Savoy, of which he speaks, must have been a very obscure event; no foreign ambassador mentioned it in his dispatches; no record of it remains except in this anti-Jacobite pamphlet. It seems more probable that the application of the fable was intended by Dryden to be more general, and that it refers, not to *one* consultation of the Catholics at the Savoy in 1686, but to almost every consultation by Catholics from the accession of James. It refers to that division of Catholic opinion which, as we have seen, existed as early as March, 1685, and became ever more marked as James unfolded his policy. Scott says further: "It is a strong instance of Dryden's prejudice against priests of all persuasions, that, in the character of the Martin, who persuaded the Swallows to postpone the flight, he decidedly appears to have designed Petre, the King's confessor and prime adviser in State matters, both spiritual and temporal." Now it is true that Dryden hated the "priests of all persuasions" both before and after he became a Catholic; and there is no doubt that Dryden in the poem betrays a personal dislike of Father Petres. But here, again, we may safely affirm that the application is broader, and that Dryden was putting into his poem some of the indignation against Petres and his influence felt by the moderate Catholics.

Fortunately we are able to corroborate this interpretation by a passage in one of the few Dryden letters extant. On February 16, 1687, at the very time when he was working on *The Hind and the*

[33] Pp. 59–61.

Panther, Dryden wrote to Etherege, who was ambassador at Ratisbon. The letter is a series of variations on the theme of idleness, in which Etherege claimed preëminence. Dryden incidentally drops a hint as to how things were going in England:

> I cannot help hearing that white sticks change their masters, and that officers of the army are not immortal in their places, because the King finds they will not vote for him in the next sessions. [Rochester had recently been dismissed from the Treasury and Lord Lumley and Shrewsbury from their colonelcies.] Oh, that our Monarch would encourage noble idleness by his own example as he of blessed memory did before him, for my mind misgives me that he will not much advance his affairs by stirring. I was going on, but am glad to be admonished by the paper.[34]

After that letter I think there can be no doubt about Dryden's position among the moderate Catholics. In its light we may safely regard the fable of the swallows as the discreet expression of Catholic disapproval of James and his policies, and the tragic end of the swallows as symbolizing what the Catholics were expecting with deep apprehension.

In conclusion, then, it does not appear so certain that conversion to Catholicism was an allurement to Dryden. The Catholics were not so happy in the reign of James II. The conversions were remarkably few, and this fact James and his advisers laid to the fear of legal oppression; no one, they said quite rightly, could turn Catholic without exposing his family and fortune to danger. It is sometimes assumed that Dryden's fortune was his pension, and that this pension would be assured by his conversion. But, in the first place, James could not have attached such weight to an office of no political consequence; had the Poet Laureate been *ex officio* a member of the House of Commons such an insinuation would have had more plausibility. In the second place, by turning Catholic Dryden made it absolutely certain that his pension would terminate with the death of James. His lot was even more precarious than that of the Catholics with estates. So that, however

[34] Sybil Rosenfeld, *The Letterbook of Sir George Etherege*, 1928, 356–357. This letter, in manuscript in the British Museum, was first mentioned by Macaulay (ed. Sir Charles Firth, p. 965), but was never published until 1928, and was never used by any editor or biographer of Dryden.

one chooses to state the matter, it appears very uncertain that Dryden improved his financial prospects by his conversion.

But those who are interested to know what Dryden himself really thought about this accusation may read it in *The Hind and the Panther*, Part III, 221–228 and 362–388. This Appendix is merely a commentary on those lines.

INDEX

ANN ARBOR PAPERBACKS

reissues of works of enduring merit

The University of Michigan Press / Ann Arbor